# Django By Example

Create your own line of successful web applications
with Django

**Antonio Melé**

**[PACKT]** open source ✳
PUBLISHING   community experience distilled

BIRMINGHAM - MUMBAI

# Django By Example

First published: November 2015

Production reference: 1261115

Published by Packt Publishing Ltd.
Livery Place
35 Livery Street
Birmingham B3 2PB, UK.

ISBN 978-1-78439-191-1

www.packtpub.com

# Credits

**Author**

Antonio Melé

**Reviewers**

Tarun Behal

Alasdair Nicol

Alex Robbins

Glen Robertson

Derek Stegelman

**Commissioning Editor**

Akram Hussain

**Acquisition Editor**

Larissa Pinto

**Content Development Editor**

Arun Nadar

**Technical Editor**

Rupali Shrawane

**Copy Editor**

Vatsal Surti

**Project Coordinator**

Neha Bhatnagar

**Proofreader**

Safis Editing

**Indexer**

Rekha Nair

**Production Coordinator**

Aparna Bhagat

**Cover Work**

Aparna Bhagat

# About the Author

**Antonio Melé** holds an MSc in Computer Science. He has been developing Django projects since 2006 and leads the django.es Spanish Django community. He has founded Zenx IT, a technology company that creates web applications for clients of several industries.

Antonio has also worked as a CTO for several technology-based start-ups. His father inspired his passion for computers and programming.

# About the Reviewers

**Tarun Behal** is a full-stack software engineer with 4 years of experience in building and delivering high-quality applications using Python, JavaScript, PHP, Ruby, and other open source technologies. He is passionate about software development and enjoys exploring open source projects. Over the years, he has provided consulting services to several organizations and has played many different roles such as cloud administrator, frontend technologies, software architect, ERP consultant, and software developer.

Tarun has a bachelors degree in computer engineering from the Uttar Pradesh Technical University, Noida, India. He currently lives in Gurgaon, India and works with Nagarro Software Pvt. Ltd. In the digital world, he can be contacted by e-mail at `tarunbehal@hotmail.com`.

> I feel very honored to have been asked to review this book. This was an amazing experience for me as I learned a lot on the way through, as I am sure you will too. I'd like to thank my family, especially my brother, Varun, and all my colleagues for their constant support and motivation.
>
> I feel honored to have been asked to review this book. This was an amazing experience as I learned a lot, as I am sure you will too.

**Alasdair Nicol** is a Python developer from Scotland. He discovered Django in 2009 while learning Python, and was instantly hooked. After 5 years with UK-based hosting provider Memset Hosting, he recently started working at SpatialBuzz, who provide SaaS for mobile network operators.

When he's not coding, Alasdair enjoys playing squash and running.

**Alex Robbins** is a programmer living in Dallas, Texas. He loves programming in Clojure and Python, doing anything from web development to data science. He has been using Django since 2008 and enjoying it the whole time. When not programming, he spends his time with his beautiful wife and amazing son.

Alex has also contributed distributed processing recipes to *Clojure Cookbook* and has technically reviewed *Enterprise Data Workflows with Cascading*.

**Glen Robertson** is a software engineer from New Zealand. He currently works at Lyft, where he builds applications in Python and PHP to help grow their transportation network and fill up more empty car seats on the road. Prior to that, he worked for Trulia, where he built heat-map visualizations with GeoDjango and PostGIS to show local information to homebuyers such as crime rates and commute times.

Glen has a bachelor in information technology, majoring in software engineering from Victoria University of Wellington.

**Derek Stegelman** is a senior web application developer at Kansas State University. He works on maintaining Python web applications written using the Django web framework. He has been working with Django for 5 years on websites and applications and actively contributes to the Django community through open source projects.

# www.PacktPub.com

## Support files, eBooks, discount offers, and more

For support files and downloads related to your book, please visit www.PacktPub.com.

Did you know that Packt offers eBook versions of every book published, with PDF and ePub files available? You can upgrade to the eBook version at www.PacktPub.com and as a print book customer, you are entitled to a discount on the eBook copy. Get in touch with us at service@packtpub.com for more details.

At www.PacktPub.com, you can also read a collection of free technical articles, sign up for a range of free newsletters and receive exclusive discounts and offers on Packt books and eBooks.

https://www2.packtpub.com/books/subscription/packtlib

Do you need instant solutions to your IT questions? PacktLib is Packt's online digital book library. Here, you can search, access, and read Packt's entire library of books.

## Why subscribe?

- Fully searchable across every book published by Packt
- Copy and paste, print, and bookmark content
- On demand and accessible via a web browser

## Free access for Packt account holders

If you have an account with Packt at www.PacktPub.com, you can use this to access PacktLib today and view 9 entirely free books. Simply use your login credentials for immediate access.

*To my parents and my sister. Thank you for always encouraging and supporting me.*

# Table of Contents

# Preface

Django is a powerful Python web framework that encourages rapid development and clean, pragmatic design, offering a relatively shallow learning curve. This makes it attractive to both novice and expert programmers.

This book will guide you through the entire process of developing professional web applications with Django. The book not only covers the most relevant aspects of the framework, it also teaches you how to integrate other popular technologies into your Django projects.

The book will walk you through the creation of real-world applications, solving common problems, and implementing best practices with a step-by-step approach that is easy to follow.

After reading this book, you will have a good understanding of how Django works and how to build practical, advanced web applications.

## What this book covers

*Chapter 1*, *Building a Blog Application*, introduces you to the framework by creating a blog application. You will create the basic blog models, views, templates, and URLs to display blog posts. You will learn how to build QuerySets with the Django ORM, and you will configure the Django administration site.

*Chapter 2*, *Enhancing Your Blog with Advanced Features*, teaches how to handle forms and modelforms, send e-mails with Django, and integrate third-party applications. You will implement a comment system for your blog posts and allow your users to share posts by e-mail. The chapter will also guide you through the process of creating a tagging system.

*Chapter 3, Extending Your Blog Application* explores how to create custom template tags and filters. The chapter will also show you how to use the sitemap framework and create an RSS feed for your posts. You will complete your blog application by building a search engine with Solr.

*Chapter 4, Building a Social Website* explains how to build a social website. You will use the Django authentication framework to create user account views. You will learn how to create a custom user profile model and build social authentication into your project using major social networks.

*Chapter 5, Sharing Content in Your Website* teaches you how to transform your social application into an image bookmarking website. You will define many-to-many relationships for models, and you will create an AJAX bookmarklet in JavaScript and integrate it into your project. The chapter will show you how to generate image thumbnails and create custom decorators for your views.

*Chapter 6, Tracking User Actions* shows you how to build a follower system for users. You will complete your image bookmarking website by creating a user activity stream application. You will learn how to optimise QuerySets, and you will work with signals. You will integrate Redis into your project to count image views.

*Chapter 7, Building an Online Shop* explores how to create an online shop. You will build the catalog models, and you will create a shopping cart using Django sessions. You will learn to manage customer orders and send asynchronous notifications to users using Celery.

*Chapter 8, Managing Payments and Orders* explains you how to integrate a payment gateway into your shop and handle payment notifications. You will also customize the administration site to export orders to CSV files, and you will generate PDF invoices dynamically.

*Chapter 9, Extending Your Shop* teaches you how to create a coupon system to apply discounts to orders. The chapter will show you how to add internationalization to your project and
how to translate models. You will also build a product recommendation engine using Redis.

*Chapter 10, Building an e-Learning Platform* guides you through creating an e-learning platform. You will add fixtures to your project, use model inheritance, create custom model fields, use class-based views, and manage groups and permissions. You will create a content management system and handle formsets.

*Chapter 11, Caching Content* shows you how to create a student registration system and manage student enrollment in courses. You will render diverse course contents and you will learn how to use the cache framework.

*Chapter 12, Building an API* explores building a RESTful API for your project using the Django REST framework.

 Additionally, *Chapter 13, Going Live,* is available for download at `https://www.packtpub.com/sites/default/files/downloads/Django_By_Example_GoingLive.pdf`. You will learn how to create a production environment using uWSGI and Nginx, and how to secure it with SSL. The chapter will explain you how to build a custom subdomain middleware and create custom management commands.

# What you need for this book

- A working installation of Python 3
- A Linux OS is recommended

# Who this book is for

This book is intended for developers with a basic knowledge of Python who wish to learn Django in a pragmatic way. Perhaps you are completely new to Django or you already know a little but you want to get the most out of it. This book will help you master the most relevant areas of the framework by building practical projects from scratch. You need to have familiarity with basic programming concepts in order to read this book. Some previous knowledge of HTML and JavaScript is assumed.

# Conventions

In this book, you will find a number of styles of text that distinguish between different kinds of information. Here are some examples of these styles, and an explanation of their meaning.

Code words in text, database table names, folder names, filenames, file extensions, pathnames, dummy URLs, user input, and Twitter handles are shown as follows: "We can include other contexts through the use of the `include` directive."

A block of code is set as follows:

```
def post_share(request, post_id):
    post = get_object_or_404(Post, id=post_id, status='published')
    if request.method == 'POST':
        form = EmailPostForm(request.POST)
```

When we wish to draw your attention to a particular part of a code block, the relevant lines or items are set in bold:

```
def post_share(request, post_id):
    post = get_object_or_404(Post, id=post_id, status='published')
    if request.method == 'POST':
        form = EmailPostForm(request.POST)
```

Any command-line input or output is written as follows:

```
python manage.py runserver
```

**New terms** and **important words** are shown in bold. Words that you see on the screen, in menus or dialog boxes for example, appear in the text like this: "Clicking the **Next** button moves you to the next screen".

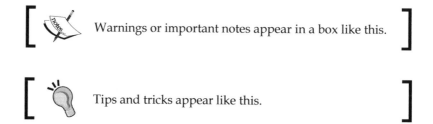

> Warnings or important notes appear in a box like this.

> Tips and tricks appear like this.

# Reader feedback

Feedback from our readers is always welcome. Let us know what you think about this book—what you liked or may have disliked. Reader feedback is important for us to develop titles that you really get the most out of.

To send us general feedback, simply send an e-mail to feedback@packtpub.com, and mention the book title via the subject of your message.

If there is a topic that you have expertise in and you are interested in either writing or contributing to a book, see our author guide on www.packtpub.com/authors.

# Customer support

Now that you are the proud owner of a Packt book, we have a number of things to help you to get the most from your purchase.

# Downloading the example code

You can download the example code files for all Packt books you have purchased from your account at `http://www.packtpub.com`. If you purchased this book elsewhere, you can visit `http://www.packtpub.com/support` and register to have the files e-mailed directly to you.

# Errata

Although we have taken every care to ensure the accuracy of our content, mistakes do happen. If you find a mistake in one of our books—maybe a mistake in the text or the code—we would be grateful if you would report this to us. By doing so, you can save other readers from frustration and help us improve subsequent versions of this book. If you find any errata, please report them by visiting `http://www.packtpub.com/submit-errata`, selecting your book, clicking on the **errata submission form** link, and entering the details of your errata. Once your errata are verified, your submission will be accepted and the errata will be uploaded on our website, or added to any list of existing errata, under the Errata section of that title. Any existing errata can be viewed by selecting your title from `http://www.packtpub.com/support`.

# Piracy

Piracy of copyright material on the Internet is an ongoing problem across all media. At Packt, we take the protection of our copyright and licenses very seriously. If you come across any illegal copies of our works, in any form, on the Internet, please provide us with the location address or website name immediately so that we can pursue a remedy.

Please contact us at `copyright@packtpub.com` with a link to the suspected pirated material.

We appreciate your help in protecting our authors, and our ability to bring you valuable content.

# Questions

You can contact us at `questions@packtpub.com` if you are having a problem with any aspect of the book, and we will do our best to address it.

# 1

# Building a Blog Application

In this book, you will learn how to build complete Django projects, ready for production use. In case you haven't installed Django yet, you will learn how to do it in the first part of this chapter. This chapter will cover how to create a simple blog application using Django. The purpose of the chapter is to get a general idea of how the framework works, understand how the different components interact with each other, and give you the skills to easily create Django projects with basic functionality. You will be guided through the creation of a complete project without elaborating upon all the details. The different framework components will be covered in detail throughout the following chapters of this book.

This chapter will cover the following points:

- Installing Django and creating your first project
- Designing models and generating model migrations
- Creating an administration site for your models
- Working with QuerySet and managers
- Building views, templates, and URLs
- Adding pagination to list views
- Using Django class-based views

## Installing Django

If you have already installed Django, you can skip this section and jump directly to *Creating your first project*. Django comes as a Python package and thus can be installed in any Python environment. If you haven't installed Django yet, here is a quick guide to installing Django for local development.

Django works well with Python versions 2.7 or 3. In the examples of this book, we are going to use Python 3. If you're using Linux or Mac OS X, you probably have Python installed. If you are not sure if Python is installed in your computer, you can verify it by typing `python` in the terminal. If you see something like the following, then Python is installed in your computer:

```
Python 3.5.0 (v3.5.0:374f501f4567, Sep 12 2015, 11:00:19)
[GCC 4.2.1 (Apple Inc. build 5666) (dot 3)] on darwin
Type "help", "copyright", "credits" or "license" for more information.
>>>
```

If your installed Python version is lower than 3, or Python is not installed on your computer, download Python 3.5.0 from `http://www.python.org/download/` and install it.

Since you are going to use Python 3, you don't have to install a database. This Python version comes with the SQLite database built-in. SQLite is a lightweight database that you can use with Django for development. If you plan to deploy your application in a production environment, you should use an advanced database such as PostgreSQL, MySQL, or Oracle. You can get more information about how to get your database running with Django in `https://docs.djangoproject.com/en/1.8/topics/install/#database-installation`.

# Creating an isolated Python environment

It is recommended that you use virtualenv to create isolated Python environments, so you can use different package versions for different projects, which is far more practical than installing Python packages system wide. Another advantage of using virtualenv is that you won't need any administration privileges to install Python packages. Run the following command in your shell to install virtualenv:

```
pip install virtualenv
```

After you install virtualenv, create an isolated environment with the following command:

```
virtualenv my_env
```

This will create a `my_env/` directory including your Python environment. Any Python libraries you install while your virtual environment is active will go into the `my_env/lib/python3.5/site-packages` directory.

If your system comes with Python 2.X and you installed Python 3.X, you have to tell virtualenv to use the latter. You can locate the path where Python 3 is installed and use it to create the virtual environment with the following commands:

```
zenx$ *which python3*
/Library/Frameworks/Python.framework/Versions/3.5/bin/python3
zenx$ *virtualenv my_env -p
/Library/Frameworks/Python.framework/Versions/3.5/bin/python3*
```

Run the following command to activate your virtual environment:

```
source my_env/bin/activate
```

The shell prompt will include the name of the active virtual environment enclosed in parentheses, like this:

```
(my_env) laptop:~ zenx$
```

You can deactivate your environment anytime with the deactivate command.

You can find more information about virtualenv at https://virtualenv.pypa.io/en/latest/.

On top of virtualenv, you can use virtualenvwrapper. This tool provides wrappers that make it easier to create and manage your virtual environments. You can download it from http://virtualenvwrapper.readthedocs.org/en/latest/.

# Installing Django with pip

pip is the preferred method for installing Django. Python 3.5 comes with pip pre-installed, but you can find pip installation instructions at https://pip.pypa.io/en/stable/installing/. Run the following command at the shell prompt to install Django with pip:

```
pip install Django==1.8.6
```

Django will be installed in the Python site-packages/ directory of your virtual environment.

Now check if Django has been successfully installed. Run python on a terminal and import Django to check its version:

```
>>> import django
>>> django.VERSION
django.VERSION(1, 8, 5, 'final', 0)
```

If you get this output, Django has been successfully installed in your machine.

Django can be installed in several other ways. You can find a complete installation guide at https://docs.djangoproject.com/en/1.8/topics/install/.

# Creating your first project

Our first Django project will be a complete blog site. Django provides a command that allows you to easily create an initial project file structure. Run the following command from your shell:

```
django-admin startproject mysite
```

This will create a Django project with the name `mysite`.

Let's take a look at the generated project structure:

```
mysite/
  manage.py
  mysite/
    __init__.py
    settings.py
    urls.py
    wsgi.py
```

These files are as follows:

- `manage.py`: A command-line utility to interact with your project. It is a thin wrapper around the `django-admin.py` tool. You don't need to edit this file.
- `mysite/`: Your project directory consist of the following files:
    - `__init__.py`: An empty file that tells Python to treat the `mysite` directory as a Python module.
    - `settings.py`: Settings and configuration for your project. Contains initial default settings.
    - `urls.py`: The place where your URL patterns live. Each URL defined here is mapped to a view.
    - `wsgi.py`: Configuration to run your project as a WSGI application.

The generated `settings.py` file includes a basic configuration to use a SQLite database and a list of Django applications that are added to your project by default. We need to create the tables in the database for the initial applications.

Open the shell and run the following commands:

```
cd mysite
```

```
python manage.py migrate
```

You will see an output that ends like this:

```
Rendering model states... DONE
Applying contenttypes.0001_initial... OK
Applying auth.0001_initial... OK
Applying admin.0001_initial... OK
Applying contenttypes.0002_remove_content_type_name... OK
Applying auth.0002_alter_permission_name_max_length... OK
Applying auth.0003_alter_user_email_max_length... OK
Applying auth.0004_alter_user_username_opts... OK
Applying auth.0005_alter_user_last_login_null... OK
Applying auth.0006_require_contenttypes_0002... OK
Applying sessions.0001_initial... OK
```

The tables for the initial applications have been created in the database. You will learn about the `migrate` management command in a bit.

# Running the development server

Django comes with a lightweight web server to run your code quickly, without needing to spend time configuring a production server. When you run the Django development server, it keeps checking for changes in your code. It reloads automatically, freeing you from manually reloading it after code changes. However, it might not notice some actions like adding new files to your project, so you will have to restart the server manually in these cases.

Start the development server by typing the following command from your project's root folder:

```
python manage.py runserver
```

You should see something like this:

```
Performing system checks...

System check identified no issues (0 silenced).
November 5, 2015 - 19:10:54
Django version 1.8.6, using settings 'mysite.settings'
Starting development server at http://127.0.0.1:8000/
Quit the server with CONTROL-C.
```

Now, open the URL `http://127.0.0.1:8000/` in your browser. You should see a page telling you the project is successfully running, as shown in the following screenshot:

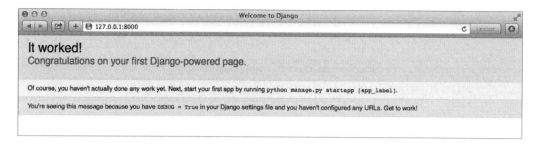

You can indicate Django to run the development server on a custom host and port, or tell it that you want to run your project loading a different settings file. For example, you can run the `manage.py` command as follows:

```
python manage.py runserver 127.0.0.1:8001 \
--settings=mysite.settings
```

This comes in handy to deal with multiple environments that require different settings. Remember, this server is only intended for development and is not suitable for production use. In order to deploy Django in a production environment, you should run it as a **Web Server Gateway Interface (WSGI)** application using a real web server such as Apache, Gunicorn, or uWSGI. You can find more information about how to deploy Django with different web servers at `https://docs.djangoproject.com/en/1.8/howto/deployment/wsgi/`.

Additional downloadable *Chapter 13, Going Live* covers setting up a production environment for your Django projects.

# Project settings

Let's open the `settings.py` file and take a look at the configuration of our project. There are several settings that Django includes in this file, but these are only a part of all the Django settings available. You can see all settings and their default values in `https://docs.djangoproject.com/en/1.8/ref/settings/`.

The following settings are worth looking at:

- DEBUG is a boolean that turns on/off the debug mode of the project. If set to True, Django will display detailed error pages when an uncaught exception is thrown by your application. When you move to a production environment, remember you have to set it to False. Never deploy a site into production with DEBUG turned on because you will expose sensitive data of your project.

- ALLOWED_HOSTS is not applied while debug mode is on or when running tests. Once you are going to move your site to production and set DEBUG to False, you will have to add your domain/host to this setting in order to allow it to serve the Django site.

- INSTALLED_APPS is a setting you will have to edit in all projects. This setting tells Django which applications are active for this site. By default, Django includes the following applications:
    - django.contrib.admin: This is an administration site.
    - django.contrib.auth: This is an authentication framework.
    - django.contrib.contenttypes: This is a framework for content types.
    - django.contrib.sessions: This is a session framework.
    - django.contrib.messages: This is a messaging framework.
    - django.contrib.staticfiles: This is a framework for managing static files.

- MIDDLEWARE_CLASSES is a tuple containing middlewares to be executed.

- ROOT_URLCONF indicates the Python module where the root URL patterns of your application are defined.

- DATABASES is a dictionary containing the settings for all the databases to be used in the project. There must always be a default database. The default configuration uses a SQLite3 database.

- LANGUAGE_CODE Defines the default language code for this Django site.

Don't worry if you don't understand much about what you are seeing. You will get more familiar with Django settings in the following chapters.

# Projects and applications

Throughout this book, you will read the terms project and application over and over. In Django, a project is considered a Django installation with some settings; and an application is a group of models, views, templates, and URLs. Applications interact with the framework to provide some specific functionalities and may be reused in various projects. You can think of the project as your website, which contains several applications like blog, wiki, or forum, which can be used in other projects.

# Creating an application

Now let's create your first Django application. We will create a blog application from scratch. From your project's root directory, run the following command:

```
python manage.py startapp blog
```

This will create the basic structure of the application, which looks like this:

```
blog/
    __init__.py
    admin.py
    migrations/
        __init__.py
    models.py
    tests.py
    views.py
```

These files are as follows:

- admin.py: This is where you register models to include them into the Django administration site. Using the Django admin site is optional.

- migrations: This directory will contain database migrations of your application. Migrations allow Django to track your model changes and synchronize the database accordingly.

- models.py: Data models of your application. All Django applications need to have a models.py file, but this file can be left empty.

- tests.py: This is where you can add tests for your application.

- views.py: The logic of your application goes here. Each view receives an HTTP request, processes it, and returns a response.

# Designing the blog data schema

We will start by defining the initial data models for our blog. A model is a Python class that subclasses django.db.models.Model, in which each attribute represents a database field. Django will create a table for each model defined in the models.py file. When you create a model, Django offers you a practical API to query the database easily.

First, we will define a Post model. Add the following lines to the models.py file of the blog application:

```python
from django.db import models
from django.utils import timezone
from django.contrib.auth.models import User

class Post(models.Model):
    STATUS_CHOICES = (
        ('draft', 'Draft'),
        ('published', 'Published'),
    )
    title = models.CharField(max_length=250)
    slug = models.SlugField(max_length=250,
                            unique_for_date='publish')
    author = models.ForeignKey(User,
                               related_name='blog_posts')
    body = models.TextField()
    publish = models.DateTimeField(default=timezone.now)
    created = models.DateTimeField(auto_now_add=True)
    updated = models.DateTimeField(auto_now=True)
    status = models.CharField(max_length=10,
                              choices=STATUS_CHOICES,
                              default='draft')

    class Meta:
        ordering = ('-publish',)

    def __str__(self):
        return self.title
```

This is our basic model for blog posts. Let's take a look at the fields we just defined for this model:

- `title`: This is the field for the post title. This field is `CharField`, which translates into a `VARCHAR` column in the SQL database.

- `slug`: This is a field intended to be used in URLs. A **slug** is a short label containing only letters, numbers, underscores, or hyphens. We will use the `slug` field to build beautiful, SEO-friendly URLs for our blog posts. We have added the `unique_for_date` parameter to this field so we can build URLs for posts using the date and slug of the post. Django will prevent from multiple posts having the same slug for the same date.

- `author`: This field is `ForeignKey`. This field defines a many-to-one relationship. We are telling Django that each post is written by a user and a user can write several posts. For this field, Django will create a foreign key in the database using the primary key of the related model. In this case, we are relying on the `User` model of the Django authentication system. We specify the name of the reverse relationship, from `User` to `Post`, with the `related_name` attribute. We are going to learn more about this later.

- `body`: This is the body of the post. This field is `TextField`, which translates into a `TEXT` column in the SQL database.

- `publish`: This datetime indicates when the post was published. We use Django's timezone `now` method as default value. This is just a timezone-aware `datetime.now`.

- `created`: This datetime indicates when the post was created. Since we are using `auto_now_add` here, the date will be saved automatically when creating an object.

- `updated`: This datetime indicates the last time the post has been updated. Since we are using `auto_now` here, the date will be updated automatically when saving an object.

- `status`: This is a field to show the status of a post. We use a `choices` parameter, so the value of this field can only be set to one of the given choices.

As you can see, Django comes with different types of fields that you can use to define your models. You can find all field types in `https://docs.djangoproject.com/en/1.8/ref/models/fields/`.

The class `Meta` inside the model contains metadata. We are telling Django to sort results by the `publish` field in descending order by default when we query the database. We specify descending order by using the negative prefix.

The \_\_str\_\_() method is the default human-readable representation of the object. Django will use it in many places such as the administration site.

 If you come from Python 2.X, note that in Python 3 all strings are natively considered unicode, therefore we only use the \_\_str\_\_() method. The \_\_unicode\_\_() method is obsolete.

Since we are going to deal with datetimes, we will install the pytz module. This module provides timezone definitions for Python and is required by SQLite to work with datetimes. Open the shell and install pytz with the following command:

```
pip install pytz
```

Django comes with support for timezone-aware datetimes. You can activate/deactivate time zone support with the USE_TZ setting in the settings.py file of your project. This setting is set to True when you create a new project using the startproject management command.

# Activating your application

In order for Django to keep track of our application and be able to create database tables for its models, we have to activate it. To do this, edit the settings.py file and add blog to the INSTALLED_APPS setting. It should look like this:

```
INSTALLED_APPS = (
    'django.contrib.admin',
    'django.contrib.auth',
    'django.contrib.contenttypes',
    'django.contrib.sessions',
    'django.contrib.messages',
    'django.contrib.staticfiles',
    'blog',
)
```

Now Django knows that our application is active for this project and will be able to introspect its models.

# Creating and applying migrations

Let's create a data table for our model in the database. Django comes with a migration system to track the changes you do to your models and propagate them into the database. The migrate command applies migrations for all applications listed in INSTALLED_APPS; it synchronizes the database with the current models and migrations.

First, we need to create a migration for the new model we just created. From the root directory of your project, enter this command:

```
python manage.py makemigrations blog
```

You should get the following output:

```
Migrations for 'blog':
  0001_initial.py:
    - Create model Post
```

Django just created a file `0001_initial.py` inside the migrations directory of the `blog` application. You can open that file to see how a migration looks like.

Let's take a look at the SQL code that Django will execute in the database to create the table for our model. The `sqlmigrate` command takes migration names and returns their SQL without running it. Run the following command to inspect its output:

```
python manage.py sqlmigrate blog 0001
```

The output should look as follows:

```
BEGIN;
CREATE TABLE "blog_post" ("id" integer NOT NULL PRIMARY KEY
AUTOINCREMENT, "title" varchar(250) NOT NULL, "slug" varchar(250) NOT
NULL, "body" text NOT NULL, "publish" datetime NOT NULL, "created"
datetime NOT NULL, "updated" datetime NOT NULL, "status" varchar(10)
NOT NULL, "author_id" integer NOT NULL REFERENCES "auth_user" ("id"));
CREATE INDEX "blog_post_2dbcba41" ON "blog_post" ("slug");
CREATE INDEX "blog_post_4f331e2f" ON "blog_post" ("author_id");
COMMIT;
```

The exact output depends on the database you are using. The output above is generated for SQLite. As you can see, Django generates the table names by combining the app name and the lowercase name of the model (`blog_post`), but you can also specify them in the `Meta` class of the models using the `db_table` attribute. Django creates a primary key automatically for each model but you can also override this specifying `primary_key=True` on one of your model fields.

Let's sync our database with the new model. Run the following command to apply existing migrations:

```
python manage.py migrate
```

You will get the following output that ends with the following line:

```
Applying blog.0001_initial... OK
```

We just applied migrations for the applications listed in INSTALLED_APPS, including our blog application. After applying migrations, the database reflects the current status of our models.

If you edit your models.py file in order to add, remove, or change fields of existing models, or if you add new models, you will have to make a new migration using the makemigrations command. The migration will allow Django to keep track of model changes. Then you will have to apply it with the migrate command to keep the database in sync with your models.

# Creating an administration site for your models

Now that we have defined the Post model, we will create a simple administration site to manage blog posts. Django comes with a built-in administration interface that is very useful for editing content. The Django admin site is built dynamically by reading your model metadata and providing a production-ready interface for editing content. You can use it out-of-the-box, configuring how you want your models to be displayed in it.

Remember that django.contrib.admin is already included in the INSTALLED_APPS setting of our project and that's why we don't have to add it.

## Creating a superuser

First, we need to create a user to manage the admin site. Run the following command:

```
python manage.py createsuperuser
```

You will see the following output. Enter your desired username, e-mail, and password:

```
Username (leave blank to use 'admin'): admin
Email address: admin@admin.com
Password: ********
Password (again): ********
Superuser created successfully.
```

# The Django administration site

Now, start the development server with the command `python manage.py runserver` and open `http://127.0.0.1:8000/admin/` in your browser. You should see the administration login page, as shown in the following screenshot:

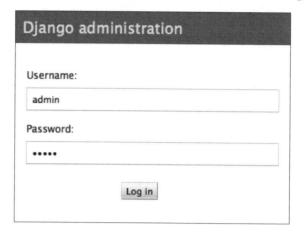

Log in using the credentials of the user you created in the previous step. You will see the admin site index page, as shown in the following screenshot:

The `Group` and `User` models you see here are part of the Django authentication framework located in `django.contrib.auth`. If you click on **Users**, you will see the user you created before. The `Post` model of your `blog` application has a relationship with this `User` model. Remember, it is a relationship defined by the `author` field.

# Adding your models to the administration site

Let's add your blog models to the administration site. Edit the `admin.py` file of your `blog` application and make it look like this:

```
from django.contrib import admin
from .models import Post

admin.site.register(Post)
```

Now, reload the admin site in your browser. You should see your `Post` model in the admin site as follows:

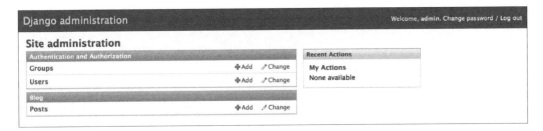

That was easy, right? When you register a model in the Django admin site, you get a user-friendly interface generated by introspecting your models that allows you to list, edit, create, and delete objects in a simple way.

Click on the **Add** link on the right of **Posts** to add a new post. You will see the create form that Django has generated dynamically for your model, as shown in the following screenshot:

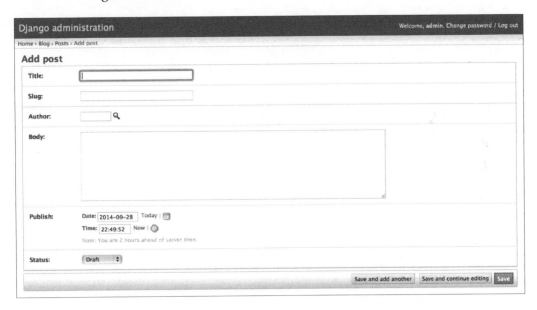

Django uses different form widgets for each type of field. Even complex fields such as `DateTimeField` are displayed with an easy interface like a JavaScript date picker.

Fill in the form and click on the **Save** button. You should be redirected to the post list page with a successful message and the post you just created, as shown in the following screenshot:

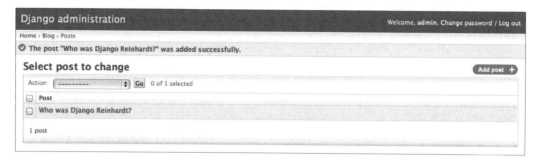

# Customizing the way models are displayed

Now we are going to see how to customize the admin site. Edit the admin.py file of your blog application and change it into this:

```python
from django.contrib import admin
from .models import Post

class PostAdmin(admin.ModelAdmin):
    list_display = ('title', 'slug', 'author', 'publish',
                    'status')
admin.site.register(Post, PostAdmin)
```

We are telling the Django admin site that our model is registered into the admin site using a custom class that inherits from ModelAdmin. In this class, we can include information about how to display the model in the admin site and how to interact with it. The list_display attribute allows you to set the fields of your model that you want to display in the admin object list page.

Let's customize the admin model with some more options, using the following code:

```python
class PostAdmin(admin.ModelAdmin):
    list_display = ('title', 'slug', 'author', 'publish',
                    'status')
    list_filter = ('status', 'created', 'publish', 'author')
    search_fields = ('title', 'body')
    prepopulated_fields = {'slug': ('title',)}
    raw_id_fields = ('author',)
    date_hierarchy = 'publish'
    ordering = ['status', 'publish']
```

Go back to your browser and reload the post list page. Now it will look like this:

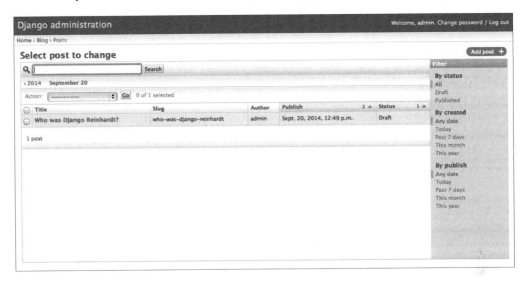

You can see that the fields displayed on the post list page are the ones you specified in the `list_display` attribute. The list page now includes a right sidebar that allows you to filter the results by the fields included in the `list_filter` attribute. A search bar has appeared on the page. This is because we have defined a list of searchable fields using the `search_fields` attribute. Just below the search bar, there is a bar to navigate quickly through a date hierarchy. This has been defined by the `date_hierarchy` attribute. You can also see that the posts are ordered by **Status** and **Publish** columns by default. You have specified the default order using the `ordering` attribute.

Now click on the **Add post** link. You will also see some changes here. As you type the title of a new post, the slug field is filled automatically. We have told Django to prepopulate the `slug` field with the input of the `title` field using the `prepopulated_fields` attribute. Also, now the `author` field is displayed with a lookup widget that can scale much better than a dropdown select input when you have thousands of users, as shown in the following screenshot:

| Author: | 1 | 🔍 admin |
|---|---|---|

With a few lines of code, we have customized the way our model is displayed in the admin site. There are plenty of ways to customize and extend the Django administration site. Later in this book, we will cover this further.

# Working with QuerySet and managers

Now that you have a fully functional administration site to manage your blog's content, it's time to learn how to retrieve information from the database and interact with it. Django comes with a powerful database-abstraction API that lets you create, retrieve, update, and delete objects easily. The Django **Object-relational Mapper (ORM)** is compatible with MySQL, PostgreSQL, SQLite, and Oracle. Remember that you can define the database of your project by editing the DATABASES setting in the settings.py file of your project. Django can work with multiple databases at a time and you can even program database routers that handle the data in any way you like.

Once you have created your data models, Django gives you a free API to interact with them. You can find the data model reference of the official documentation at https://docs.djangoproject.com/en/1.8/ref/models/.

## Creating objects

Open the terminal and run the following command to open the Python shell:

```
python manage.py shell
```

Then type the following lines:

```
>>> from django.contrib.auth.models import User
>>> from blog.models import Post
>>> user = User.objects.get(username='admin')
>>> Post.objects.create(title='One more post',
                slug='one-more-post',
                body='Post body.',
                author=user)
>>> post.save()
```

Let's analyze what this code does. First, we retrieve the user object that has the username admin:

```
user = User.objects.get(username='admin')
```

The get() method allows you to retrieve a single object from the database. Note that this method expects one result that matches the query. If no results are returned by the database, this method will raise a DoesNotExist exception, and if the database returns more than one result, it will raise a MultipleObjectsReturned exception. Both exceptions are attributes of the model class that the query is being performed on.

Then we create a `Post` instance with a custom title, slug, and body; and we set the user we previously retrieved as author of the post:

```
post = Post(title='Another post', slug='another-post', body='Post
body.', author=user)
```

 This object is in memory and is not persisted to the database.

Finally, we save the `Post` object to the database using the `save()` method:

```
post.save()
```

This action performs an INSERT SQL statement behind the scenes. We have seen how to create an object in memory first and then persist it to the database, but we can also create the object into the database directly using the `create()` method as follows:

```
Post.objects.create(title='One more post', slug='one-more-post',
body='Post body.', author=user)
```

# Updating objects

Now, change the title of the post into something different and save the object again:

```
>>> post.title = 'New title'
>>> post.save()
```

This time, the `save()` method performs an UPDATE SQL statement.

 The changes you make to the object are not persisted to the database until you call the `save()` method.

# Retrieving objects

The Django **Object-relational mapping (ORM)** is based on QuerySet. A QuerySet is a collection of objects from your database that can have several filters to limit the results. You already know how to retrieve a single object from the database using the `get()` method. As you have seen, we have accessed this method using `Post.objects.get()`. Each Django model has at least one manager, and the default manager is called `objects`. You get a `QuerySet` object by using your models manager. To retrieve all objects from a table, you just use the `all()` method on the default `objects` manager, like this:

```
>>> all_posts = Post.objects.all()
```

This is how we create a QuerySet that returns all objects in the database. Note that this QuerySet has not been executed yet. Django QuerySets are *lazy*; they are only evaluated when they are forced to do it. This behavior makes QuerySets very efficient. If we don't set the QuerySet to a variable, but instead write it directly on the Python shell, the SQL statement of the QuerySet is executed because we force it to output results:

```
>>> Post.objects.all()
```

## Using the filter() method

To filter a QuerySet, you can use the `filter()` method of the manager. For example, we can retrieve all posts published in the year 2015 using the following QuerySet:

```
Post.objects.filter(publish__year=2015)
```

You can also filter by multiple fields. For example, we can retrieve all posts published in 2015 by the author with the username `admin`:

```
Post.objects.filter(publish__year=2015, author__username='admin')
```

This equals to building the same QuerySet chaining multiple filters:

```
Post.objects.filter(publish__year=2015)\
        filter(author__username='admin')
```

 We are building queries with field lookup methods using two underscores (`publish__year`), but we are also accessing fields of related models using two underscores (`author__username`).

## Using exclude()

You can exclude certain results from your QuerySet using the `exclude()` method of the manager. For example, we can retrieve all posts published in 2015 whose titles don't start by `Why`:

```
Post.objects.filter(publish__year=2015)\
        .exclude(title__startswith='Why')
```

## Using order_by()

You can order results by different fields using the `order_by()` method of the manager. For example, you can retrieve all objects ordered by their title:

```
Post.objects.order_by('title')
```

Ascending order is implied. You can indicate descending order with a negative sign prefix, like this:

```
Post.objects.order_by('-title')
```

# Deleting objects

If you want to delete an object, you can do it from the object instance:

```
post = Post.objects.get(id=1)
post.delete()
```

 Note that deleting objects will also delete any dependent relationships.

# When QuerySet are evaluated

You can concatenate as many filters as you like to a QuerySet and you will not hit the database until the QuerySet is evaluated. Querysets are only evaluated in the following cases:

- The first time you iterate over them
- When you slice them. for instance: `Post.objects.all()[:3]`
- When you pickle or cache them
- When you call `repr()` or `len()` on them
- When you explicitly call `list()` on them
- When you test it in a statement such as `bool()`, `or` , `and`, or `if`

# Creating model managers

As we previously mentioned, `objects` is the default manager of every model, which retrieves all objects in the database. But we can also define custom managers for our models. We are going to create a custom manager to retrieve all posts with `published` status.

There are two ways to add managers to your models: You can add extra manager methods or modify initial manager QuerySets. The first one turns up something like `Post.objects.my_manager()` and the later like `Post.my_manager.all()`. Our manager will allow us to retrieve posts using `Post.published`.

Edit the `models.py` file of your `blog` application to add the custom manager:

```python
class PublishedManager(models.Manager):
    def get_queryset(self):
        return super(PublishedManager,
                     self).get_queryset()\
                          .filter(status='published')

class Post(models.Model):
    # ...
    objects = models.Manager() # The default manager.
    published = PublishedManager() # Our custom manager.
```

`get_queryset()` is the method that returns the QuerySet to be executed. We use it to include our custom filter in the final QuerySet. We have defined our custom manager and added it to the `Post` model; we can now use it to perform queries. For example, we can retrieve all published posts whose title starts with `Who` using:

```python
Post.published.filter(title__startswith='Who')
```

# Building list and detail views

Now that you have some knowledge about how to use the ORM, you are ready to build the views of the blog application. A Django view is just a Python function that receives a web request and returns a web response. Inside the view goes all the logic to return the desired response.

First, we will create our application views, then we will define an URL pattern for each view; and finally, we will create HTML templates to render the data generated by the views. Each view will render a template passing variables to it and will return an HTTP response with the rendered output.

# Creating list and detail views

Let's start by creating a view to display the list of posts. Edit the `views.py` file of your `blog` application and make it look like this:

```python
from django.shortcuts import render, get_object_or_404
from .models import Post

def post_list(request):
    posts = Post.published.all()
    return render(request,
                  'blog/post/list.html',
                  {'posts': posts})
```

You just created your first Django view. The `post_list` view takes the `request` object as the only parameter. Remember that this parameter is required by all views. In this view, we are retrieving all the posts with the `published` status using the `published` manager we created previously.

Finally, we are using the `render()` shortcut provided by Django to render the list of posts with the given template. This function takes the `request` object as parameter, the template path and the variables to render the given template. It returns an `HttpResponse` object with the rendered text (normally HTML code). The `render()` shortcut takes the request context into account, so any variable set by template context processors is accessible by the given template. Template context processors are just callables that set variables into the context. You will learn how to use them in *Chapter 3, Extending Your Blog* Application.

Let's create a second view to display a single post. Add the following function to the `views.py` file:

```
def post_detail(request, year, month, day, post):
    post = get_object_or_404(Post, slug=post,
                                   status='published',
                                   publish__year=year,
                                   publish__month=month,
                                   publish__day=day)
    return render(request,
                  'blog/post/detail.html',
                  {'post': post})
```

This is the post detail view. This view takes `year`, `month`, `day`, and `post` parameters to retrieve a published post with the given slug and date. Notice that when we created the `Post` model, we added the `unique_for_date` parameter to the `slug` field. This way we ensure that there will be only one post with a slug for a given date, and thus, we can retrieve single posts by date and slug. In the detail view, we are using the `get_object_or_404()` shortcut to retrieve the desired `Post`. This function retrieves the object that matches with the given parameters, or launches an HTTP 404 (Not found) exception if no object is found. Finally, we use the `render()` shortcut to render the retrieved post using a template.

# Adding URL patterns for your views

An URL pattern is composed of a Python regular expression, a view, and a name that allows you to name it project-wide. Django runs through each URL pattern and stops at the first one that matches the requested URL. Then, Django imports the view of the matching URL pattern and executes it, passing an instance of the `HttpRequest` class and keyword or positional arguments.

If you haven't worked with regular expressions before, you might want to take a look at `https://docs.python.org/3/howto/regex.html` first.

Create an `urls.py` file in the directory of the `blog` application and add the following lines:

```
from django.conf.urls import url
from . import views

urlpatterns = [
    # post views
    url(r'^$', views.post_list, name='post_list'),
    url(r'^(?P<year>\d{4})/(?P<month>\d{2})/(?P<day>\d{2})/'\
        r'(?P<post>[-\w]+)/$',
        views.post_detail,
        name='post_detail'),
]
```

The first URL pattern doesn't take any arguments and is mapped to the `post_list` view. The second pattern takes the following four arguments and is mapped to the `post_detail` view. Let's take a look at the regular expression of the URL pattern:

- `year`: Requires four digits.
- `month`: Requires two digits. We will only allow months with leading zeros.
- `day`: Requires two digits. We will only allow days with leading zeros.
- `post`: Can be composed by words and hyphens.

 Creating an `urls.py` file for each app is the best way to make your applications reusable by other projects.

Now you have to include the URL patterns of your blog application into the main URL patterns of the project. Edit the `urls.py` file located in the `mysite` directory of your project and make it look like the following:

```
from django.conf.urls import include, url
from django.contrib import admin

urlpatterns = [
    url(r'^admin/', include(admin.site.urls)),
    url(r'^blog/', include('blog.urls',
                    namespace='blog',
                    app_name='blog')),
]
```

This way, you are telling Django to include the URL patterns defined in the blog urls.py under the blog/ path. You are giving them a namespace called blog so you can refer to this group of URLs easily.

# Canonical URLs for models

You can use the post_detail URL that you have defined in the previous section to build the canonical URL for Post objects. The convention in Django is to add a get_absolute_url() method to the model that returns the canonical URL of the object. For this method, we will use the reverse() method that allows you to build URLs by their name and passing optional parameters. Edit your models.py file and add the following:

```
from django.core.urlresolvers import reverse
Class Post(models.Model):
    # ...
    def get_absolute_url(self):
        return reverse('blog:post_detail',
                    args=[self.publish.year,
                        self.publish.strftime('%m'),
                        self.publish.strftime('%d'),
                        self.slug])
```

Note that we are using the strftime() function to build the URL using month and day with leading zeros. We will use the get_absolute_url() method in our templates.

# Creating templates for your views

We have created views and URL patterns for our application. Now it's time to add templates to display posts in a user-friendly way.

Create the following directories and files inside your blog application directory:

```
templates/
    blog/
        base.html
        post/
            list.html
            detail.html
```

This will be the file structure for our templates. The `base.html` file will include the main HTML structure of the website and divide the content into a main content area and a sidebar. The `list.html` and `detail.html` files will inherit from the `base.html` file to render the blog post list and detail views respectively.

Django has a powerful template language that allows you to specify how data is displayed. It is based on template tags, which look like `{% tag %}` template variables, which look like `{{ variable }}` and template filters, which can be applied to variables and look like `{{ variable|filter }}`. You can see all built-in template tags and filters in `https://docs.djangoproject.com/en/1.8/ref/templates/builtins/`.

Let's edit the `base.html` file and add the following code:

```
{% load staticfiles %}
<!DOCTYPE html>
<html>
<head>
  <title>{% block title %}{% endblock %}</title>
  <link href="{% static "css/blog.css" %}" rel="stylesheet">
</head>
<body>
  <div id="content">
    {% block content %}
    {% endblock %}
  </div>
  <div id="sidebar">
    <h2>My blog</h2>
      <p>This is my blog.</p>
  </div>
</body>
</html>
```

`{% load staticfiles %}` tells Django to load the `staticfiles` template tags that are provided by the `django.contrib.staticfiles` application. After loading it, you are able to use the `{% static %}` template filter throughout this template. With this template filter, you can include static files such as the `blog.css` file that you will find in the code of this example, under the `static/` directory of the blog application. Copy this directory into the same location of your project to use the existing static files.

You can see that there are two {% block %} tags. These tell Django that we want to define a block in that area. Templates that inherit from this template can fill the blocks with content. We have defined a block called title and a block called content.

Let's edit the post/list.html file and make it look like the following:

```
{% extends "blog/base.html" %}

{% block title %}My Blog{% endblock %}

{% block content %}
  <h1>My Blog</h1>
  {% for post in posts %}
    <h2>
      <a href="{{ post.get_absolute_url }}">
        {{ post.title }}
      </a>
    </h2>
    <p class="date">
      Published {{ post.publish }} by {{ post.author }}
    </p>
    {{ post.body|truncatewords:30|linebreaks }}
  {% endfor %}
{% endblock %}
```

With the {% extends %} template tag, we are telling Django to inherit from the blog/base.html template. Then we are filling the title and content blocks of the base template with content. We iterate through the posts and display their title, date, author, and body, including a link in the title to the canonical URL of the post. In the body of the post, we are applying two template filters: truncatewords truncates the value to the number of words specified, and linebreaks converts the output into HTML line breaks. You can concatenate as many template filters as you wish; each one will be applied to the output generated by the previous one.

Open the shell and execute the command `python manage.py runserver` to start the development server. Open `http://127.0.0.1:8000/blog/` in your browser and you will see everything running. Note that you need to have some posts with status **Published** in order to see them here. You should see something like this:

Then, let's edit the `post/detail.html` file and make it look like the following:

```
{% extends "blog/base.html" %}

{% block title %}{{ post.title }}{% endblock %}

{% block content %}
  <h1>{{ post.title }}</h1>
  <p class="date">
    Published {{ post.publish }} by {{ post.author }}
  </p>
  {{ post.body|linebreaks }}
{% endblock %}
```

Now, you can go back to your browser and click on one of the post titles to see the detail view of a post. You should see something like this:

Take a look at the URL. It should look like /blog/2015/09/20/who-was-django-reinhardt/. We have created a SEO friendly URL for our blog posts.

# Adding pagination

When you start adding content to your blog, you will soon realize you need to split the list of posts across several pages. Django has a built-in pagination class that allows you to manage paginated data easily.

Edit the views.py file of the blog application to import the Django paginator classes and modify the post_list view as follows:

```
from django.core.paginator import Paginator, EmptyPage,\
                                  PageNotAnInteger


def post_list(request):
    object_list = Post.published.all()
    paginator = Paginator(object_list, 3) # 3 posts in each page
    page = request.GET.get('page')
    try:
        posts = paginator.page(page)
    except PageNotAnInteger:
        # If page is not an integer deliver the first page
        posts = paginator.page(1)
    except EmptyPage:
        # If page is out of range deliver last page of results
        posts = paginator.page(paginator.num_pages)
    return render(request,
                  'blog/post/list.html',
                  {'page': page,
                   'posts': posts})
```

This is how pagination works:

1. We instantiate the `Paginator` class with the number of objects we want to display in each page.

2. We get the `page` GET parameter that indicates the current page number.

3. We obtain the objects for the desired page calling the `page()` method of `Paginator`.

4. If the `page` parameter is not an integer, we retrieve the first page of results. If this parameter is a number higher than the last page of results, we retrieve the last page.

5. We pass the page number and retrieved objects to the template.

Now, we have to create a template to display the paginator, so that it can be included in any template that uses pagination. In the templates folder of the `blog` application, create a new file and name it `pagination.html`. Add the following HTML code to the file:

```html
<div class="pagination">
  <span class="step-links">
    {% if page.has_previous %}
      <a href="?page={{ page.previous_page_number }}">Previous</a>
    {% endif %}
    <span class="current">
      Page {{ page.number }} of {{ page.paginator.num_pages }}.
    </span>
      {% if page.has_next %}
        <a href="?page={{ page.next_page_number }}">Next</a>
      {% endif %}
  </span>
</div>
```

The pagination template expects a `Page` object in order to render previous and next links and display the current page and total pages of results. Let's go back to the `blog/post/list.html` template and include the `pagination.html` template at the bottom of the `{% content %}` block, like this:

```html
{% block content %}
  . . .
    {% include "pagination.html" with page=posts %}
{% endblock %}
```

Since the `Page` object we are passing to the template is called `posts`, we are including the pagination template into the post list template specifying the parameters to render it correctly. This is the method you can use to reuse your pagination template in paginated views of different models.

Now, open `http://127.0.0.1:8000/blog/` in your browser. You should see the pagination at the bottom of the post list and you should be able to navigate through pages:

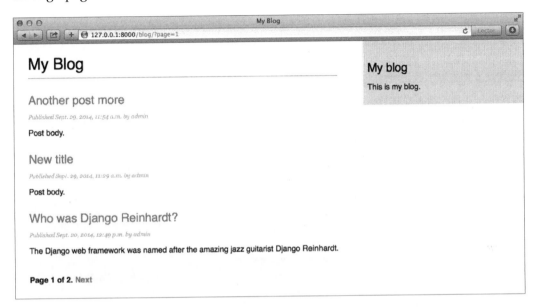

# Using class-based views

Since a view is a callable that takes a web request and returns a web response, you can also define your views as class methods. Django provides base view classes for this. All of them inherit from the `View` class, which handles HTTP method dispatching and other functionality. This is an alternate method to create your views.

We are going to change our `post_list` view into a class-based view to use the generic `ListView` offered by Django. This base view allows you to list objects of any kind.

Edit the `views.py` file of your `blog` application and add the following code:

```
from django.views.generic import ListView

class PostListView(ListView):
    queryset = Post.published.all()
    context_object_name = 'posts'
    paginate_by = 3
    template_name = 'blog/post/list.html'
```

This class-based view is analogous to the previous `post_list` view. Here, we are telling `ListView` to:

- Use a specific QuerySet instead of retrieving all objects. Instead of defining a `queryset` attribute, we could have specified `model = Post` and Django would have built the generic `Post.objects.all()` QuerySet for us.

- Use the context variable `posts` for the query results. The default variable is `object_list` if we don't specify any `context_object_name`.

- Paginate the result displaying three objects per page.

- Use a custom template to render the page. If we don't set a default template, `ListView` will use `blog/post_list.html`.

Now, open the `urls.py` file of your `blog` application, comment the previous `post_list` URL pattern, and add a new URL pattern using the `PostListView` class as follows:

```
urlpatterns = [
    # post views
    # url(r'^$', views.post_list, name='post_list'),
    url(r'^$', views.PostListView.as_view(), name='post_list'),
    url(r'^(?P<year>\d{4})/(?P<month>\d{2})/(?P<day>\d{2})/'\
        r'(?P<post>[-\w]+)/$',
        views.post_detail,
        name='post_detail'),
]
```

In order to keep pagination working, we have to use the right page object that is passed to the template. Django's `ListView` passes the selected page in a variable called `page_obj`, so you have to edit your `post_list.html` template accordingly to include the paginator using the right variable, like this:

```
{% include "pagination.html" with page=page_obj %}
```

Open `http://127.0.0.1:8000/blog/` in your browser and check that everything works the same way as with the previous `post_list` view. This is a simple example of a class-based view that uses a generic class provided by Django. You will learn more about class-based views in *Chapter 10, Building an e-Learning Platform* and successive chapters.

# Summary

In this chapter, you have learned the basics of the Django web framework by creating a basic blog application. You have designed the data models and applied migrations to your project. You have created the views, templates, and URLs for your blog, including object pagination.

In the next chapter, you will learn how to enhance your blog application with a comment system, tagging functionality, and allowing your users to share posts by e-mail.

# 2

# Enhancing Your Blog with Advanced Features

In the previous chapter, you created a basic blog application. Now you will turn your application into a fully functional blog with advanced features such as sharing posts by e-mail, adding comments, tagging posts, and retrieving posts by similarity. In this chapter, you will learn the following topics:

- Sending e-mails with Django
- Creating forms and handling them in views
- Creating forms from models
- Integrating third-party applications
- Building complex QuerySets

## Sharing posts by e-mail

First, we will allow users to share posts by sending them by e-mail. Take a short time to think how you would use **views**, **URL's**, and **templates** to create this functionality using what you have learned in the previous chapter. Now, check what you need to allow your users to send posts by e-mail. You will need to:

- Create a form for users to fill in their name and e-mail, the e-mail recipient, and optional comments
- Create a view in the `views.py` file that handles the posted data and sends the e-mail
- Add an URL pattern for the new view in the `urls.py` file of the blog application
- Create a template to display the form

# Creating forms with Django

Let's start by building the form to share posts. Django has a built-in forms framework that allows you to create forms in an easy manner. The forms framework allows you to define the fields of your form, specify the way they have to be displayed, and indicate how they have to validate input data. Django forms framework also offers a flexible way to render forms and handle the data.

Django comes with two base classes to build forms:

- `Form`: Allows you to build standard forms
- `ModelForm`: Allows you to build forms to create or update model instances

First, create a `forms.py` file inside the directory of your `blog` application and make it look like this:

```python
from django import forms

class EmailPostForm(forms.Form):
    name = forms.CharField(max_length=25)
    email = forms.EmailField()
    to = forms.EmailField()
    comments = forms.CharField(required=False,
                               widget=forms.Textarea)
```

This is your first Django form. Take a look at the code: we have created a form by inheriting the base `Form` class. We use different field types for Django to validate fields accordingly.

 Forms can reside anywhere in your Django project but the convention is to place them inside a `forms.py` file for each application.

The `name` field is a `CharField`. This type of field is rendered as an `<input type="text">` HTML element. Each field type has a default widget that determines how the field is displayed in HTML. The default widget can be overridden with the `widget` attribute. In the `comments` field, we use a `Textarea` widget to display it as a `<textarea>` HTML element instead of the default `<input>` element.

Field validation also depends on the field type. For example, the email and to fields are EmailField. Both fields require a valid e-mail address, otherwise the field validation will raise a forms.ValidationError exception and the form will not validate. Other parameters are also taken into account for form validation: we define a maximum length of 25 characters for the name field and make the comments field optional with required=False. All of this is also taken into account for field validation. The field types used in this form are only a part of Django form fields. For a list of all form fields available, you can visit https://docs.djangoproject.com/en/1.8/ref/forms/fields/.

# Handling forms in views

You have to create a new view that handles the form and sends an e-mail when it's successfully submitted. Edit the views.py file of your blog application and add the following code to it:

```
from .forms import EmailPostForm

def post_share(request, post_id):
    # Retrieve post by id
    post = get_object_or_404(Post, id=post_id, status='published')

    if request.method == 'POST':
        # Form was submitted
        form = EmailPostForm(request.POST)
        if form.is_valid():
            # Form fields passed validation
            cd = form.cleaned_data
            # ... send email
    else:
        form = EmailPostForm()
    return render(request, 'blog/post/share.html', {'post': post,
                                                    'form': form})
```

This view works as follows:

- We define the `post_share` view that takes the `request` object and the `post_id` as parameters.

- We use the `get_object_or_404()` shortcut to retrieve the post by ID and make sure the retrieved post has a `published` status.

- We use the same view for both displaying the initial form and processing the submitted data. We differentiate if the form was submitted or not based on the request method. We are going to submit the form using POST. We assume that if we get a GET request, an empty form has to be displayed, and if we get a POST request, the form was submitted and needs to be processed. Therefore, we use `request.method == 'POST'` to distinguish between the two scenarios.

The following is the process to display and handle the form:

1. When the view is loaded initially with a GET request, we create a new form instance that will be used to display the empty form in the template:

   ```
   form = EmailPostForm()
   ```

2. The user fills in the form and submits it via POST. Then, we create a form instance using the submitted data that is contained in `request.POST`:

   ```
   if request.method == 'POST':
       # Form was submitted
       form = EmailPostForm(request.POST)
   ```

3. After this, we validate the submitted data using the form's `is_valid()` method. This method validates the data introduced in the form and returns `True` if all fields contain valid data. If any field contains invalid data, then `is_valid()` returns `False`. You can see a list of validation errors by accessing `form.errors`.

4. If the form is not valid, we render the form in the template again with the submitted data. We will display validation errors in the template.

5. If the form is valid, we retrieve the validated data accessing `form.cleaned_data`. This attribute is a dictionary of form fields and their values.

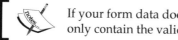 If your form data does not validate, `cleaned_data` will only contain the valid fields.

Now, you need to learn how to send e-mails with Django to put everything together.

# Sending e-mails with Django

Sending e-mails with Django is pretty straightforward. First, you need to have a local SMTP server or define the configuration of an external SMTP server by adding the following settings in the `settings.py` file of your project:

- `EMAIL_HOST`: The SMTP server host. Default `localhost`.
- `EMAIL_PORT`: The SMTP port Default 25.
- `EMAIL_HOST_USER`: Username for the SMTP server.
- `EMAIL_HOST_PASSWORD`: Password for the SMTP server.
- `EMAIL_USE_TLS`: Whether to use a TLS secure connection.
- `EMAIL_USE_SSL`: Whether to use an implicit TLS secure connection.

If you don't have a local SMTP server, you can probably use the SMTP server of your e-mail provider. The sample configuration below is valid for sending e-mails via Gmail servers using a Google account:

```
EMAIL_HOST = 'smtp.gmail.com'
EMAIL_HOST_USER = 'your_account@gmail.com'
EMAIL_HOST_PASSWORD = 'your_password'
EMAIL_PORT = 587
EMAIL_USE_TLS = True
```

Run the command `python manage.py shell` to open the Python shell and send an e-mail like this:

```
>>> from django.core.mail import send_mail
>>> send_mail('Django mail', 'This e-mail was sent with Django.',
'your_account@gmail.com', ['your_account@gmail.com'], fail_
silently=False)
```

`send_mail()` takes the subject, message, sender, and list of recipients as required arguments. By setting the optional argument `fail_silently=False`, we are telling it to raise an exception if the e-mail couldn't be sent correctly. If the output you see is `1`, then your e-mail was successfully sent. If you are sending e-mails by Gmail with the preceding configuration, you might have to enable access for less secured apps at `https://www.google.com/settings/security/lesssecureapps`.

Now, we are going to add this to our view. Edit the `post_share` view in the `views.py` file of your `blog` application and make it look like this:

```
from django.core.mail import send_mail


def post_share(request, post_id):
    # Retrieve post by id
```

```
post = get_object_or_404(Post, id=post_id, status='published')
sent = False

if request.method == 'POST':
    # Form was submitted
    form = EmailPostForm(request.POST)
    if form.is_valid():
        # Form fields passed validation
        cd = form.cleaned_data
        post_url = request.build_absolute_uri(
                                 post.get_absolute_url())
        subject = '{} ({}) recommends you reading "{}"'.
format(cd['name'], cd['email'], post.title)
        message = 'Read "{}" at {}\n\n{}\'s comments: {}'.
format(post.title, post_url, cd['name'], cd['comments'])
        send_mail(subject, message, 'admin@myblog.com',
[cd['to']])
        sent = True
else:
    form = EmailPostForm()
return render(request, 'blog/post/share.html', {'post': post,
                                                'form': form,
                                                'sent': sent})
```

Note that we declare a `sent` variable and set it to `True` when the post was sent. We are going to use that variable later in the template to display a success message when the form is successfully submitted. Since we have to include a link to the post in the e-mail, we retrieve the absolute path of the post using its `get_absolute_url()` method. We use this path as input for `request.build_absolute_uri()` to build a complete URL including HTTP schema and hostname. We build the subject and the message body of the e-mail using the cleaned data of the validated form and finally send the e-mail to the e-mail address contained in the `to` field of the form.

Now that your view is complete, remember to add a new URL pattern for it. Open the `urls.py` file of your `blog` application and add the `post_share` URL pattern, as follows:

```
urlpatterns = [
    # ...
    url(r'^(?P<post_id>\d+)/share/$', views.post_share,
        name='post_share'),
]
```

# Rendering forms in templates

After creating the form, programming the view, and adding the URL pattern, we are only missing the template for this view. Create a new file into the `blog/templates/blog/post/` directory and name it `share.html`. Add the following code to it:

```
{% extends "blog/base.html" %}

{% block title %}Share a post{% endblock %}

{% block content %}
  {% if sent %}
    <h1>E-mail successfully sent</h1>
    <p>
      "{{ post.title }}" was successfully sent to {{ cd.to }}.
    </p>
  {% else %}
    <h1>Share "{{ post.title }}" by e-mail</h1>
    <form action="." method="post">
      {{ form.as_p }}
      {% csrf_token %}
      <input type="submit" value="Send e-mail">
    </form>
  {% endif %}
{% endblock %}
```

This is the template to display the form or a success message when it's sent. As you can see, we create the HTML form element indicating that it has to be submitted by the POST method:

```
<form action="." method="post">
```

Then we include the actual form instance. We tell Django to render its fields in HTML paragraph `<p>` elements with the as_p method. We can also render the form as an unordered list with `as_ul` or as a HTML table with `as_table`. If we want to render each field, we can also iterate through the fields like in the following example:

```
{% for field in form %}
  <div>
    {{ field.errors }}
    {{ field.label_tag }} {{ field }}
  </div>
{% endfor %}
```

The {% csrf_token %} template tag introduces a hidden field with an auto-generated token to avoid **Cross-Site request forgery (CSRF)** attacks. These attacks consist of a malicious website or program performing an unwanted action for a user on your site. You can find more information about this at https://en.wikipedia.org/wiki/Cross-site_request_forgery.

The preceding tag generates a hidden field that looks like this:

```
<input type='hidden' name='csrfmiddlewaretoken'
value='26JjKo2lcEtYkGoV9z4XmJIEHLXN5LDR' />
```

 By default, Django checks for the CSRF token in all POST requests. Remember to include the csrf_token tag in all forms that are submitted via POST.

Edit your blog/post/detail.html template and add a the following link to the share post URL after the {{ post.body|linebreaks }} variable:

```
<p>
  <a href="{% url "blog:post_share" post.id %}">
    Share this post
  </a>
</p>
```

Remember that we are building the URL dynamically using the {% url %} template tag provided by Django. We are using the namespace called blog and the URL named post_share, and we are passing the post ID as parameter to build the absolute URL.

Now, start the development server with the command python manage.py runserver, and open http://127.0.0.1:8000/blog/ in your browser. Click on any post title to view the detail page. Under the post body, you should see the link we just added, as shown in the following image:

## Who was Django Reinhardt?

Published Sept. 20, 2014, 12:49 p.m. by admin

The Django web framework was named after the amazing jazz guitarist Django Reinhardt.

Share this post

**My blog**

This is my blog.

Click on **Share this post** and you should see the page including the form to share this post by e-mail. It has to look like the following:

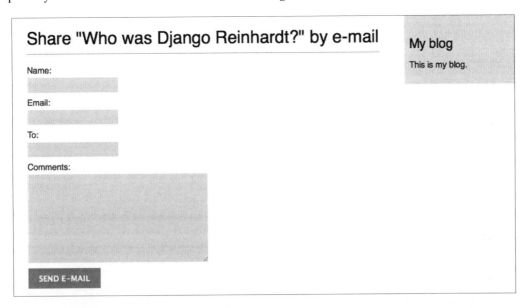

CSS styles for the form are included in the example code in the `static/css/blog.css` file. When you click on the **Send e-mail** button, the form is submitted and validated. If all fields contain valid data, you will get a success message like the following:

If you input invalid data, you will see that the form is rendered again, including all validation errors:

# Creating a comment system

Now we are going to build a comment system for the blog, wherein the users will be able to comment on posts. To build the comment system, you will need to:

- Create a model to save comments
- Create a form to submit comments and validate the input data
- Add a view that processes the form and saves the new comment into the database
- Edit the post detail template to display the list of comments and the form for adding a new comment

First, let's build a model to store comments. Open the `models.py` file of your `blog` application and add the following code:

```python
class Comment(models.Model):
    post = models.ForeignKey(Post, related_name='comments')
    name = models.CharField(max_length=80)
    email = models.EmailField()
    body = models.TextField()
    created = models.DateTimeField(auto_now_add=True)
    updated = models.DateTimeField(auto_now=True)
    active = models.BooleanField(default=True)

    class Meta:
        ordering = ('created',)

    def __str__(self):
        return 'Comment by {} on {}'.format(self.name, self.post)
```

This is our `Comment` model. It contains a `ForeignKey` to associate the comment with a single post. This many-to-one relationship is defined in the `Comment` model because each comment will be made on one post, and each post might have multiple comments. The `related_name` attribute allows us to name the attribute that we use for the relation from the related object back to this one. After defining this, we can retrieve the post of a comment object using `comment.post` and retrieve all comments of a post using `post.comments.all()`. If you don't define the `related_name` attribute, Django will use the undercase name of the model followed by _set (that is, `comment_set`) to name the manager of the related object back to this one.

You can learn more about many-to-one relationships at `https://docs. djangoproject.com/en/1.8/topics/db/examples/many_to_one/`.

We have included an `active` boolean field that we will use to manually deactivate inappropriate comments. We use the `created` field to sort comments in chronological order by default.

The new `Comment` model you just created is not yet synchronized into the database. Run the following command to generate a new migration that reflects the creation of the new model:

**python manage.py makemigrations blog**

You should see this output:

```
Migrations for 'blog':
  0002_comment.py:
    - Create model Comment
```

Django has generated a file `0002_comment.py` inside the `migrations/` directory of the `blog` application. Now, you need to create the related database schema and apply the changes to the database. Run the following command to apply existing migrations:

```
python manage.py migrate
```

You will get an output that includes the following line:

```
Applying blog.0002_comment... OK
```

The migration we just created has been applied and now a `blog_comment` table exists in the database.

Now, we can add our new model to the administration site in order to manage comments through a simple interface. Open the `admin.py` file of the `blog` application and add an import for the `Comment` model and the following `ModelAdmin`:

```python
from .models import Post, Comment

class CommentAdmin(admin.ModelAdmin):
    list_display = ('name', 'email', 'post', 'created', 'active')
    list_filter = ('active', 'created', 'updated')
    search_fields = ('name', 'email', 'body')
admin.site.register(Comment, CommentAdmin)
```

Start the development server with the command `python manage.py runserver` and open `http://127.0.0.1:8000/admin/` in your browser. You should see the new model included in the **Blog** section, as shown in the following screenshot:

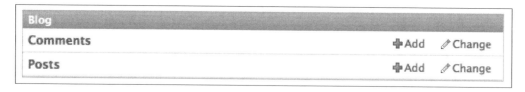

Our model is now registered into the admin site and we can manage `Comment` instances using a simple interface.

# Creating forms from models

We still need to build a form to let our users comment on blog posts. Remember that Django has two base classes to build forms: Form and ModelForm. You used the first one previously to let your users share posts by e-mail. In the present case, you will need to use ModelForm because you have to build a form dynamically from your Comment model. Edit the forms.py of your blog application and add the following lines:

```
from .models import Comment

class CommentForm(forms.ModelForm):
    class Meta:
        model = Comment
        fields = ('name', 'email', 'body')
```

To create a form from a model, we just need to indicate which model to use to build the form in the Meta class of the form. Django introspects the model and builds the form dynamically for us. Each model field type has a corresponding default form field type. The way we define our model fields is taken into account for form validation. By default, Django builds a form field for each field contained in the model. However, you can explicitly tell the framework which fields you want to include in your form using a fields list, or define which fields you want to exclude using an exclude list of fields. For our CommentForm, we will just use the name, email, and body fields for the form because those are the only fields our users will be able to fill in.

# Handling ModelForms in views

We will use the post detail view to instantiate the form, and process it in order to keep it simple. Edit the models.py file, add imports for the Comment model and the CommentForm form, and modify the post_detail view to make it look like the following:

```
from .models import Post, Comment
from .forms import EmailPostForm, CommentForm

def post_detail(request, year, month, day, post):
    post = get_object_or_404(Post, slug=post,
                                   status='published',
                                   publish__year=year,
                                   publish__month=month,
                                   publish__day=day)
```

```
    # List of active comments for this post
    comments = post.comments.filter(active=True)

    if request.method == 'POST':
        # A comment was posted
        comment_form = CommentForm(data=request.POST)
        if comment_form.is_valid():
            # Create Comment object but don't save to database
yet
            new_comment = comment_form.save(commit=False)
            # Assign the current post to the comment
            new_comment.post = post
            # Save the comment to the database
            new_comment.save()
    else:
        comment_form = CommentForm()
    return render(request,
                    'blog/post/detail.html',
                    {'post': post,
                     'comments': comments,
                     'comment_form': comment_form})
```

Let's review what we have added to our view. We are using the post_detail view to display the post and its comments. We add a QuerySet to retrieve all active comments for this post:

```
comments = post.comments.filter(active=True)
```

We are building this QuerySet starting from the post object. We are using the manager for related objects we defined as comments using the related_name attribute of the relationship in the Comment model.

We also use the same view to let our users add a new comment. Therefore we build a form instance with comment_form = CommentForm() if the view is called by a GET request. If the request is done via POST, we instantiate the form using the submitted data and validate it using the is_valid() method. If the form is invalid, we render the template with the validation errors. If the form is valid, we take the following actions:

1. We create a new Comment object by calling the form's save() method like this:

```
new_comment = comment_form.save(commit=False)
```

The `save()` method creates an instance of the model that the form is linked to and saves it to the database. If you call it with `commit=False`, you create the model instance, but you don't save it to the database. This comes very handy when you want to modify the object before finally saving, which is what we do next. The `save()` method is available for `ModelForm` but not for `Form` instances, since they are not linked to any model.

2. We assign the current post to the comment we just created:

```
new_comment.post = post
```

By doing this, we are specifying that the new comment belongs to the given post.

3. Finally, we save the new comment to the database with the following code:

```
new_comment.save()
```

Our view is now ready to display and process new comments.

# Adding comments to the post detail template

We have created the functionality to manage comments for a post. Now we need to adapt our `post_detail.html` template to do the following:

- Display the total number of comments for the post
- Display the list of comments
- Display a form for users to add a new comment

First, we will add the total comments. Open the `blog_detail.html` template and append the following code inside the `content` block:

```
{% with comments.count as total_comments %}
  <h2>
    {{ total_comments }} comment{{ total_comments|pluralize }}
  </h2>
{% endwith %}
```

We are using the Django ORM in the template executing the QuerySet `comments.count()`. Note that Django template language doesn't use parentheses for calling methods. The `{% with %}` tag allows us to assign a value to a new variable that will be available to be used until the `{% endwith %}` tag.

 The `{% with %}` template tag is useful to avoid hitting the database or accessing *expensive* methods multiple times.

We use the `pluralize` template filter to display a plural suffix for the word *comment* depending on the `total_comments` value. Template filters take the value of the variable they are applied to as input and return a computed value. We will discuss template filters in *Chapter 3, Extending Your Blog Application*.

The `pluralize` template filter displays an "s" if the value is different than 1. The preceding text will be rendered as *0 comments, 1 comment,* or *N comments.* Django includes plenty of template tags and filters that help you display information in the way you want.

Now, let's include the list of comments. Append the following lines to the template after the preceding code:

```
{% for comment in comments %}
  <div class="comment">
    <p class="info">
      Comment {{ forloop.counter }} by {{ comment.name }}
      {{ comment.created }}
    </p>
    {{ comment.body|linebreaks }}
  </div>
{% empty %}
  <p>There are no comments yet.</p>
{% endfor %}
```

We use the `{% for %}` template tag to loop through comments. We display a default message if the `comments` list is empty, telling our users there are no comments for this post yet. We enumerate comments with the `{{ forloop.counter }}` variable, which contains the loop counter in each iteration. Then we display the name of the user who posted the comment, the date, and the body of the comment.

Finally, you need to render the form or display a successful message instead when it is successfully submitted. Add the following lines just below the previous code:

```
{% if new_comment %}
  <h2>Your comment has been added.</h2>
{% else %}
  <h2>Add a new comment</h2>
  <form action="." method="post">
    {{ comment_form.as_p }}
    {% csrf_token %}
    <p><input type="submit" value="Add comment"></p>
  </form>
{% endif %}
```

The code is pretty straightforward: If the `new_comment` object exists, we display a success message because the comment was successfully created. Otherwise, we render the form with a paragraph `<p>` element for each field and include the CSRF token required for POST requests. Open `http://127.0.0.1:8000/blog/` in your browser and click on a post title to see its detail page. You will see something like the following:

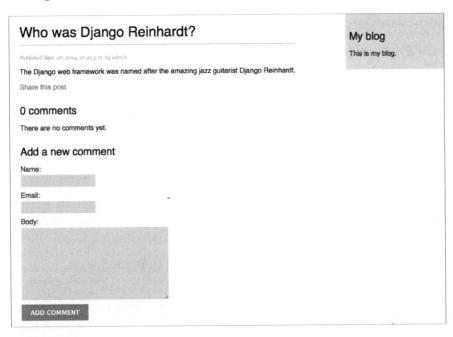

Add a couple of comments using the form. They should appear under your post in chronological order, like this:

Open `http://127.0.0.1:8000/admin/blog/comment/` in your browser. You will see the admin page with the list of comments you created. Click on one of them to edit it, uncheck the **Active** checkbox, and click the **Save** button. You will be redirected to the list of comments again and the **Active** column will display an inactive icon for the comment. It should look like the first comment in the following screenshot:

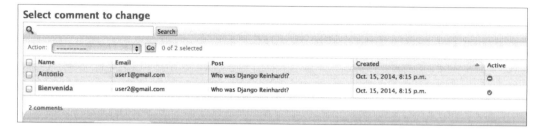

If you go back to the post detail view, you will notice that the deleted comment is not displayed anymore; neither is it being counted for the total number of comments. Thanks to the `active` field, you can deactivate inappropriate comments and avoid showing them in your posts.

# Adding tagging functionality

After implementing our comment system, we are going to create a way to tag our posts. We are going to do this by integrating a third-party Django tagging application in our project. `django-taggit` is a reusable application that primarily offers you a `Tag` model and a manager to easily add tags to any model. You can take a look at its source code at `https://github.com/alex/django-taggit`.

First, you need to install django-taggit via pip, running the following command:

**`pip install django-taggit==0.17.1`**

Then open the `settings.py` file of the `mysite` project and add `taggit` to your `INSTALLED_APPS` setting like this:

```
INSTALLED_APPS = (
    # ...
    'blog',
    'taggit',
)
```

Open the `models.py` file of your blog application and add the `TaggableManager` manager provided by django-taggit to the `Post` model using the following code:

```
from taggit.managers import TaggableManager
class Post(models.Model):
    # ...
    tags = TaggableManager()
```

The `tags` manager will allow you to add, retrieve, and remove tags from `Post` objects.

Run the following command to create a migration for your model changes:

```
python manage.py makemigrations blog
```

You should get the following output:

```
Migrations for 'blog':
  0003_post_tags.py:
    - Add field tags to post
```

Now, run the following command to create the required database tables for django-taggit models and to synchronize your model changes:

```
python manage.py migrate
```

You will see an output indicating that migrations have been applied, as follows:

```
Applying taggit.0001_initial... OK
Applying taggit.0002_auto_20150616_2121... OK
Applying blog.0003_post_tags... OK
```

Your database is now ready to use `django-taggit` models. Open the terminal with the command `python manage.py shell` and learn how to use the `tags` manager. First, we retrieve one of our posts (the one with ID 1):

```
>>> from blog.models import Post
>>> post = Post.objects.get(id=1)
```

Then add some tags to it and retrieve its tags back to check that they were successfully added:

```
>>> post.tags.add('music', 'jazz', 'django')
>>> post.tags.all()
[<Tag: jazz>, <Tag: django>, <Tag: music>]
```

Finally, remove a tag and check the list of tags again:

```
>>> post.tags.remove('django')
>>> post.tags.all()
[<Tag: jazz>, <Tag: music>]
```

That was easy, right? Run the command `python manage.py runserver` to start the development server again and open `http://127.0.0.1:8000/admin/taggit/tag/` in your browser. You will see the admin page with the list of `Tag` objects of the `taggit` application:

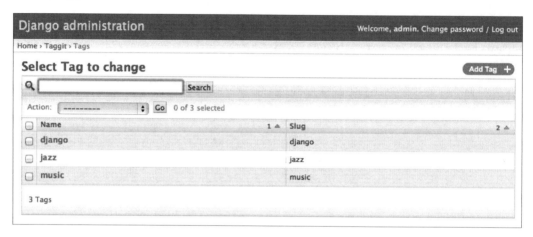

Navigate to `http://127.0.0.1:8000/admin/blog/post/` and click on a post to edit it. You will see that posts now include a new **Tags** field like the following where you can easily edit tags:

Now, we are going to edit our blog posts to display the tags. Open the `blog/post/list.html` template and add the following HTML code below the post title:

```
<p class="tags">Tags: {{ post.tags.all|join:", " }}</p>
```

The `join` template filter works as the Python string `join()` method to concatenate elements with the given string. Open `http://127.0.0.1:8000/blog/` in your browser. You should see the list of tags under each post title:

## Who was Django Reinhardt?

Tags: jazz, music

*Published Sept. 20, 2014, 12:49 p.m. by admin*

The Django web framework was named after the amazing jazz guitarist Django Reinhardt.

Now, we are going to edit our `post_list` view to let users list all posts tagged with a specific tag. Open the `views.py` file of your `blog` application, import the `Tag` model form `django-taggit`, and change the `post_list` view to optionally filter posts by tag like this:

```python
from taggit.models import Tag

def post_list(request, tag_slug=None):
    object_list = Post.published.all()
    tag = None

    if tag_slug:
        tag = get_object_or_404(Tag, slug=tag_slug)
        object_list = object_list.filter(tags__in=[tag])
    # ...
```

The view now works as follows:

1.  The view takes an optional `tag_slug` parameter that has a `None` default value. This parameter will come in the URL.

2.  Inside the view, we build the initial QuerySet, retrieving all published posts, and if there is a given tag slug, we get the `Tag` object with the given slug using the `get_object_or_404()` shortcut.

3.  Then we filter the list of posts by the ones that contain the given tag. Since this is a many-to-many relationship, we have to filter by tags contained in a given list, which in our case contains only one element.

Remember that Querysets are lazy. The QuerySets to retrieve posts will only be evaluated when we loop over the post list when rendering the template.

Finally, modify the `render()` function at the bottom of the view to pass the `tag` variable to the template The view should finally look like this:

```
def post_list(request, tag_slug=None):
    object_list = Post.published.all()
    tag = None

    if tag_slug:
        tag = get_object_or_404(Tag, slug=tag_slug)
        object_list = object_list.filter(tags__in=[tag])

    paginator = Paginator(object_list, 3) # 3 posts in each page
    page = request.GET.get('page')
    try:
        posts = paginator.page(page)
    except PageNotAnInteger:
        # If page is not an integer deliver the first page
        posts = paginator.page(1)
    except EmptyPage:
        # If page is out of range deliver last page of results
        posts = paginator.page(paginator.num_pages)
    return render(request, 'blog/post/list.html', {'page': page,
                                                    'posts': posts,
                                                    'tag': tag})
```

Open the `urls.py` file of your `blog` application, comment out the class-based `PostListView` URL pattern, and uncomment the `post_list` view like this:

```
url(r'^$', views.post_list, name='post_list'),
# url(r'^$', views.PostListView.as_view(), name='post_list'),
```

Add the following additional URL pattern to list posts by tag:

```
url(r'^tag/(?P<tag_slug>[-\w]+)/$', views.post_list,
    name='post_list_by_tag'),
```

As you can see, both patterns point to the same view, but we are naming them differently. The first pattern will call the `post_list` view without any optional parameters, while the second pattern will call the view with the `tag_slug` parameter.

Since we are using the `post_list` view, edit the `blog/post/list.html` template and modify the pagination to use the `posts` object like this:

```
{% include "pagination.html" with page=posts %}
```

Add the following lines above the {% for %} loop:

```
{% if tag %}
  <h2>Posts tagged with "{{ tag.name }}"</h2>
{% endif %}
```

If the user is accessing the blog, he will see the list of all posts. If he is filtering by posts tagged with a specific tag, he will see this information. Now, change the way tags are displayed into the following:

```
<p class="tags">
  Tags:
  {% for tag in post.tags.all %}
    <a href="{% url "blog:post_list_by_tag" tag.slug %}">
      {{ tag.name }}
    </a>
    {% if not forloop.last %}, {% endif %}
  {% endfor %}
</p>
```

Now, we loop through all the tags of a post displaying a custom link to the URL to filter posts by that tag. We build the URL with {% url "blog:post_list_by_tag" tag.slug %}, using the name of the URL and the tag slug as parameter. We separate the tags by commas.

Open http://127.0.0.1:8000/blog/ in your browser and click on any tag link. You will see the list of posts filtered by that tag like this:

## My Blog

### Posts tagged with "jazz"

### Who was Django Reinhardt?

**Tags:** jazz , music

*Published Sept. 20, 2014, 12:49 p.m. by admin*

The Django web framework was named after the amazing jazz guitarist Django Reinhardt.

**Page 1 of 1.**

# Retrieving posts by similarity

Now that we have tagging for our blog posts, we can do many interesting things with them. Using tags, we can classify our blog posts very well. Posts about similar topics will have several tags in common. We are going to build a functionality to display similar posts by the number of tags they share. In this way, when a user reads a post, we can suggest them to read other related posts.

In order to retrieve similar posts for a specific post, we need to:

- Retrieve all tags for the current post.
- Get all posts that are tagged with any of those tags.
- Exclude the current post from that list to avoid recommending the same post.
- Order the results by the number of tags shared with the current post.
- In case of two or more posts with the same number of tags, recommend the most recent post.
- Limit the query to the number of posts we want to recommend.

These steps are translated into a complex QuerySet that we are going to include in our `post_detail` view. Open the `views.py` file of your blog application and add the following import at the top of it:

```
from django.db.models import Count
```

This is the `Count` aggregation function of the Django ORM. This function will allow us to perform aggregated counts. Then add the following lines inside the `post_detail` view before the `render()` function:

```
# List of similar posts
post_tags_ids = post.tags.values_list('id', flat=True)
similar_posts = Post.published.filter(tags__in=post_tags_ids)\
                              .exclude(id=post.id)
similar_posts = similar_posts.annotate(same_tags=Count('tags'))\
                             .order_by('-same_tags','-publish')[:4]
```

This code is as follows:

1. We retrieve a Python list of ID'S for the tags of the current post. The `values_list()` QuerySet returns tuples with the values for the given fields. We are passing it `flat=True` to get a flat list like `[1, 2, 3, ...]`.

2. We get all posts that contain any of these tags excluding the current post itself.

3. We use the `Count` aggregation function to generate a calculated field `same_tags` that contains the number of tags shared with all the tags queried.

4. We order the result by the number of shared tags (descendant order) and by the `publish` to display recent posts first for the posts with the same number of shared tags. We slice the result to retrieve only the first four posts.

Add the `similar_posts` object to the context dictionary for the `render()` function as follows:

```
return render(request,
              'blog/post/detail.html',
              {'post': post,
              'comments': comments,
              'comment_form': comment_form,
              'similar_posts': similar_posts})
```

Now, edit the `blog/post/detail.html` template and add the following code before the post comments list:

```
<h2>Similar posts</h2>
{% for post in similar_posts %}
  <p>
    <a href="{{ post.get_absolute_url }}">{{ post.title }}</a>
  </p>
{% empty %}
  There are no similar posts yet.
{% endfor %}
```

It's also recommended that you add the list of tags to your post detail template the same way we did in the post list template. Now, your post detail page should look like this:

# Who was Django Reinhardt?

Published Sept. 20, 2014, 12:49 p.m. by admin

**Tags:** jazz , music

The Django web framework was named after the amazing jazz guitarist Django Reinhardt.

Share this post

## Similar posts

Another post more

New title

You are successfully recommending similar posts to your users. `django-taggit` also includes a a `similar_objects()` manager that you can use to retrieve objects by shared tags. You can see all django-taggit managers at `http://django-taggit.readthedocs.org/en/latest/api.html`.

# Summary

In this chapter, you learned how to work with Django forms and model forms. You created a system to share your site's content by e-mail and you created a comment system for your blog. You added tagging to your blog posts, integrating a reusable application, and you built complex QuerySets to retrieve objects by similarity.

In the next chapter, you will learn how to create custom template tags and filters. You will also build a custom sitemap and feed for your blog posts, and integrate an advanced search engine into your application.

# 3

# Extending Your Blog Application

The previous chapter went through the basics of forms, and you learned how to integrate third-party applications into your project. This chapter will cover the following points:

- Creating custom template tags and filters
- Adding a sitemap and a post feed
- Building a search engine with Solr and Haystack

## Creating custom template tags and filters

Django offers a variety of built-in template tags such as `{% if %}` or `{% block %}`. You have used several in your templates. You can find a complete reference of built-in template tags and filters at `https://docs.djangoproject.com/en/1.8/ref/templates/builtins/`.

However, Django also allows you to create your own template tags to perform custom actions. Custom template tags come in very handy when you need to add functionality to your templates that is not covered by the core set of Django template tags.

# Creating custom template tags

Django provides the following helper functions that allow you to create your own template tags in an easy manner:

- `simple_tag`: Processes the data and returns a string
- `inclusion_tag`: Processes the data and returns a rendered template
- `assignment_tag`: Processes the data and sets a variable in the context

Template tags must live inside Django applications.

Inside your `blog` application directory, create a new directory, name it `templatetags` and add an empty `__init__.py` file to it. Create another file in the same folder and name it `blog_tags.py`. The file structure of the blog application should look like the following:

```
blog/
    __init__.py
    models.py
    ...
    templatetags/
        __init__.py
        blog_tags.py
```

The name of the file is important. You are going to use the name of this module to load your tags in templates.

We will start by creating a simple tag to retrieve the total posts published in the blog. Edit the `blog_tags.py` file you just created and add the following code:

```python
from django import template

register = template.Library()

from ..models import Post

@register.simple_tag
def total_posts():
    return Post.published.count()
```

We have created a simple template tag that returns the number of posts published so far. Each template tags module needs to contain a variable called `register` to be a valid tag library. This variable is an instance of `template.Library` and it's used to register your own template tags and filters. Then we are defining a tag called `total_posts` with a Python function and using `@register.simple_tag` to define the function as a simple tag and register it. Django will use the function's name as the tag name. If you want to register it with a different name, you can do it by specifying a `name` attribute like `@register.simple_tag(name='my_tag')`.

 After adding a new template tags module, you will need to restart the Django development server in order to use the new template tags and filters.

Before using custom template tags, you have to make them available for the template using the `{% load %}` tag. As mentioned before, you need to use the name of the Python module containing your template tags and filters. Open the `blog/base.html` template and add `{% load blog_tags %}` at the top of it to load your template tags module. Then use the tag you created to display your total posts. Just add `{% total_posts %}` to your template. The template should finally look like this:

```
{% load blog_tags %}
{% load staticfiles %}
<!DOCTYPE html>
<html>
<head>
  <title>{% block title %}{% endblock %}</title>
  <link href="{% static "css/blog.css" %}" rel="stylesheet">
</head>
<body>
  <div id="content">
    {% block content %}
    {% endblock %}
  </div>
  <div id="sidebar">
    <h2>My blog</h2>
    <p>This is my blog. I've written {% total_posts %} posts so far.</p>
  </div>
</body>
</html>
```

We need to restart the server to keep track of the new files added to the project. Stop the development server with *Ctrl+C* and run it again using this command:

```
python manage.py runserver
```

Open `http://127.0.0.1:8000/blog/` in your browser. You should see the number of total posts in the sidebar of the site, like this:

## My blog

This is my blog. I've written 4 posts so far.

The power of custom template tags is that you can process any data and add it to any template regardless of the view executed. You can perform QuerySets or process any data to display results in your templates.

Now, we are going to create another tag to display the latest posts in the sidebar of our blog. This time we are going to use an inclusion tag. Using an inclusion tag, you can render a template with context variables returned by your template tag. Edit the `blog_tags.py` file and add the following code:

```
@register.inclusion_tag('blog/post/latest_posts.html')
def show_latest_posts(count=5):
    latest_posts = Post.published.order_by('-publish')[:count]
    return {'latest_posts': latest_posts}
```

In this code, we register the template tag with `@register.inclusion_tag` and we specify the template that has to be rendered with the returned values with `blog/post/latest_posts.html`. Our template tag will accept an optional `count` parameter that defaults to 5 and allows us to specify the number of comments we want to display. We use this variable to limit the results of the query `Post.published.order_by('-publish')[:count]`. Notice that the function returns a dictionary of variables instead of a simple value. Inclusion tags have to return a dictionary of values that is used as the context to render the specified template. Inclusion tags return a dictionary. The template tag we just created can be used passing the optional number of comments to display like `{% show_latest_posts 3 %}`.

Now, create a new template file under `blog/post/` and name it `latest_posts.html`. Add the following code to it:

```
<ul>
{% for post in latest_posts %}
  <li>
    <a href="{{ post.get_absolute_url }}">{{ post.title }}</a>
```

```
    </li>
{% endfor %}
</ul>
```

Here, we display an unordered list of posts using the `latest_posts` variable returned by our template tag. Now, edit the `blog/base.html` template and add the new template tag to display the last 3 comments. The sidebar block should look like the following:

```
<div id="sidebar">
  <h2>My blog</h2>
  <p>This is my blog. I've written {% total_posts %} posts so far.</p>

  <h3>Latest posts</h3>
  {% show_latest_posts 3 %}
</div>
```

The `template` tag is called passing the number of comments to display and the template is rendered in place with the given context.

Now, go back to your browser and refresh the page. The sidebar should now look like this:

Finally, we are going to create an assignment tag. Assignment tags are like simple tags but they store the result in a given variable. We will create an assignment tag to display the most commented posts. Edit the `blog_tags.py` file and add the following import and template tag in it:

```
from django.db.models import Count

@register.assignment_tag
def get_most_commented_posts(count=5):
    return Post.published.annotate(
            total_comments=Count('comments')
        ).order_by('-total_comments')[:count]
```

This QuerySet uses the `annotate()` function for query aggregation, using the `Count` aggregation function. We build a QuerySet aggregating the total number of comments for each post in a `total_comments` field and we order the QuerySet by this field. We also provide an optional `count` variable to limit the total number of objects returned to a given value.

In adition to `Count`, Django offers the aggregation functions `Avg`, `Max`, `Min`, and `Sum`. You can read more about aggregation functions at `https://docs.djangoproject.com/en/1.8/topics/db/aggregation/`.

Edit the `blog/base.html` template and append the following code to the sidebar `<div>` element:

```
<h3>Most commented posts</h3>
{% get_most_commented_posts as most_commented_posts %}
<ul>
{% for post in most_commented_posts %}
  <li>
    <a href="{{ post.get_absolute_url }}">{{ post.title }}</a>
  </li>
{% endfor %}
</ul>
```

The notation for assignment template tags is `{% template_tag as variable %}`. For our template tag, we use `{% get_most_commented_posts as most_commented_posts %}`. This way, we are storing the result of the template tag in a new variable named `most_commented_posts`. Then, we display the returned posts with an unordered list.

Now, open your browser and refresh the page to see the final result. It should look like the following:

You can read more about custom template tags at `https://docs.djangoproject.com/en/1.8/howto/custom-template-tags/`.

# Creating custom template filters

Django has a variety of built-in template filters that allow you to modify variables in templates. These are Python functions that take one or two parameters—the value of the variable it's being applied to, and an optional argument. They return a value that can be displayed or treated by another filter. A filter looks like `{{ variable|my_filter }}` or passing an argument, it looks like `{{ variable|my_filter:"foo" }}`. You can apply as many filters as you like to a variable like `{{ variable|filter1|filter2 }}`, and each of them will be applied to the output generated by the previous filter.

We are going to create a custom filter to be able to use markdown syntax in our blog posts and then convert the post contents to HTML in the templates. Markdown is a plain text formatting syntax that is very simple to use and it's intended to be converted into HTML. You can learn the basics of this format at `http://daringfireball.net/projects/markdown/basics`.

First, install the Python markdown module via pip using the following command:

```
pip install Markdown==2.6.2
```

Then edit the `blog_tags.py` file and include the following code:

```python
from django.utils.safestring import mark_safe
import markdown

@register.filter(name='markdown')
def markdown_format(text):
    return mark_safe(markdown.markdown(text))
```

We register template filters in the same way as we do with template tags. To avoid collision between our function name and the `markdown` module, we name our function `markdown_format` and name the filter `markdown` for usage in templates like `{{ variable|markdown }}`. Django escapes the HTML code generated by filters. We use the `mark_safe` function provided by Django to mark the result as safe HTML to be rendered in the template. By default, Django will not trust any HTML code and will escape it before placing it into the output. The only exception are variables that are marked safe from escaping. This behavior prevents Django from outputting potentially dangerous HTML and allows you to create exceptions when you know you are returning safe HTML.

Now, load your template tags module in the post list and detail templates. Add the following line at the top of the post/list.html and post/detail.html template after the {% extends %} tag:

```
{% load blog_tags %}
```

In the post/detail.html templates, replace the following line:

```
{{ post.body|linebreaks }}
```

...with the following one:

```
{{ post.body|markdown }}
```

Then, in the post/list.html file, replace this line:

```
{{ post.body|truncatewords:30|linebreaks }}
```

...with the following one:

```
{{ post.body|markdown|truncatewords_html:30 }}
```

The truncatewords_html filter truncates a string after a certain number of words, avoiding unclosed HTML tags.

Now, open http://127.0.0.1:8000/admin/blog/post/add/ in your browser and add a post with the following body:

```
This is a post formatted with markdown
--------------------------------------

*This is emphasized* and **this is more emphasized**.

Here is a list:

* One
* Two
* Three

And a [link to the Django website](https://www.djangoproject.com/)
```

Open your browser and see how the post is rendered. You should see the following:

Markdown post

**Tags:** markdown

*Published Nov. 4, 2014, 1:29 a.m. by admin*

## This is a post formatted with markdown

*This is emphasized* and **this is more emphasized**.

Here is a list:

- One
- Two
- Three

**And a** link to the Django website

As you can see, custom template filters are very useful to customize formatting. You can find more information about custom filters at `https://docs.djangoproject.com/en/1.8/howto/custom-template-tags/#writing-custom-template-filters`.

# Adding a sitemap to your site

Django comes with a sitemap framework, which allows you to generate sitemaps for your site dynamically. A sitemap is an XML file that tells search engines the pages of your website, their relevance, and how frequently they are updated. By using a sitemap, you will help crawlers indexing your website's content.

The Django sitemap framework depends on `django.contrib.sites`, which allows you to associate objects to particular websites that are running with your project. This comes handy when you want to run multiple sites using a single Django project. To install the sitemap framework, we need to activate both the sites and the sitemap applications in our project. Edit the `settings.py` file of your project and add `django.contrib.sites` and `django.contrib.sitemaps` to the INSTALLED_APPS setting. Also define a new setting for the site ID, as follows:

```
SITE_ID = 1

# Application definition
INSTALLED_APPS = (
```

```
# ...
'django.contrib.sites',
'django.contrib.sitemaps',
)
```

Now, run the following command to create the tables of the Django sites application in the database:

```
python manage.py migrate
```

You should see an output that contains this line:

```
Applying sites.0001_initial... OK
```

The `sites` application is now synced with the database. Now, create a new file inside your `blog` application directory and name it `sitemaps.py`. Open the file and add the following code to it:

```
from django.contrib.sitemaps import Sitemap
from .models import Post

class PostSitemap(Sitemap):
    changefreq = 'weekly'
    priority = 0.9

    def items(self):
        return Post.published.all()

    def lastmod(self, obj):
        return obj.publish
```

We create a custom sitemap by inheriting the `Sitemap` class of the `sitemaps` module. The `changefreq` and `priority` attributes indicate the change frequency of your post pages and their relevance in your website (maximum value is 1). The `items()` method returns the QuerySet of objects to include in this sitemap. By default, Django calls the `get_absolute_url()` method on each object to retrieve its URL. Remember that we created this method in *Chapter 1, Building a Blog Application*, to retrieve the canonical URL for posts. If you want to specify the URL for each object, you can add a `location` method to your sitemap class. The `lastmod` method receives each object returned by `items()` and returns the last time the object was modified. Both `changefreq` and `priority` method can also be either methods or attributes. You can see the complete sitemap reference in the official Django documentation located at `https://docs.djangoproject.com/en/1.8/ref/contrib/sitemaps/`.

Finally, we just need to add our sitemap URL. Edit the main `urls.py` file of your project and add the sitemap like this:

```python
from django.conf.urls import include, url
from django.contrib import admin
from django.contrib.sitemaps.views import sitemap
from blog.sitemaps import PostSitemap

sitemaps = {
    'posts': PostSitemap,
}

urlpatterns = [
    url(r'^admin/', include(admin.site.urls)),
    url(r'^blog/',
        include('blog.urls'namespace='blog', app_name='blog')),
    url(r'^sitemap\.xml$', sitemap, {'sitemaps': sitemaps},
        name='django.contrib.sitemaps.views.sitemap'),
]
```

Here, we include the required imports and define a dictionary of sitemaps. We define a URL pattern that matches with `sitemap.xml` and uses the sitemap view. The `sitemaps` dictionary is passed to the `sitemap` view. Now open `http://127.0.0.1:8000/sitemap.xml` in your browser. You should see XML code like the following:

```xml
<?xml version="1.0" encoding="UTF-8"?>
<urlset xmlns="http://www.sitemaps.org/schemas/sitemap/0.9">
  <url>
    <loc>http://example.com/blog/2015/09/20/another-post/</loc>
    <lastmod>2015-09-29</lastmod>
    <changefreq>weekly</changefreq>
    <priority>0.9</priority>
  </url>
  <url>
    <loc>http://example.com/blog/2015/09/20/who-was-django-
reinhardt/</loc>
    <lastmod>2015-09-20</lastmod>
    <changefreq>weekly</changefreq>
    <priority>0.9</priority>
  </url>
</urlset>
```

The URL for each post has been built calling its `get_absolute_url()` method. The `lastmod` attribute corresponds to the post `publish` date field as we specified in our sitemap, and the `changefreq` and `priority` attributes are also taken from our `PostSitemap` class. You can see that the domain used to build the URLs is `example.com`. This domain comes from a `Site` object stored in the database. This default object has been created when we synced the sites framework with our database. Open `http://127.0.0.1:8000/admin/sites/site/` in your browser. You should see something like this:

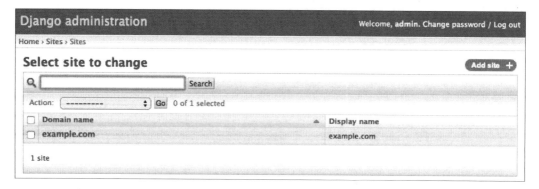

This is the list display admin view for the sites framework. Here, you can set the domain or host to be used by the sites framework and the applications that depend on it. In order to generate URLs that exist in our local environment, change the domain name to `127.0.0.1:8000` as shown in the following screenshot and save it:

We point to our local host for development purposes. In a production environment, you will have to use your own domain name for the sites framework.

# Creating feeds for your blog posts

Django has a built-in syndication feed framework that you can use to dynamically generate RSS or Atom feeds in a similar manner to creating sitemaps using the sites framework.

Create a new file in your `blog` application directory and name it `feeds.py`. Add the following lines to it:

```python
from django.contrib.syndication.views import Feed
from django.template.defaultfilters import truncatewords
from .models import Post

class LatestPostsFeed(Feed):
    title = 'My blog'
    link = '/blog/'
    description = 'New posts of my blog.'

    def items(self):
        return Post.published.all()[:5]

    def item_title(self, item):
        return item.title

    def item_description(self, item):
        return truncatewords(item.body, 30)
```

First, we subclass the `Feed` class of the syndication framework. The `title`, `link`, and `description` attributes correspond to the `<title>`, `<link>`, and `<description>` RSS elements respectively.

The `items()` method retrieves the objects to be included in the feed. We are retrieving only the last five published posts for this feed. The `item_title()` and `item_description()` methods receive each object returned by `items()` and return the title and description for each item. We use the truncatewords built-in template filter to build the description of the blog post with the first 30 words.

Now, edit the `urls.py` file of your `blog` application, import the `LatestPostsFeed` you just created, and instantiate the feed in a new URL pattern:

```python
from .feeds import LatestPostsFeed

urlpatterns = [
    # ...
    url(r'^feed/$', LatestPostsFeed(), name='post_feed'),
]
```

Navigate to `http://127.0.0.1:8000/blog/feed/` in your browser. You should now see the RSS feedincluding the last five blog posts:

```xml
<?xml version="1.0" encoding="utf-8"?>
<rss xmlns:atom="http://www.w3.org/2005/Atom" version="2.0">
  <channel>
    <title>My blog</title>
    <link>http://127.0.0.1:8000/blog/</link>
    <description>New posts of my blog.</description>
    <atom:link href="http://127.0.0.1:8000/blog/feed/" rel="self"/>
    <language>en-us</language>
    <lastBuildDate>Sun, 20 Sep 2015 20:40:55 -0000</lastBuildDate>
    <item>
      <title>Who was Django Reinhardt?</title>
      <link>http://127.0.0.1:8000/blog/2015/09/20/who-was-django-
reinhardt/</link>
      <description>The Django web framework was named after the
amazing jazz guitarist Django Reinhardt.</description>
      <guid>http://127.0.0.1:8000/blog/2015/09/20/who-was-django-
reinhardt/</guid>
    </item>
    ...
  </channel>
</rss>
```

If you open the same URL in a RSS client, you will be able to see your feed with a user-friendly interface.

Last step is adding a feed subscription link to the blog's sidebar. Open the `blog/base.html` template and add the following line under the number of total posts inside the sidebar `div`:

```
<p><a href="{% url "blog:post_feed" %}">Subscribe to my RSS feed</a></
p>
```

Now, open `http://127.0.0.1:8000/blog/` in your browser and take a look at the sidebar. The new link should take you to your blog's feed:

**My blog**

This is my blog. I've written 4 posts so far.

Subscribe to my RSS feed

# Adding a search engine with Solr and Haystack

Now, we are going to add search capabilities to our blog. The Django ORM allows you to perform case-insensitive lookups using the `icontains` filter. For example, you can use the following query to find posts that contain the word `framework` in their body:

```
Post.objects.filter(body__icontains='framework')
```

However, if you need more powerful search functionalities, you have to use a proper search engine. We are going to use Solr in conjunction with Django to build a search engine for our blog. Solr is a popular open-source search platform that offers full-text search, term boosting, hit highlighting, faceted search, and dynamic clustering, among other advanced search features.

In order to integrate Solr in our project, we are going to use Haystack. Haystack is a Django application that works as an abstraction layer for multiple search engines. It offers a simple search API very similar to Django QuerySets. Let's start by installing and configuring Solr and Haystack.

## Installing Solr

You will need the Java Runtime Environment version 1.7 or higher to install Solr. You can check your java version using the command `java -version` in the shell prompt. The output might vary but you need to make sure the installed version is at least 1.7:

```
java version "1.7.0_25"
Java(TM) SE Runtime Environment (build 1.7.0_25-b15)
Java HotSpot(TM) 64-Bit Server VM (build 23.25-b01, mixed mode)
```

If you don't have Java installed or your version is lower than the required one, then you can download Java from `http://www.oracle.com/technetwork/java/javase/downloads/index.html`.

After checking your Java version, download Solr version 4.10.4 from `http://archive.apache.org/dist/lucene/solr/`. Unzip the downloaded file and go to the `example` directory within the Solr installation directory (that is, `cd solr-4.10.4/example/`). This directory contains a ready to use Solr configuration. From this directory, run Solr with the built-in Jetty web server using the command:

```
java -jar start.jar
```

Open your browser and enter the URL `http://127.0.0.1:8983/solr/`. You should see something like the following:

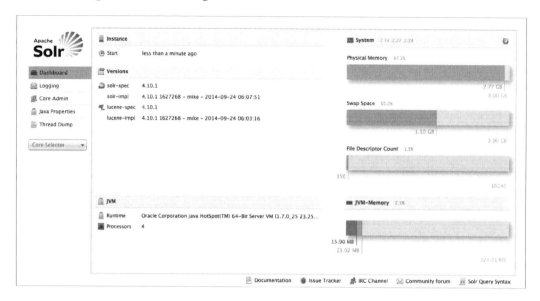

This is the Solr administration console. This console shows you usage statistics and allows you to manage your search backend, check the indexed data, and perform queries.

# Creating a Solr core

Solr allows you to isolate instances in cores. Each Solr **core** is a **Lucene** instance along with a Solr configuration, a data schema, and other required configuration to use it. Solr allows you to create and manage cores on the fly. The example configuration includes a core called `collection1`. You can see the information of this core if you click on the **Core Admin** menu tab, as shown in the following screenshot:

We are going to create a core for our blog application. First, we need to create the file structure for our core. Inside the example directory within the solr-4.10.4/ directory, create a new directory and name it blog. Then create the following empty files and directories inside it:

```
blog/
    data/
    conf/
        protwords.txt
        schema.xml
        solrconfig.xml
        stopwords.txt
        synonyms.txt
        lang/
            stopwords_en.txt
```

Add the following XML code to the solrconfig.xml file:

```xml
<?xml version="1.0" encoding="utf-8" ?>
<config>
  <luceneMatchVersion>LUCENE_36</luceneMatchVersion>
  <requestHandler name="/select" class="solr.StandardRequestHandler"
default="true" />
  <requestHandler name="/update" class="solr.UpdateRequestHandler" />
  <requestHandler name="/admin" class="solr.admin.AdminHandlers" />
  <requestHandler name="/admin/ping" class="solr.PingRequestHandler">
    <lst name="invariants">
      <str name="qt">search</str>
      <str name="q">*:*</str>
    </lst>
  </requestHandler>
</config>
```

You can also copy this file from the code that comes along with this chapter. This is a minimal Solr configuration. Edit the schema.xml file and add the following XML code:

```xml
<?xml version="1.0" ?>
<schema name="default" version="1.5">
</schema>
```

This is an empty **schema**. The schema defines the fields and their types for the data that will be indexed in the search engine. We are going to use a custom schema later.

Now, click on the **Core Admin** menu tab and then click on the **Add Core** button. You will see a form like the following that allows you to specify the information for your core:

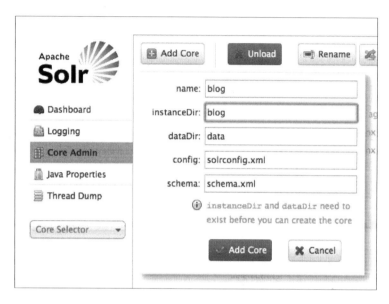

Fill the form with the following data:

- **name**: blog
- **instanceDir**: blog
- **dataDir**: data
- **config**: solrconfig.xml
- **schema**: schema.xml

The **name** field is the name you want to give to this core. The **instanceDir** field is the directory of your core. The **dataDir** is the directory where indexed data will reside. It is located inside the **instanceDir**. The **config** field is the name of your Solr XML configuration file and the **schema** field is the name of your Solr XML data schema file.

Now, click the **Add Core** button. If you see the following, then your new core has been successfully added to Solr:

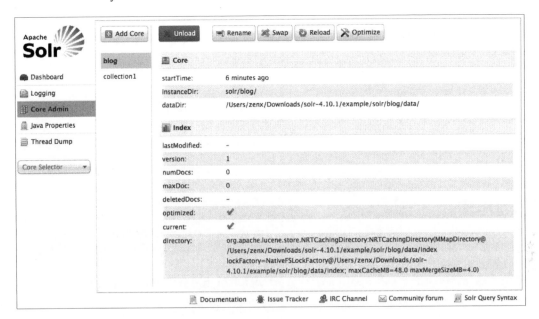

# Installing Haystack

To use Solr with Django, we need Haystack. Install Haystack via pip using the following command:

```
pip install django-haystack==2.4.0
```

Haystack can interact with several search engine backends. To use the Solr backend, you also need to install the pysolr module. Run the following command to install it:

```
pip install pysolr==3.3.2
```

After installing django-haystack and pysolr, you need to activate Haystack in your project. Open the settings.py file and add haystack to the INSTALLED_APPS setting like this:

```
INSTALLED_APPS = (
    # ...
    'haystack',
)
```

You need to define the search engine backends for haystack. You can do this by adding a HAYSTACK_CONNECTIONS setting. Add the following into your settings.py file:

```
HAYSTACK_CONNECTIONS = {
    'default': {
        'ENGINE': 'haystack.backends.solr_backend.SolrEngine',
        'URL': 'http://127.0.0.1:8983/solr/blog'
    },
}
```

Notice that the URL points to our blog core. Haystack is now installed and ready to be used with Solr.

# Building indexes

Now, we have to register the models we want to store in the search engine. The convention for Haystack is to create a search_indexes.py file into your application and register your models there. Create a new file into your blog application directory and name it search_indexes.py. Add the following code to it:

```
from haystack import indexes
from .models import Post

class PostIndex(indexes.SearchIndex, indexes.Indexable):
    text = indexes.CharField(document=True, use_template=True)
    publish = indexes.DateTimeField(model_attr='publish')

    def get_model(self):
        return Post

    def index_queryset(self, using=None):
        return self.get_model().published.all()
```

This is a custom SearchIndex for the Post model. With this index, we tell Haystack which data from this model has to be indexed in the search engine. The index is built by subclassing indexes.SearchIndex and indexes.Indexable. Every SearchIndex requires that one of its fields has document=True. The convention is to name this field text. This field is the primary search field. With use_template=True, we are telling Haystack that this field will be rendered to a data template to build the document the search engine will index. The publish field is a datetime field that will be also indexed. We indicate that this field corresponds to the publish field of the Post model by using the model_attr parameter. The field will be indexed with the content of the publish field of the indexed Post object.

Additional fields like this one are useful to provide additional filters to searches. The `get_model()` method has to return the model for the documents that will be stored in this index. The `index_queryset()` method returns the QuerySet for the objects that will be indexed. Notice that we are only including published posts.

Now, create the path and file `search/indexes/blog/post_text.txt` in the templates directory of the `blog` application and add the following code to it:

```
{{ object.title }}
{{ object.tags.all|join:", " }}
{{ object.body }}
```

This is the default path for the document template for the `text` field of our index. Haystack uses the application name and the model name to build the path dynamically. Every time we are going to index an object, Haystack will build a document based on this template and then index the document in the Solr search engine.

Now that we have a custom search index, we have to create the appropriate Solr schema. Solr's configuration is XML-based, so we have to generate an XML schema for the data we are going to index. Fortunately, Haystack offers a way to generate the schema dynamically, based on our search indexes. Open the terminal and run the following command:

```
python manage.py build_solr_schema
```

You should see an XML output. If you take a look at the bottom of the generated XML code, you will see that Haystack generated fields for your `PostIndex` automatically:

```
<field name="text" type="text_en" indexed="true" stored="true"
  multiValued="false" />
<field name="publish" type="date" indexed="true" stored="true"
  multiValued="false" />
```

Copy the whole XML output from the initial tag `<?xml version="1.0" ?>` to the last tag `</schema>`, including both tags.

This XML is the schema to index data into Solr. Paste the new schema into the `blog/conf/schema.xml` file inside the `example` directory of your Solr installation. The `schema.xml` file is included in the code that comes along with this chapter, so you can also copy it directly from this file.

Open `http://127.0.0.1:8983/solr/` in your browser and click on **Core Admin** menu tab, then click on the **blog** core, and then click the **Reload** button:

We reload the core so that it takes into account the `schema.xml` changes. When the core finishes reloading, the new schema is ready to index new data.

# Indexing data

Let's index the posts of our blog into Solr. Open the terminal and execute the following command:

```
python manage.py rebuild_index
```

You should see the following warning:

```
WARNING: This will irreparably remove EVERYTHING from your search
index in connection 'default'.
Your choices after this are to restore from backups or rebuild via the
`rebuild_index` command.
Are you sure you wish to continue? [y/N]
```

Enter y for yes. Haystack will clear the search index and insert all published blog posts. You should see an output like this:

```
Removing all documents from your index because you said so.
All documents removed.
Indexing 4 posts
```

Open `http://127.0.0.1:8983/solr/#/blog` in your browser. Under **Statistics**, you should be able to see the number of indexed documents as follows:

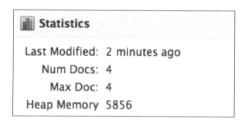

Now, open `http://127.0.0.1:8983/solr/#/blog/query` in your browser. This is a query interface provided by Solr. Click the **Execute query** button. The default query requests all documents indexed in your core. You will see a JSON output with the results of the query. The outputted documents look like the following:

```
{
    "id": "blog.post.1",
    "text": "Who was Django Reinhardt?\njazz, music\nThe Django
web framework was named after the amazing jazz guitarist Django
Reinhardt.",
    "django_id": "1",
    "publish": "2015-09-20T12:49:52Z",
    "django_ct": "blog.post"
},
```

This is the data stored for each post in the search index. The `text` field contains the title, tags separated by commas, and the body of the post, as this field is built with the template we defined before.

You have used `python manage.py rebuild_index` to remove everything in the index and to index the documents again. To update your index without removing all objects, you can use `python manage.py update_index`. Alternatively, you can use the parameter `--age=<num_hours>` to update less objects. You can set up a Cron job for this in order to keep your Solr index updated.

# Creating a search view

Now, we are going to create a custom view to allow our users to search posts. First, we need a search form. Edit the `forms.py` file of your `blog` application and add the following form:

```
class SearchForm(forms.Form):
    query = forms.CharField()
```

We will use the `query` field to let the users introduce search terms. Edit the `views.py` file of your `blog` application and add the following code to it:

```
from .forms import EmailPostForm, CommentForm, SearchForm
from haystack.query import SearchQuerySet

def post_search(request):
    form = SearchForm()
    if 'query' in request.GET:
        form = SearchForm(request.GET)
        if form.is_valid():
```

```
            cd = form.cleaned_data
            results = SearchQuerySet().models(Post)\
                        .filter(content=cd['query']).load_all()
            # count total results
            total_results = results.count()
    return render(request,
                'blog/post/search.html',
                {'form': form,
                 'cd': cd,
                 'results': results,
                 'total_results': total_results})
```

In this view, first we instantiate the SearchForm that we created before. We are going to submit the form using the GET method so that the resulting URL includes the query parameter. To see if the form has been submitted, we look for the query parameter in the request.GET dictionary. When the form is submitted, we instantiate it with the submitted GET data and we check that the given data is valid. If the form is valid, we use the we use SearchQuerySet to perform a search for indexed Post objects whose main content contains the given query. The load_all() method loads all related Post objects from the database at once. With this method, we populate the search results with the database objects to avoid per-object access to the database when iterating over results to access object data. Finally, we store the total number of results in a total_results variable and pass the local variables as context to render a template.

The search view is ready. We need to create a template to display the form and the results when the user performs a search. Create a new file inside the templates/ blog/post/ directory, name it search.html, and add the following code to it:

```
{% extends "blog/base.html" %}

{% block title %}Search{% endblock %}

{% block content %}
  {% if "query" in request.GET %}
    <h1>Posts containing "{{ cd.query }}"</h1>
    <h3>Found {{ total_results }} result{{ total_results|pluralize
}}</h3>
      {% for result in results %}
        {% with post=result.object %}
          <h4><a href="{{ post.get_absolute_url }}">{{ post.title }}</
a></h4>
            {{ post.body|truncatewords:5 }}
        {% endwith %}
      {% empty %}
```

```
    <p>There are no results for your query.</p>
   {% endfor %}
   <p><a href="{% url "blog:post_search" %}">Search again</a></p>
  {% else %}
   <h1>Search for posts</h1>
   <form action="." method="get">
    {{ form.as_p }}
    <input type="submit" value="Search">
   </form>
  {% endif %}
 {% endblock %}
```

As in the search view, we distinguish if the form has been submitted based on the presence of the `query` parameter. Before the post is submitted, we display the form and a submit button. After the post is submitted, we display the query performed, the total number of results, and the list of results. Each `result` is a document returned by Solr and encapsulated by Haystack. We need to use `result.object` to access the actual `Post` object related to this result.

Finally, edit the `urls.py` file of your `blog` application and add the following URL pattern:

```
url(r'^search/$', views.post_search, name='post_search'),
```

Now, open `http://127.0.0.1:8000/blog/search/` in your browser. You should see a search form like this:

Now, enter a query and click the **Search** button. You will see the results of the search query like the this:

Now, you have a powerful search engine built into your project, but starting from here there are a plenty of things you can do with Solr and Haystack. Haystack includes search views, forms, and advanced functionalities for search engines. You can read the Haystack documentation at `http://django-haystack.readthedocs.org/en/latest/`.

The Solr search engine can be adapted to any need by customizing your schema. You can combine analyzers, tokenizers, and token filters that are executed at index or search time to provide a more accurate search for your site's content. You can see all possibilities for this at `https://wiki.apache.org/solr/AnalyzersTokenizersTokenFilters`.

# Summary

In this chapter, you learned how to create custom Django template tags and filters to provide templates with custom functionality. You also created a sitemap for search engines to crawl your site and an RSS feed for users to subscribe to. You also built a search engine for your blog by integrating Solr with Haystack into your project.

In the next chapter, you will learn how to build a social website by using the Django authentication framework, creating custom user profiles, and building social authentication.

# 4
# Building a Social Website

In the previous chapter, you learned how to create sitemaps and feeds, and you built a search engine for your blog application. In this chapter, you will develop a social application. You will create functionality for users to login, logout, edit, and reset their password. You will learn how to create a custom profile for your users, and you will add social authentication to your site.

This chapter will cover the following points:

- Using the authentication framework
- Creating user registration views
- Extending the User model with a custom profile model
- Adding social authentication with python-social-auth

Let's start by creating our new project.

## Creating a social website project

We are going to create a social application that will allow users to share images they find on the Internet. We will need to build the following elements for this project:

- An authentication system for users to register, log in, edit their profile, and change or reset their password
- A followers' system to allow users to follow each other
- Functionality to display shared images and implement a bookmarklet for users to share images from any website
- An activity stream for each user that allows users to see the content uploaded by the people they follow

This chapter addresses the first point.

# Starting your social website project

Open the terminal and use the following commands to create a virtual environment for your project and activate it:

```
mkdir env
virtualenv env/bookmarks
source env/bookmarks/bin/activate
```

The shell prompt will display your active virtual environment as follows:

```
(bookmarks) laptop:~ zenx$
```

Install Django in your virtual environment with the following command:

```
pip install Django==1.8.6
```

Run the following command to create a new project:

```
django-admin startproject bookmarks
```

After creating the initial project structure, use the following commands to get into your project directory and create a new application named `account`:

```
cd bookmarks/
django-admin startapp account
```

Remember to activate the new application in your project by adding it to the INSTALLED_APPS setting in the settings.py file. Place it in the INSTALLED_APPS list before any of the other installed apps:

```
INSTALLED_APPS = (
    'account',
    # ...
)
```

Run the next command to sync the database with the models of the default applications included in the INSTALLED_APPS setting:

```
python manage.py migrate
```

We are going to build an authentication system into our project using the authentication framework.

# Using the Django authentication framework

Django comes with a built-in authentication framework that can handle user authentication, sessions, permissions, and user groups. The authentication system includes views for common user actions such as login, logout, change password, and reset password.

The authentication framework is located at `django.contrib.auth` and is used by other Django `contrib` packages. Remember that you already used the authentication framework in *Chapter 1, Building a Blog Application* to create a superuser for your blog application to access the administration site.

When you create a new Django project using the `startproject` command, the authentication framework is included in the default settings of your project. It consists of the `django.contrib.auth` application and the following two middleware classes found in the `MIDDLEWARE_CLASSES` setting of your project:

- `AuthenticationMiddleware`: Associates users with requests using sessions
- `SessionMiddleware`: Handles the current session across requests

A middleware is a class with methods that are globally executed during the request or response phase. You will use middleware classes on several occasions throughout this book. You will learn to create custom middlewares in *Chapter 13, Going Live*.

The authentication framework also includes the following models:

- `User`: A user model with basic fields; the main fields of this model are: `username`, `password`, `email`, `first_name`, `last_name`, and `is_active`.
- `Group`: A group model to categorize users.
- `Permission`: Flags to perform certain actions.

The framework also includes default authentication views and forms that we will use later.

# Creating a log-in view

We will start by using the Django authentication framework to allow users to log in into our website. Our view should perform the following actions to log in a user:

1. Get the username and password by posting a form.

2. Authenticate the user against the data stored in the database.

3. Check if the user is active.

4. Log the user into the website and start an authenticated session.

First, we are going to create a log in form. Create a new `forms.py` file into your `account` application directory and add the following lines to it:

```
from django import forms

class LoginForm(forms.Form):
    username = forms.CharField()
    password = forms.CharField(widget=forms.PasswordInput)
```

This form will be used to authenticate users against the database. Note that we use the `PasswordInput` widget to render its HTML `input` element, including a `type="password"` attribute. Edit the `views.py` file of your `account` application and add the following code to it:

```
from django.http import HttpResponse
from django.shortcuts import render
from django.contrib.auth import authenticate, login
from .forms import LoginForm

def user_login(request):
    if request.method == 'POST':
        form = LoginForm(request.POST)
        if form.is_valid():
            cd = form.cleaned_data
            user = authenticate(username=cd['username'],
                                password=cd['password'])
            if user is not None:
                if user.is_active:
                    login(request, user)
                    return HttpResponse('Authenticated '\
                                        'successfully')
                else:
                    return HttpResponse('Disabled account')
```

```
        else:
            return HttpResponse('Invalid login')
    else:
        form = LoginForm()
    return render(request, 'account/login.html', {'form': form})
```

This is what our basic log in view does: when the `user_login` view is called with a GET request, we instantiate a new log in form with `form = LoginForm()` to display it in the template. When the user submits the form via POST, we perform the following actions:

1.  Instantiate the form with the submitted data with `form = LoginForm(request.POST)`.

5.  Check if the form is valid. If it is not valid, we display the form errors in our template (for example, if user did not fill one of the fields).

6.  If the submitted data is valid, we authenticate the user against the database by using the `authenticate()` method. This method takes a `username` and a `password` and returns a `User` object if the user has been successfully authenticated, or `None` otherwise. If the user has not been authenticated, we return a raw `HttpResponse` displaying a message.

7.  If the user was successfully authenticated, we check if the user is active accessing its `is_active` attribute. This is an attribute of Django's `User` model. If the user is not active, we return an `HttpResponse` displaying the information.

8.  If the user is active, we log the user into the website. We set the user in the session by calling the `login()` method and return a success message.

>  Note the difference between `authenticate` and `login`: `authenticate()` checks user credentials and returns a user object if they are right; `login()` sets the user in the current session.

Now, you need to create an URL pattern for this view. Create a new `urls.py` file into your `account` application directory and add the following code to it:

```
from django.conf.urls import url
from . import views

urlpatterns = [
    # post views
    url(r'^login/$', views.user_login, name='login'),
]
```

Edit the main `urls.py` file located in your `bookmarks` project directory and include the URL patterns of the `account` application as follows:

```
from django.conf.urls import include, url
from django.contrib import admin

urlpatterns = [
    url(r'^admin/', include(admin.site.urls)),
    url(r'^account/', include('account.urls')),
]
```

The log in view can now be accessed by a URL. It is time to create a template for this view. Since you don't have any templates for this project, you can start by creating a base template that can be extended by the log in template. Create the following files and directories inside the `account` application directory:

```
templates/
    account/
        login.html
    base.html
```

Edit the `base.html` file and add the following code to it:

```
{% load staticfiles %}
<!DOCTYPE html>
<html>
<head>
  <title>{% block title %}{% endblock %}</title>
  <link href="{% static "css/base.css" %}" rel="stylesheet">
</head>
<body>
  <div id="header">
    <span class="logo">Bookmarks</span>
  </div>
  <div id="content">
    {% block content %}
    {% endblock %}
  </div>
</body>
</html>
```

This will be the base template for the website. As we did in our previous project, we include the CSS styles in the main template. You can find these static files in the code that comes along with this chapter. Copy the `static/` directory of the `account` application to the same location in your project, so that you can use the static files.

The base template defines a `title` and a `content` block that can be filled with content by the templates that extend from it.

Let's create the template for our log-in form. Open the `account/login.html` template and add the following code to it:

```
{% extends "base.html" %}

{% block title %}Log-in{% endblock %}

{% block content %}
  <h1>Log-in</h1>
  <p>Please, use the following form to log-in:</p>
  <form action="." method="post">
    {{ form.as_p }}
    {% csrf_token %}
    <p><input type="submit" value="Log-in"></p>
  </form>
{% endblock %}
```

This template includes the form that is instantiated in the view. Since our form will be submitted via POST, we include the `{% csrf_token %}` template tag for CSRF protection. You learned about CSRF protection in *Chapter 2, Enhancing Your Blog with Advanced Features*.

There are no users in your database yet. You will need to create a superuser first in order to be able to access the administration site to manage other users. Open the command line and execute `python manage.py createsuperuser`. Fill in the desired username, e-mail, and password. Then run the development server using the command `python manage.py runserver` and open `http://127.0.0.1:8000/admin/` in your browser. Access the administration site using the username and password of the user you just created. You will see the Django administration site, including the `User` and `Group` models of the Django authentication framework. It will look as follows:

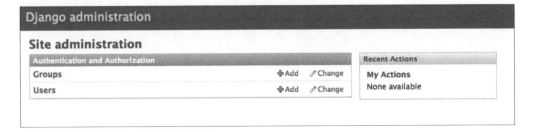

Create a new user using the administration site and open `http://127.0.0.1:8000/account/login/` in your browser. You should see the rendered template, including the log-in form:

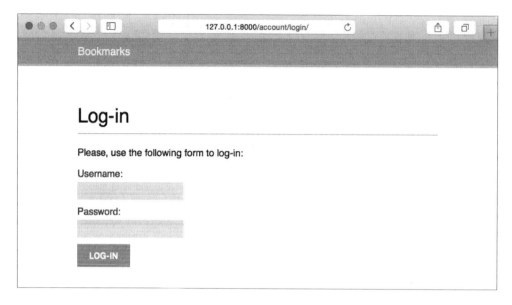

Now, submit the form leaving one of the fields empty. In this case, you will see that the form is not valid and it displays errors as follows:

If you enter an non-existing user or a wrong password, you will get an **Invalid login** message.

If you enter valid credentials, you get an **Authenticated successfully** message like this:

# Using Django authentication views

Django includes several forms and views in the authentication framework that you can use straightaway. The login view you have created is a good exercise to understand the process of user authentication in Django. However, you can use the default Django authentication views in most cases.

Django provides the following views to deal with authentication:

- login: Handles a log in form and logs in a user
- logout: Logs out a user
- logout_then_login: Logs out a user and redirects him to the log-in page

Django provides the following views to handle password changes:

- password_change: Handles a form to change user password
- password_change_done: The success page shown to the user after changing his password

Django also includes the following views to allow users to reset their password:

- password_reset: Allows the user to reset his password. It generates a one-time use link with a token and sends it to the user's e-mail account.
- password_reset_done: Shows the user that the e-mail to reset his password has been sent to his e-mail account.
- password_reset_confirm: Lets the user set a new password.
- password_reset_complete: The success page shown to the user after he resets their password.

The views listed here can save you a lot of time when creating a website with user accounts. The views use default values that you can override, such as the location of the template to be rendered or the form to be used by the view.

You can get more information about built-in authentication views at https://docs. djangoproject.com/en/1.8/topics/auth/default/#module-django.contrib. auth.views.

# Log in and log out views

Edit the urls.py of your account application and make it look like this:

```
from django.conf.urls import url
from . import views

urlpatterns = [
    # previous login view
    # url(r'^login/$', views.user_login, name='login'),

    # login / logout urls
    url(r'^login/$',
        'django.contrib.auth.views.login',
        name='login'),
    url(r'^logout/$',
        'django.contrib.auth.views.logout',
        name='logout'),
    url(r'^logout-then-login/$',
        'django.contrib.auth.views.logout_then_login',
        name='logout_then_login'),
]
```

We comment out the URL pattern for the user_login view we have created previously to use the login view of Django's authentication framework.

Create a new directory inside the templates directory of your account application and name it registration. This is the default path where the Django authentication views expect your authentication templates to be. Create a new file inside the new directory, name it login.html, and add the following code to it:

```
{% extends "base.html" %}

{% block title %}Log-in{% endblock %}

{% block content %}
  <h1>Log-in</h1>
  {% if form.errors %}
    <p>
      Your username and password didn't match.
      Please try again.
    </p>
  {% else %}
    <p>Please, use the following form to log-in:</p>
  {% endif %}
```

```
<div class="login-form">
  <form action="{% url 'login' %}" method="post">
    {{ form.as_p }}
    {% csrf_token %}
    <input type="hidden" name="next" value="{{ next }}" />
    <p><input type="submit" value="Log-in"></p>
  </form>
</div>
{% endblock %}
```

This login template is quite similar to the one we created before. Django uses the `AuthenticationForm` located at `django.contrib.auth.forms` by default. This form tries to authenticate the user and raises a validation error if the login was not successful. In this case, we can look for errors using `{% if form.errors %}` in the template to check if the provided credentials are wrong. Notice that we have added a hidden HTML `<input>` element to submit the value of a variable called `next`. This variable is first set by the log in view when you pass a `next` parameter in the request (for example. `http://127.0.0.1:8000/account/login/?next=/account/`).

The `next` parameter has to be a URL. If this parameter is given, the Django login view will redirect to the given URL after the user logs in.

Now, create a `logged_out.html` template inside the `registration` template directory and make it look like this:

```
{% extends "base.html" %}

{% block title %}Logged out{% endblock %}

{% block content %}
  <h1>Logged out</h1>
  <p>You have been successfully logged out. You can <a href="{% url
"login" %}">log-in again</a>.</p>
{% endblock %}
```

This is the template that Django will display after the user logs out.

After adding the URL patterns and the templates for log in and log out views, your website is ready for users to log in using the Django authentication views.

Note that the `logout_then_login` view we included in our urlconf does not need any template since it performs a redirect to the log in view.

Now, we are going to create a new view to display a dashboard to the user when he or she logs in their `account`. Open the `views.py` file of your account application and add the following code to it:

```python
from django.contrib.auth.decorators import login_required

@login_required
def dashboard(request):
    return render(request,
                  'account/dashboard.html',
                  {'section': 'dashboard'})
```

We decorate our view with the `login_required` decorator of the authentication framework. The `login_required` decorator checks if the current user is authenticated. If the user is authenticated, it executes the decorated view; if the user is not authenticated, it redirects him to the login URL with the URL he was trying to access as a GET parameter named `next`. By doing so, the log in view redirects the user back to the URL he was trying to access after he is successfully logged in. Remember that we added a hidden input in the form of our log in template for this purpose.

We also define a `section` variable. We are going to use this variable to track which section of the site the user is watching. Multiple views may correspond to the same section. This is a simple way to define which section each view corresponds to.

Now, you need to create a template for the dashboard view. Create a new file inside the `templates/account/` directory and name it `dashboard.html`. Make it look like this:

```html
{% extends "base.html" %}

{% block title %}Dashboard{% endblock %}

{% block content %}
  <h1>Dashboard</h1>
  <p>Welcome to your dashboard.</p>
{% endblock %}
```

Then, add the following URL pattern for this view in the `urls.py` file of the `account` application:

```python
urlpatterns = [
    # ...
    url(r'^$', views.dashboard, name='dashboard'),
]
```

Edit the `settings.py` file of your project and add the following code to it:

```
from django.core.urlresolvers import reverse_lazy

LOGIN_REDIRECT_URL = reverse_lazy('dashboard')
LOGIN_URL = reverse_lazy('login')
LOGOUT_URL = reverse_lazy('logout')
```

These settings are:

- `LOGIN_REDIRECT_URL`: Tells Django which URL to redirect after login if the `contrib.auth.views.login` view gets no next parameter
- `LOGIN_URL`: Is the URL to redirect the user to log in (e.g. using the `login_required` decorator)
- `LOGOUT_URL`: Is the URL to redirect the user to log out

We are using `reverse_lazy()` to build the URLs dynamically by their name. The `reverse_lazy()` function reverses URLs just like `reverse()` does, but you can use it when you need to reverse URLs before your project's URL configuration is loaded.

Let's summarize what you have done so far:

- You added the built-in Django authentication log in and log out views to your project
- You created custom templates for both views and defined a simple view to redirect users after they log in
- Finally, you configured your settings for Django to use these URLs by default

Now, we are going to add log in and log out links to our base template to put everything together.

In order to do this, we have to determine whether the current user is logged in or not, to display the appropriate link in each case. The current user is set in the Http `Request` object by the authentication middleware. You can access it with `request.user`. You will find a user object in the request even if the user is not authenticated. A non-authenticated user is set in the request as an instance of `AnonymousUser`. The best way to check if the current user is authenticated is by calling `request.user.is_authenticated()`.

Edit your `base.html` and modify the `<div>` element with ID `header`, like this:

```
<div id="header">
  <span class="logo">Bookmarks</span>
  {% if request.user.is_authenticated %}
    <ul class="menu">
      <li {% if section == "dashboard" %}class="selected"{% endif %}>
        <a href="{% url "dashboard" %}">My dashboard</a>
      </li>
      <li {% if section == "images" %}class="selected"{% endif %}>
        <a href="#">Images</a>
      </li>
      <li {% if section == "people" %}class="selected"{% endif %}>
        <a href="#">People</a>
      </li>
    </ul>
  {% endif %}

  <span class="user">
    {% if request.user.is_authenticated %}
      Hello {{ request.user.first_name }},
      <a href="{% url "logout" %}">Logout</a>
    {% else %}
      <a href="{% url "login" %}">Log-in</a>
    {% endif %}
  </span>
</div>
```

As you can see, we only display the site's menu to authenticated users. We also check the current section to add a `selected` class attribute to the corresponding `<li>` item in order to highlight the current section in the menu using CSS. We also display the user's first name and a link to log out if the user is authenticated, or a link to log in otherwise.

Now, open `http://127.0.0.1:8000/account/login/` in your browser. You should see the log in page. Enter a valid username and password and click the **Log-in** button. You should see something like this:

You can see that the **My dashboard** section is highlighted with CSS because it has a `selected` class. Since the user is authenticated the first name of the user is displayed in the right side of the header. Click on the **Logout** link. You should see the following page:

In this page, you can see that the user is logged out, and therefore, you cannot see the menu of the website anymore. The link on the right side of the header is shows now **Log-in**.

If you are seeing the log out page of the Django administration site instead of your own log out page, check the `INSTALLED_APPS` setting of your project and make sure that `django.contrib.admin` comes after the `account` application. Both templates are located in the same relative path and the Django template loader will use the first one it finds.

# Change password views

We also need our users to be able to change their password after they log in to our site. We are going to integrate Django authentication views for password change. Open the `urls.py` file of the `account` application and add the following URL patterns to it:

```
# change password urls
url(r'^password-change/$',
    'django.contrib.auth.views.password_change',
    name='password_change'),
url(r'^password-change/done/$',
    'django.contrib.auth.views.password_change_done',
    name='password_change_done'),
```

The `password_change` view will handle the form to change the password and the `password_change_done` will display a success message after the user has successfully changed his password. Let's create a template for each view.

Add a new file inside the `templates/registration/` directory of your `account` application and name it `password_change_form.html`. Add the following code to it:

```
{% extends "base.html" %}

{% block title %}Change you password{% endblock %}

{% block content %}
  <h1>Change you password</h1>
  <p>Use the form below to change your password.</p>
  <form action="." method="post">
    {{ form.as_p }}
    <p><input type="submit" value="Change"></p>
    {% csrf_token %}
  </form>
{% endblock %}
```

This template includes the form to change the password. Now, create another file in the same directory and name it `password_change_done.html`. Add the following code to it:

```
{% extends "base.html" %}

{% block title %}Password changed{% endblock %}

{% block content %}
  <h1>Password changed</h1>
  <p>Your password has been successfully changed.</p>
{% endblock %}
```

This template only contains the success message to be displayed when the user has successfully changed their password.

Open `http://127.0.0.1:8000/account/password-change/` in your browser. If your user is not logged in, the browser will redirect you to the login page. After you are successfully authenticated, you will see the following change password page:

Fill in the form with your current password and your new password and click the **Change** button. You will see the following success page:

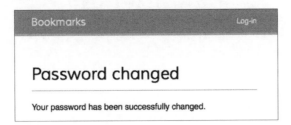

Log out and log in again using your new password to verify that everything works as expected.

# Reset password views

Add the following URL patterns for password restoration to the `urls.py` file of the `account` application:

```
# restore password urls
url(r'^password-reset/$',
    'django.contrib.auth.views.password_reset',
    name='password_reset'),
url(r'^password-reset/done/$',
    'django.contrib.auth.views.password_reset_done',
    name='password_reset_done'),
url(r'^password-reset/confirm/(?P<uidb64>[-\w]+)/(?P<token>[-\w]+)/$',
    'django.contrib.auth.views.password_reset_confirm',
    name='password_reset_confirm'),
url(r'^password-reset/complete/$',
    'django.contrib.auth.views.password_reset_complete',
    name='password_reset_complete'),
```

Add a new file in the `templates/registration/` directory of your `account` application and name it `password_reset_form.html`. Add the following code to it:

```
{% extends "base.html" %}

{% block title %}Reset your password{% endblock %}

{% block content %}
  <h1>Forgotten your password?</h1>
  <p>Enter your e-mail address to obtain a new password.</p>
  <form action="." method="post">
    {{ form.as_p }}
    <p><input type="submit" value="Send e-mail"></p>
    {% csrf_token %}
  </form>
{% endblock %}
```

Now, create another file in the same directory and name it `password_reset_email.html`. Add the following code to it:

```
Someone asked for password reset for email {{ email }}. Follow the
link below:
{{ protocol }}://{{ domain }}{% url "password_reset_confirm"
uidb64=uid token=token %}
Your username, in case you've forgotten: {{ user.get_username }}
```

This is the template that will be used to render the e-mail sent to the user to reset their password.

Create another file in the same directory and name it `password_reset_done.html`. Add the following code to it:

```
{% extends "base.html" %}

{% block title %}Reset your password{% endblock %}

{% block content %}
  <h1>Reset your password</h1>
  <p>We've emailed you instructions for setting your password.</p>
  <p>If you don't receive an email, please make sure you've entered
the address you registered with.</p>
{% endblock %}
```

Create another template and name it `password_reset_confirm.html`. Add the following code to it:

```
{% extends "base.html" %}

{% block title %}Reset your password{% endblock %}

{% block content %}
  <h1>Reset your password</h1>
  {% if validlink %}
    <p>Please enter your new password twice:</p>
    <form action="." method="post">
      {{ form.as_p }}
      {% csrf_token %}
      <p><input type="submit" value="Change my password" /></p>
    </form>
  {% else %}
    <p>The password reset link was invalid, possibly because it has
already been used. Please request a new password reset.</p>
  {% endif %}
{% endblock %}
```

We check if the provided link is valid. Django reset password view sets this variable and puts it in the context of this template. If the link is valid, we display the user password reset form.

Create another template and name it `password_reset_complete.html`. Enter the following code into it:

```
{% extends "base.html" %}

{% block title %}Password reset{% endblock %}

{% block content %}
  <h1>Password set</h1>
  <p>Your password has been set. You can <a href="{% url "login"
%}">log in now</a></p>
{% endblock %}
```

Finally, edit the `registration/login.html` template of the `account` application and add the following code after the `<form>` element:

```
<p><a href="{% url "password_reset" %}">Forgotten your
password?</a></p>
```

Now, open `http://127.0.0.1:8000/account/login/` in your browser and click the **Forgotten your password?** link. You should see the following page:

At this point, you need to add an SMTP configuration to the `settings.py` file of your project, so that Django is able to send e-mails. We have seen how to add e-mail settings to your project in *Chapter 2, Enhancing Your Blog with Advanced Features*. However, during development, you can configure Django to write e-mails to the standard output instead of sending them through an SMTP server. Django provides an e-mail backend to write e-mails to the console. Edit the `settings.py` file of your project and add the following line:

```
EMAIL_BACKEND = 'django.core.mail.backends.console.EmailBackend'
```

The EMAIL_BACKEND setting indicates the class to use to send e-mails.

Go back to your browser, enter the e-mail address of an existing user, and click the **Send e-mail** button. You should see the following page:

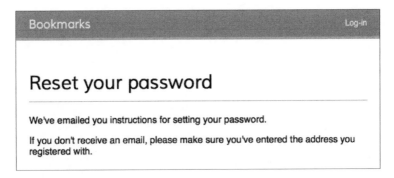

Take a look at the console where you are running the development server. You will see the generated e-mail as follows:

```
IME-Version: 1.0
Content-Type: text/plain; charset="utf-8"
Content-Transfer-Encoding: 7bit
Subject: Password reset on 127.0.0.1:8000
From: webmaster@localhost
To: user@domain.com
Date: Thu, 24 Sep 2015 14:35:08 -0000
Message-ID: <20150924143508.62996.55653@zenx.local>


Someone asked for password reset for email user@domain.com. Follow the
link below:
http://127.0.0.1:8000/account/password-reset/confirm/MQ/45f-
9c3f30caafd523055fcc/
Your username, in case you've forgotten: zenx
```

The e-mail is rendered using the `password_reset_email.html` template we created earlier. The URL to reset your password includes a token that was generated dynamically by Django. Open the link in your browser. You should see the following page:

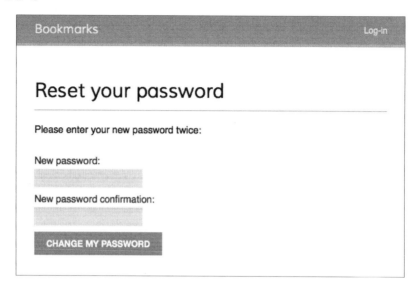

The page to set a new password corresponds to the `password_reset_confirm.html` template. Fill in a new password and click the **Change my password** button. Django creates a new encrypted password and saves it in the database. You will see a success page like this one:

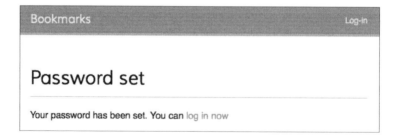

Now, you can log in back to your account using your new password. Each token to set a new password can be used only once. If you open the link you received again, you will get a message telling you the token is invalid.

You have integrated the views of the Django authentication framework in your project. These views are suitable for most cases. However, you can create your own views if you need a different behavior.

# User registration and user profiles

Existing users can now log in, log out, change their password, and reset the password if they forgot it. Now, we need to build a view to allow visitors to create a user account.

## User registration

Let's create a simple view to allow user registration in our website. Initially, we have to create a form to let the user enter a username, their real name, and a password. Edit the `forms.py` file located inside the `account` application directory and add the following code to it:

```python
from django.contrib.auth.models import User

class UserRegistrationForm(forms.ModelForm):
    password = forms.CharField(label='Password',
                               widget=forms.PasswordInput)
    password2 = forms.CharField(label='Repeat password',
                               widget=forms.PasswordInput)

    class Meta:
        model = User
        fields = ('username', 'first_name', 'email')

    def clean_password2(self):
        cd = self.cleaned_data
        if cd['password'] != cd['password2']:
            raise forms.ValidationError('Passwords don\'t match.')
        return cd['password2']
```

We have created a model form for the `User` model. In our form we include only the `username`, `first_name`, and `email` fields of the model. These fields will be validated based on their corresponding model fields. For example, if the user chooses a username that already exists, their will get a validation error. We have added two additional fields `password` and `password2` for the user to set his or her password and confirm it. We have defined a `clean_password2()` method to check the second password against the first one and not let the form validate if the passwords don't match. This check is done when we validate the form calling its `is_valid()` method. You can provide a `clean_<fieldname>()` method to any of your form fields in order to clean the value or raise form validation errors for the specific field. Forms also include a general `clean()` method to validate the entire form, which is useful to validate fields that depend on each other.

Django also provides a `UserCreationForm` form that you can use, which resides in `django.contrib.auth.forms` and is very similar to the one we have created.

Edit the `views.py` file of the `account` application and add the following code to it:

```python
from .forms import LoginForm, UserRegistrationForm

def register(request):
    if request.method == 'POST':
        user_form = UserRegistrationForm(request.POST)
        if user_form.is_valid():
            # Create a new user object but avoid saving it yet
            new_user = user_form.save(commit=False)
            # Set the chosen password
            new_user.set_password(
                user_form.cleaned_data['password'])
            # Save the User object
            new_user.save()
            return render(request,
                          'account/register_done.html',
                          {'new_user': new_user})
    else:
        user_form = UserRegistrationForm()
    return render(request,
                  'account/register.html',
                  {'user_form': user_form})
```

The view for creating user accounts is quite simple. Instead of saving the raw password entered by the user, we use the `set_password()` method of the `User` model that handles encryption to save for safety.

Now, edit the `urls.py` file of your `account` application and add the following URL pattern:

```python
url(r'^register/$', views.register, name='register'),
```

Finally, create a new template in the `account/` template directory, name it `register.html`, and make it look as follows:

```html
{% extends "base.html" %}

{% block title %}Create an account{% endblock %}

{% block content %}
  <h1>Create an account</h1>
  <p>Please, sign up using the following form:</p>
```

```
<form action="." method="post">
  {{ user_form.as_p }}
  {% csrf_token %}
  <p><input type="submit" value="Create my account"></p>
</form>
{% endblock %}
```

Add a template file in the same directory and name it `register_done.html`. Add the following code to it:

```
{% extends "base.html" %}

{% block title %}Welcome{% endblock %}

{% block content %}
  <h1>Welcome {{ new_user.first_name }}!</h1>
  <p>Your account has been successfully created. Now you can <a
href="{% url "login" %}">log in</a>.</p>
{% endblock %}
```

Now, open `http://127.0.0.1:8000/account/register/` in your browser. You will see the registration page you created:

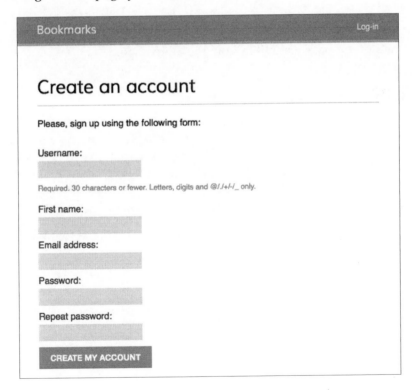

Fill in the details for a new user and click the **Create my account** button. If all fields are valid, the user will be created and you will get the following success message:

Click the **log in** link and enter your username and password to verify that you can access your account.

Now, you can also add a link for registration to your login template. Edit the `registration/login.html` template and replace this line:

```
<p>Please, use the following form to log-in:</p>
```

...with this one:

```
<p>Please, use the following form to log-in. If you don't have an
account <a href="{% url "register" %}">register here</a></p>
```

We made the sign up page accessible from the login page.

# Extending the User model

When you have to deal with user accounts, you will find out that the User model of the Django authentication framework is suitable for common cases. However, the User model comes with very basic fields. You may wish to extend the User model to include additional data. The best way to do this is by creating a profile model that contains all additional fields and a one-to-one relationship with the Django User model.

Edit the `models.py` file of your `account` application and add the following code to it:

```
from django.db import models
from django.conf import settings

class Profile(models.Model):
    user = models.OneToOneField(settings.AUTH_USER_MODEL)
    date_of_birth = models.DateField(blank=True, null=True)
```

```
photo = models.ImageField(upload_to='users/%Y/%m/%d',
                          blank=True)

def __str__(self):
    return 'Profile for user {}'.format(self.user.username)
```

 In order to keep your code generic, use the get_user_model() method to retrieve the user model and the AUTH_USER_MODEL setting to refer to it when defining model's relations to the user model, instead of referring to the auth User model directly.

The user one-to-one field allows us to associate profiles with users. The photo field is an ImageField field. You will need to install one of the Python packages to manage images, which are **PIL (Python Imaging Library)** or **Pillow**, which is a PIL fork. Install Pillow by running the following command in your shell:

**pip install Pillow==2.9.0**

For Django to serve media files uploaded by users with the development server, add the following settings to the settings.py file of your project:

```
MEDIA_URL = '/media/'
MEDIA_ROOT = os.path.join(BASE_DIR, 'media/')
```

MEDIA_URL is the base URL to serve the media files uploaded by users, and MEDIA_ROOT is the local path where they reside. We build the path dynamically relative to our project path to make our code more generic.

Now, edit the main urls.py file of the bookmarks project and modify the code as follows:

```
from django.conf.urls import include, url
from django.contrib import admin
from django.conf import settings
from django.conf.urls.static import static

urlpatterns = [
    url(r'^admin/', include(admin.site.urls)),
    url(r'^account/', include('account.urls')),
]

if settings.DEBUG:
    urlpatterns += static(settings.MEDIA_URL,
                          document_root=settings.MEDIA_ROOT)
```

In this way, the Django development server will be in charge of serving the media files during development.

> The static() helper function is suitable for development but not for production use. Never serve your static files with Django in a production environment.

Open the shell and run the following command to create the database migration for the new model:

**python manage.py makemigrations**

You will get this output:

```
Migrations for 'account':
  0001_initial.py:
    - Create model Profile
```

Next, sync the database with the following command:

**python manage.py migrate**

You will see an output that includes the following line:

```
Applying account.0001_initial... OK
```

Edit the admin.py file of the account application and register the Profile model in the administration site, like this:

```
from django.contrib import admin
from .models import Profile

class ProfileAdmin(admin.ModelAdmin):
    list_display = ['user', 'date_of_birth', 'photo']

admin.site.register(Profile, ProfileAdmin)
```

Run the development server again using the python manage.py runserver command. Now, you should be able to see the Profile model in the administration site of your project, as follows:

Now, we are going to let users edit their `profile` in the website. Add the following model forms to the `forms.py` file of the `account` application:

```python
from .models import Profile

class UserEditForm(forms.ModelForm):
    class Meta:
        model = User
        fields = ('first_name', 'last_name', 'email')

class ProfileEditForm(forms.ModelForm):
    class Meta:
        model = Profile
        fields = ('date_of_birth', 'photo')
```

These forms are as follows:

- `UserEditForm`: Will allow users to edit their first name, last name, and e-mail, which are stored in the built-in `User` model.
- `ProfileEditForm`: Will allow users to edit the extra data we save in the custom `Profile` model. Users will be able to edit their date of birth and upload a picture for their profile.

Edit the `views.py` file of the `account` application and import the Profile model like this:

```python
from .models import Profile
```

And add the following lines to the `register` view below `new_user.save()`:

```python
# Create the user profile
profile = Profile.objects.create(user=new_user)
```

When users register in our site, we create an empty profile associated to them. You should create a `Profile` object manually using the administration site for the users you created before.

Now, we are going to let users edit their profile. Add the following code to the same file:

```python
from .forms import LoginForm, UserRegistrationForm, \
                    UserEditForm, ProfileEditForm


@login_required
def edit(request):
    if request.method == 'POST':
```

```
        user_form = UserEditForm(instance=request.user,
                                     data=request.POST)
        profile_form = ProfileEditForm(
                               instance=request.user.profile,
                               data=request.POST,
                               files=request.FILES)
        if user_form.is_valid() and profile_form.is_valid():
            user_form.save()
            profile_form.save()
    else:
        user_form = UserEditForm(instance=request.user)
        profile_form = ProfileEditForm(
                               instance=request.user.profile)
    return render(request,
                  'account/edit.html',
                  {'user_form': user_form,
                   'profile_form': profile_form})
```

We use the `login_required` decorator because users have to be authenticated to edit their profile. In this case, we are using two model forms: `UserEditForm` to store the data of the built-in User model and `ProfileEditForm` to store the additional profile data. To validate the submitted data, we check that the `is_valid()` method of both forms returns `True`. In this case, we save both forms to update the corresponding object in the database.

Add the following URL pattern to the `urls.py` file of the `account` application:

```
url(r'^edit/$', views.edit, name='edit'),
```

Finally, create a template for this view in `templates/account/` and name it `edit.html`. Add the following code to it:

```
{% extends "base.html" %}

{% block title %}Edit your account{% endblock %}

{% block content %}
  <h1>Edit your account</h1>
  <p>You can edit your account using the following form:</p>
  <form action="." method="post" enctype="multipart/form-data">
    {{ user_form.as_p }}
    {{ profile_form.as_p }}
    {% csrf_token %}
    <p><input type="submit" value="Save changes"></p>
  </form>
{% endblock %}
```

We include enctype="multipart/form-data" in our form to enable file uploads. We use one HTML form to submit both the user_form and the profile_form forms.

Register a new user and open http://127.0.0.1:8000/account/edit/. You should see the following page:

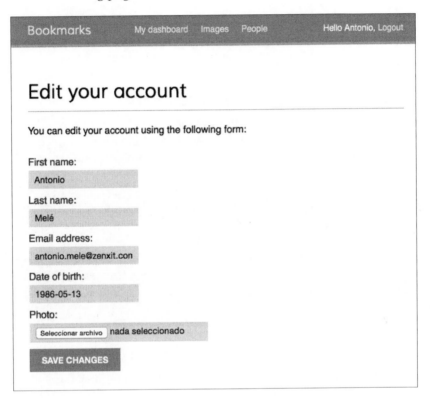

Now, you can also edit the dashboard page and include links to edit profile and change password pages. Open the account/dashboard.html template and replace this line:

```
<p>Welcome to your dashboard.</p>
```

...with this one:

```
<p>Welcome to your dashboard. You can <a href="{% url "edit" %}">edit
your profile</a> or <a href="{% url "password_change" %}">change your
password</a>.</p>
```

Users can now access the form to edit their profile from their dashboard.

# Using a custom User model

Django also offers a way to substitute the whole User model with your own custom model. Your user class should inherit from Django's AbstractUser class, which provides the full implementation of the default user as an abstract model. You can read more about this method at https://docs.djangoproject.com/en/1.8/topics/auth/customizing/#substituting-a-custom-user-model.

Using a custom user model will give you more flexibility, but it might also result in more difficult integration with pluggable applications that interact with the User model.

# Using the messages framework

When dealing with user actions, you might want to inform your users about the result of their actions. Django has a built-in messages framework that allows you to display one-time notifications to your users. The messages framework is located at django.contrib.messages and it is included in the default INSTALLED_APPS list of the settings.py file when you create new projects using python manage.py startproject. You will notice that your settings file contains a middleware named django.contrib.messages.middleware.MessageMiddleware in the list of MIDDLEWARE_CLASSES of your settings. The messages framework provides a simple way to add messages to users. Messages are stored in the database and displayed in the next request the user does. You can use the messages framework in your views by importing the messages module and adding new messages with simple shortcuts like this:

```
from django.contrib import messages
messages.error(request, 'Something went wrong')
```

You can create new messages using the add_message() method or any of the following shortcut methods:

- success(): Success messages to display after an action was successful
- info(): Informational messages
- warning(): Something has not yet failed but may fail imminently
- error(): An action was not successful or something failed
- debug(): Debug messages that will be removed or ignored in a production environment

Let's display messages to users. Since the messages framework applies globally to the project, we can display messages for the user in our base template. Open the base.html template and add the following code between the <div> element with the id header and the <div> element with the id content:

```
{% if messages %}
  <ul class="messages">
    {% for message in messages %}
      <li class="{{ message.tags }}">
        {{ message|safe }}
          <a href="#" class="close">X</a>
      </li>
    {% endfor %}
  </ul>
{% endif %}
```

The messages framework includes a context processor that adds a messages variable to the request context. So you can use this variable in your templates to display current messages to the user.

Now, let's modify our edit view to use the messages framework. Edit the views.py file of your application and make the edit view look as follows:

```
from django.contrib import messages

@login_required
def edit(request):
    if request.method == 'POST':
    # ...
        if user_form.is_valid() and profile_form.is_valid():
            user_form.save()
            profile_form.save()
            messages.success(request, 'Profile updated '\
                                    'successfully')
        else:
            messages.error(request, 'Error updating your profile')
    else:
        user_form = UserEditForm(instance=request.user)
        # ...
```

We add a success message when the user successfully updates their profile. If any of the forms are invalid, we add an error message instead.

Open `http://127.0.0.1:8000/account/edit/` in your browser and edit your profile. When the profile is successfully updated, you should see the following message:

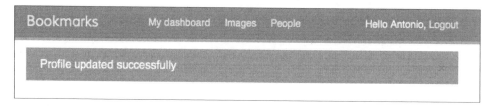

When the form is not valid, you should see the following message:

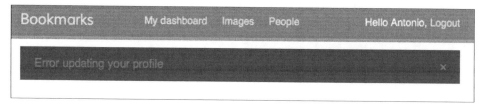

# Building a custom authentication backend

Django allows you to authenticate against different sources. The AUTHENTICATION_ BACKENDS setting includes the list of authentication backends for your project. By default, this setting is set to the following:

```
('django.contrib.auth.backends.ModelBackend',)
```

The default `ModelBackend` authenticates users against the database using the `User` model of `django.contrib.auth`. This will suit most of your projects. However, you can create custom backends to authenticate your user against other sources like a LDAP directory or any other system.

You can read more information about customizing authentication at `https://docs.djangoproject.com/en/1.8/topics/auth/customizing/#other-authentication-sources`.

Whenever you use the `authenticate()` function of `django.contrib.auth`, Django tries to authenticate the user against each of the backends defined in AUTHENTICATION_BACKENDS one by one, until one of them successfully authenticates the user. Only if all of the backends fail to authenticate the user, he or she will not be authenticated into your site.

Django provides a simple way to define your own authentication backends. An authentication backend is a class that provides the following two methods:

- `authenticate()`: Takes user credentials as parameters. Has to return `True` if the user has been successfully authenticated, or `False` otherwise.

- `get_user()`: Takes a user ID parameter and has to return a `User` object.

Creating a custom authentication backend is as simple as writing a Python class that implements both methods. We are going to create an authentication backend to let users authenticate in our site using their e-mail address instead of their username.

Create a new file inside your `account` application directory and name it `authentication.py`. Add the following code to it:

```python
from django.contrib.auth.models import User

class EmailAuthBackend(object):
    """
    Authenticate using e-mail account.
    """
    def authenticate(self, username=None, password=None):
        try:
            user = User.objects.get(email=username)
            if user.check_password(password):
                return user
            return None
        except User.DoesNotExist:
            return None

    def get_user(self, user_id):
        try:
            return User.objects.get(pk=user_id)
        except User.DoesNotExist:
            return None
```

This is a simple authentication backend. The `authenticate()` method receives the `username` and `password` optional parameters. We could use different parameters, but we use `username` and `password` to make our backend work with the authentication framework views straightaway. The preceding code works as follows:

- `authenticate()`: We try to retrieve a user with the given e-mail address and check the password using the built-in `check_password()` method of the `User` model. This method handles the password hashing to compare the given password against the password stored in the database.

- `get_user()`: We get a user by the ID set in the `user_id` parameter. Django uses the backend that authenticated the user to retrieve the `User` object for the duration of the user session.

Edit the `settings.py` file of your project and add the following setting:

```
AUTHENTICATION_BACKENDS = (
    'django.contrib.auth.backends.ModelBackend',
    'account.authentication.EmailAuthBackend',
)
```

We keep the default `ModelBackend` that is used to authenticate with username and password, and we include our own email-based authentication backend. Now, open `http://127.0.0.1:8000/account/login/` in your browser. Remember that Django will try to authenticate the user against each of the backends, so now you should be able to log in using your username or e-mail account seamlessly.

> The order of the backends listed in the `AUTHENTICATION_BACKENDS` setting matters. If the same credentials are valid for multiple backends, Django will stop at the first backend that successfully authenticates the user.

# Adding social authentication to your site

You might also want to add social authentication to your site using services such as Facebook, Twitter, or Google. Python-social-auth is a Python module that simplifies the process of adding social authentication to your website. By using this module, you can let your users log in to your website using their account of other services. You can find the code of this module at `https://github.com/omab/python-social-auth`.

This module comes with authentication backends for different Python frameworks, including Django.

To install the package via pip, open the console and run the following command:

```
pip install python-social-auth==0.2.12
```

Then add `social.apps.django_app.default` to the `INSTALLED_APPS` setting in the `settings.py` file of your project:

```
INSTALLED_APPS = (
    #...
    'social.apps.django_app.default',
)
```

This is the default application to add python-social-auth to Django projects. Now, run the following command to sync python-social-auth models with your database:

```
python manage.py migrate
```

You should see that the migrations for the `default` application are applied as follows:

```
Applying default.0001_initial... OK
Applying default.0002_add_related_name... OK
Applying default.0003_alter_email_max_length... OK
```

Python-social-auth includes backends for multiple services. You can see a list of all backends at `https://python-social-auth.readthedocs.org/en/latest/backends/index.html#supported-backends`.

We are going to include authentication backends for Facebook, Twitter, and Google.

You need to add social login URL patterns to your project. Open the main `urls.py` file of the `bookmarks` project and add the following URL pattern to it:

```
url('social-auth/',
    include('social.apps.django_app.urls', namespace='social')),
```

In order to make social authentication work, you will need a hostname, because several services will not allow redirecting to `127.0.0.1` or `localhost`. In order to fix this, under Linux or Mac OS X, edit your `/etc/hosts` file and add the following line to it:

```
127.0.0.1 mysite.com
```

This will tell your computer to point the `mysite.com` hostname to your own machine. If you are using Windows, your hosts file is located at `C:\Winwows\System32\Drivers\etc\hosts`.

To verify that your host redirection worked, open `http://mysite.com:8000/account/login/` in your browser. If you see the log in page of your application, everything was done correctly.

# Authentication using Facebook

In order to let your users log in with their Facebook account to your site, add the following line to the `AUTHENTICATION_BACKENDS` setting in the `settings.py` file of your project:

```
'social.backends.facebook.Facebook2OAuth2',
```

In order to add social authentication with Facebook, you need a Facebook developer account, and you have to to create a new Facebook application. Open `https://developers.facebook.com/apps/?action=create` in your browser and click on the **Add new app** button. Click on **Website** platform and enter *Bookmarks* for your app name. When asked, enter `http://mysite.com:8000/` as your Site URL. Follow the quickstart and click on **Create App ID**.

Go to the Dashboard of your site. You will see something similar to the following:

Copy the **App ID** and **App Secret** keys and add them to the `settings.py` file of your project as follows:

```
SOCIAL_AUTH_FACEBOOK_KEY = 'XXX' # Facebook App ID
SOCIAL_AUTH_FACEBOOK_SECRET = 'XXX' # Facebook App Secret
```

Optionally, you can define a `SOCIAL_AUTH_FACEBOOK_SCOPE` setting with the extra permissions you want to ask Facebook users for:

```
SOCIAL_AUTH_FACEBOOK_SCOPE = ['email']
```

Finally, open your `registration/login.html` template and append the following code to the `content` block:

```
<div class="social">
  <ul>
    <li class="facebook"><a href="{% url "social:begin" "facebook" %}">Sign in with Facebook</a></li>
  </ul>
</div>
```

Open `http://mysite.com:8000/account/login/` in your browser. Now your login page will look as follows:

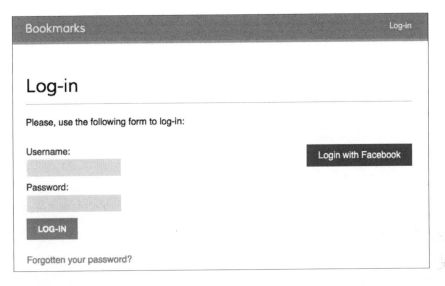

Click the **Login with Facebook** button. You will be redirected to Facebook, and you will see a modal dialog asking for your permission to let the *Bookmarks* application access your public Facebook profile:

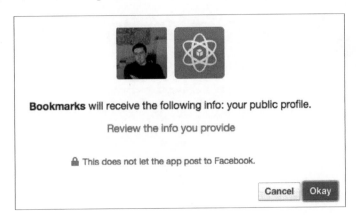

Click the **Okay** button. Python-social-auth handles the authentication. If everything goes well, you will be logged in and redirected to the dashboard page of your site. Remember that we have used this URL in the `LOGIN_REDIRECT_URL` setting. As you can see, adding social authentication to your site is pretty straightforward.

# Authentication using Twitter

For social authentication using Twitter, add the following line to the
AUTHENTICATION_BACKENDS setting in the settings.py file of your project:

```
'social.backends.twitter.TwitterOAuth',
```

You need to create a new application in your Twitter account. Open https://apps.
twitter.com/app/new in your browser and enter the details of your application
including the following settings:

- **Website**: http://mysite.com:8000/
- **Callback URL**: http://mysite.com:8000/social-auth/complete/
  twitter/

Make sure you mark the checkbox **Allow this application to be used to Sign in
with Twitter**. Then click on **Keys and Access Tokens**. You should see the following
information:

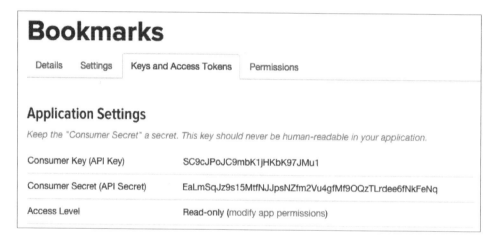

Copy the **Consumer Key** and **Consumer Secret** keys into the following settings in
the settings.py file of your project:

```
SOCIAL_AUTH_TWITTER_KEY = 'XXX' # Twitter Consumer Key
SOCIAL_AUTH_TWITTER_SECRET = 'XXX' # Twitter Consumer Secret
```

Now, edit the login.html template and add the following code in the `<ul>` element:

```
<li class="twitter"><a href="{% url "social:begin" "twitter"
%}">Login with Twitter</a></li>
```

Open `http://mysite.com:8000/account/login/` in your browser and click the
**Login with Twitter** link. You will be redirected to Twitter and it will ask you to
authorize the application:

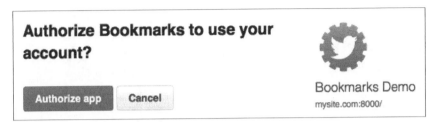

Click on **Authorize app** button. You will be logged in and redirected to the
dashboard page of your site.

# Authentication using Google

Google offers OAuth2 authentication. You can read about Google's OAuth2
implementation at `https://developers.google.com/accounts/docs/OAuth2`.

First, you need to create an API key in your Google Developer Console. Open
`https://console.developers.google.com/project` in your browser and click
the **Create project** button. Give it a name and click the **Create** button as follows:

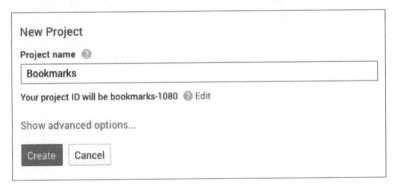

After the project is created, click the **APIs & auth** link on the left menu and then click on **Credentials** section. Click the **Add credentials** button and choose **OAuth 2.0 client ID** as follows:

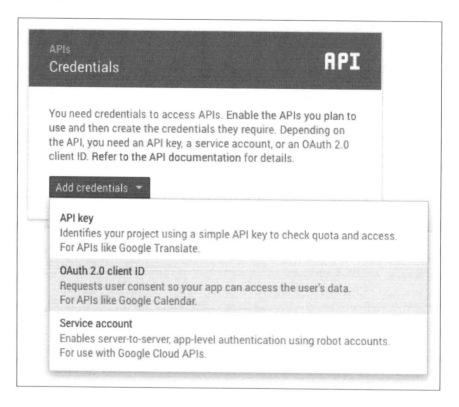

Google will ask you to configure the consent screen first. This is the page that will be shown to users to give their consent to access your site with their Google account. Click the **Configure consent screen** button. Select your e-mail address, enter *Bookmarks* as **Product name**, and click the **Save** button. The consent screen for your application will be configured and you will be redirected to finish creating your Client ID.

Fill in the form with the following information:

- **Application type**: Select **Web application**
- **Name**: Enter *Bookmarks*.
- **Authorized redirect URIs**: Add `http://mysite.com:8000/social-auth/complete/google-oauth2/`

The form should look as follows:

Click the **Create** button. You will get the **Client ID** and **Client Secret** keys. Add them to your `settings.py` file, like this:

```
SOCIAL_AUTH_GOOGLE_OAUTH2_KEY = '' # Google Consumer Key
SOCIAL_AUTH_GOOGLE_OAUTH2_SECRET = '' # Google Consumer Secret
```

In the left menu of the Google Developers Console, under the **APIs & auth** section, click the **APIs** link. You will see a list that contains all Google APIs. Click on **Google+ API** and then click the **Enable API** button in the following page:

Edit the `login.html` template and add the following code to the `<ul>` element:

```
<li class="google"><a href="{% url "social:begin" "google" %}">Login
with Google</a></li>
```

Open `http://mysite.com:8000/account/login/` in your browser. The login page should now look as follows:

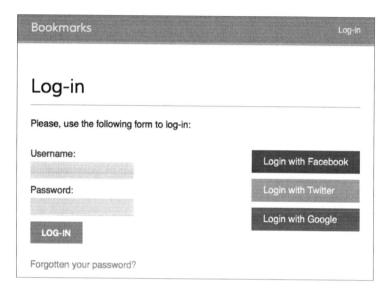

Click the **Login with Google** button. You should be redirected to Google and asked for permissions with the consent screen we previously configured:

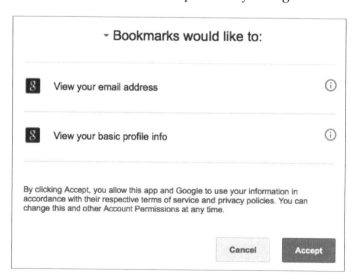

Click the **Accept** button. You will be logged in and redirected to the dashboard page of your website.

We have added social authentication to our project. The python-social-auth module contains backends for other popular on-line services.

# Summary

In this chapter, you learned how to build an authentication system into your site and created custom user profiles. You also added social authentication to your site.

In the next chapter, you will learn how to create an image bookmarking system, generate image thumbnails, and create AJAX views.

# 5
# Sharing Content in Your Website

In the previous chapter, you built user registration and authentication into your website. You learned how to create a custom profile model for your users and you added social authentication to your site with major social networks.

In this chapter, you will learn how to create a JavaScript bookmarklet to share content from other sites into your website, and you will implement AJAX features into your project using jQuery and Django.

This chapter will cover the following points:

- Creating many-to-many relationships
- Customizing behavior for forms
- Using jQuery with Django
- Building a jQuery bookmarklet
- Generating image thumbnails using sorl-thumbnail
- Implementing AJAX views and integrating them with jQuery
- Creating custom decorators for views
- Building AJAX pagination

# Creating an image bookmarking website

We are going to allow users to bookmark and share images they find in other websites and share them in our site. For this, we will need to do the following tasks:

1. Define a model to store images and their information.
2. Create a form and a view to handle image uploads.
3. Build a system for users to be able to post images they find in external websites.

First, create a new application inside your bookmarks project directory with the following command:

```
django-admin startapp images
```

Add `'images'` to the `INSTALLED_APPS` setting in the `settings.py` file as follows:

```
INSTALLED_APPS = (
    # ...
    'images',
)
```

Now Django knows that the new application is active.

# Building the image model

Edit the `models.py` file of the `images` application and add the following code to it:

```python
from django.db import models
from django.conf import settings

class Image(models.Model):
    user = models.ForeignKey(settings.AUTH_USER_MODEL,
                             related_name='images_created')
    title = models.CharField(max_length=200)
    slug = models.SlugField(max_length=200,
                            blank=True)
    url = models.URLField()
    image = models.ImageField(upload_to='images/%Y/%m/%d')
    description = models.TextField(blank=True)
    created = models.DateField(auto_now_add=True,
                               db_index=True)

    def __str__(self):
        return self.title
```

This is the model we are going to use to store images bookmarked from different sites. Let's take a look at the fields of this model:

- `user`: The `User` object that bookmarked this image. This is a `ForeignKey` field because it specifies a one-to-many relationship: A user can post multiple images, but each image is posted by a single user.

- `title`: A title for the image.

- `slug`: A short label containing only letters, numbers, underscores, or hyphens to be used for building beautiful SEO-friendly URLs.

- `url`: The original URL for this image.

- `image`: The image file.

- `description`: An optional description for the image.

- `created`: The datetime that indicates when the object has been created in the database. Since we use `auto_now_add`, this datetime is automatically set when the object is created. We use `db_index=True` so that Django creates an index in the database for this field.

> Database indexes improve query performance. Consider setting db_ index=True for fields that you frequently query using `filter()`, `exclude()`, or `order_by()`. ForeignKey fields or fields with `unique=True` imply the creation of an index. You can also use `Meta.index_together` to create indexes for multiple fields.

We are going to override the `save()` method of the `Image` model to automatically generate the slug field based on the value of the `title` field. Import the `slugify()` function and add a `save()` method to the `Image` model as follows:

```
from django.utils.text import slugify

class Image(models.Model):
    # ...
    def save(self, *args, **kwargs):
        if not self.slug:
            self.slug = slugify(self.title)
        super(Image, self).save(*args, **kwargs)
```

In this code, we use the `slufigy()` function provided by Django to automatically generate the image `slug` for the given title when no slug is provided. Then, we save the object. We will generate slugs for images automatically so that users don't have to enter a `slug` for each image.

# Creating many-to-many relationships

We are going to add another field to the `Image` model to store the users that like an image. We will need a many-to-many relationship in this case, because a user might like multiple images and each image can be liked by multiple users.

Add the following field to the `Image` model:

```
users_like = models.ManyToManyField(settings.AUTH_USER_MODEL,
                                     related_name='images_liked',
                                     blank=True)
```

When you define a `ManyToManyField`, Django creates an intermediary join table using the primary keys of both models. The `ManyToManyField` can be defined in any of the two related models.

As with `ForeignKey` fields, the `related_name` attribute of `ManyToManyField` allows us to name the relationship from the related object back to this one. `ManyToManyField` fields provide a many-to-many manager that allows us to retrieve related objects such as `image.users_like.all()` or from a user object such as `user.images_liked.all()`.

Open the command line and run the following command to create an initial migration:

**python manage.py makemigrations images**

You should see the following output:

```
Migrations for 'images':
  0001_initial.py:
    - Create model Image
```

Now run this command to apply your migration:

**python manage.py migrate images**

You will get an output that includes the following line:

```
Applying images.0001_initial... OK
```

The `Image` model is now synced to the database.

# Registering the image model in the administration site

Edit the `admin.py` file of the `images` application and register the `Image` model into the administration site as follows:

```
from django.contrib import admin
from .models import Image

class ImageAdmin(admin.ModelAdmin):
    list_display = ['title', 'slug', 'image', 'created']
    list_filter = ['created']

admin.site.register(Image, ImageAdmin)
```

Start the development server with the command `python manage.py runserver`. Open `http://127.0.0.1:8000/admin/` in your browser and you will see the `Image` model in the administration site, like this:

# Posting content from other websites

We are going to allow users to bookmark `images` from external websites. The user will provide the URL of the image, a title, and optional description. Our application will download the image and create a new `Image` object in the database.

Let's start by building a form to submit new images. Create a new `forms.py` file inside the images application directory and add the following code to it:

```
from django import forms
from .models import Image

class ImageCreateForm(forms.ModelForm):
    class Meta:
        model = Image
        fields = ('title', 'url', 'description')
        widgets = {
            'url': forms.HiddenInput,
        }
```

As you can see, this form is a `ModelForm` built from the `Image` model including only the `title`, `url`, and `description` fields. Our users are not going to enter the image URL directly in the form. Instead, they are going to use a JavaScript tool to choose an image from an external site and our form will receive its URL as a parameter. We override the default widget of the `url` field to use a `HiddenInput` widget. This widget is rendered as an HTML input element with a `type="hidden"` attribute. We use this widget because we don't want this field to be visible to users.

# Cleaning form fields

In order to verify that the provided image URL is valid, we are going to check that the filename ends with a `.jpg` or `.jpeg` extension to only allow JPG files. Django allows you to define form methods to clean specific fields using the notation `clean_<fieldname>()`. This method is executed for each field, if present, when you call `is_valid()` on a form instance. In the clean method, you can alter the field's value or raise any validation errors for this specific field when needed. Add the following method to the `ImageCreateForm`:

```
def clean_url(self):
    url = self.cleaned_data['url']
    valid_extensions = ['jpg', 'jpeg']
    extension = url.rsplit('.', 1)[1].lower()
    if extension not in valid_extensions:
        raise forms.ValidationError('The given URL does not ' \
                                    'match valid image extensions.')
    return url
```

In this code, we define a `clean_url()` method to clean the `url` field. The code works as follows:

1. We get the value of the `url` field by accessing the `cleaned_data` dictionary of the form instance.

2. We split the URL to get the file extension and check if it is one of the valid extensions. If it is not a valid extension, we raise a `ValidationError` and the form instance will not be validated. We are performing a very simple validation. You could use more advanced methods to check whether the given URL provides a valid image file or not.

In addition to validating the given URL, we will also need to download the image file and save it. We could, for example, use the view that handles the form to download the image file. Instead, we are going to take a more general approach by overriding the `save()` method of our model form to perform this task every time the form is saved.

# Overriding the save() method of a ModelForm

As you know, `ModelForm` provides a `save()` method to save the current model instance to the database and return the object. This method receives a boolean `commit` parameter, which allows you to specify whether the object has to be persisted to the database. If `commit` is `False`, the `save()` method will return a model instance but will not save it to the database. We are going to override the `save()` method of our form in order to retrieve the given image and save it.

Add the following imports at the top of the `forms.py` file:

```
from urllib import request
from django.core.files.base import ContentFile
from django.utils.text import slugify
```

Then add the following `save()` method to the `ImageCreateForm`:

```
def save(self, force_insert=False,
                force_update=False,
                commit=True):
    image = super(ImageCreateForm, self).save(commit=False)
    image_url = self.cleaned_data['url']
    image_name = '{}.{}'.format(slugify(image.title),
                                image_url.rsplit('.', 1)[1].lower())

    # download image from the given URL
    response = request.urlopen(image_url)
    image.image.save(image_name,
                    ContentFile(response.read()),
                    save=False)
    if commit:
        image.save()
    return image
```

We override the `save()` method keeping the parameters required by `ModelForm`. This code is as follows:

1.  We create a new `image` instance by calling the `save()` method of the form with `commit=False`.
2.  We get the URL from the `cleaned_data` dictionary of the form.
3.  We generate the image name by combining the `image` title slug with the original file extension.

4. We use the Python `urllib` module to download the image and then we call the `save()` method of the image field passing it a `ContentFile` object that is instantiated with the downloaded file contents. In this way we save the file to the media directory of our project. We also pass the parameter `save=False` to avoid saving the object to database yet.

5. In order to maintain the same behavior as the `save()` method we override, we save the form to the database only when the commit parameter is `True`.

Now we need a view for handling the form. Edit the `views.py` file of the images application and add the following code to it:

```
from django.shortcuts import render, redirect
from django.contrib.auth.decorators import login_required
from django.contrib import messages
from .forms import ImageCreateForm


@login_required
def image_create(request):
    if request.method == 'POST':
        # form is sent
        form = ImageCreateForm(data=request.POST)
        if form.is_valid():
            # form data is valid
            cd = form.cleaned_data
            new_item = form.save(commit=False)

            # assign current user to the item
            new_item.user = request.user
            new_item.save()
            messages.success(request, 'Image added successfully')

            # redirect to new created item detail view
            return redirect(new_item.get_absolute_url())
    else:
        # build form with data provided by the bookmarklet via GET
        form = ImageCreateForm(data=request.GET)

    return render(request,
                  'images/image/create.html',
                  {'section': 'images',
                   'form': form})
```

We add a `login_required` decorator to the `image_create` view to prevent access for non-authenticated users. This is how this view works:

1.  We expect initial data via GET in order create an instance of the form. This data will consist of the `url` and `title` attributes of an image from an external website and will be provided via GET by the JavaScript tool we will create later. For now we just assume that this data will be there initially.

2.  If the form is submitted we check if it is valid. If the form is valid we create a new `Image` instance, but we prevent the object from being saved into the database yet by passing `commit=False`.

3.  We assign the current user to the new `image` object. This is how we can know who uploaded each `image`.

4.  We save the image object to the database.

5.  Finally, we create a success message using the Django messaging framework and redirect the user to the canonical URL of the new image. We haven't implemented the `get_absolute_url()` method of the Image model yet, we will do that later.

Create a new `urls.py` file inside your `images` application and add the following code to it:

```python
from django.conf.urls import url
from . import views

urlpatterns = [
    url(r'^create/$', views.image_create, name='create'),
]
```

Edit the main `urls.py` file of your project to include the patterns we just created for the images application as follows:

```python
urlpatterns = [
    url(r'^admin/', include(admin.site.urls)),
    url(r'^account/', include('account.urls')),
    url(r'^images/', include('images.urls', namespace='images')),
]
```

Finally, you need to create a template to render the form. Create the following directory structure inside the `images` application directory:

```
templates/
    images/
        image/
            create.html
```

Edit the new `create.html` template and add the following code to it:

```
{% extends "base.html" %}

{% block title %}Bookmark an image{% endblock %}

{% block content %}
  <h1>Bookmark an image</h1>
  <img src="{{ request.GET.url }}" class="image-preview">
  <form action="." method="post">
    {{ form.as_p }}
    {% csrf_token %}
    <input type="submit" value="Bookmark it!">
  </form>
{% endblock %}
```

Now open `http://127.0.0.1:8000/images/create/?title=...&url=...` in your browser, including a `title` and `url` GET parameters providing an existing JPG image URL in the latter.

For example, you can use the following URL: `http://127.0.0.1:8000/images/create/?title=%20Django%20and%20Duke&url=http://upload.wikimedia.org/wikipedia/commons/8/85/Django_Reinhardt_and_Duke_Ellington_%28Gottlieb%29.jpg`.

You will see the form with an image preview like the following one:

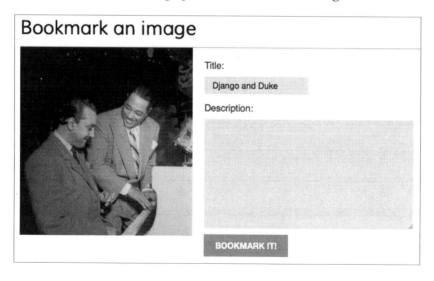

Add a description and click the **Bookmark it!** button. A new `Image` object will be saved into your database. You will get an error indicating that the `Image` model has no `get_absolute_url()` method. Don't worry about this for now, we are going to add this method later. Open `http://127.0.0.1:8000/admin/images/image/` in your browser and verify that the new image object has been saved.

# Building a bookmarklet with jQuery

A bookmarklet is a bookmark stored in a web browser that contains JavaScript code to extend the browser's functionality. When you click the bookmark, the JavaScript code is executed on the website being displayed in the browser. This is very useful for building tools that interact with other websites.

Some online services such as Pinterest implement their own bookmarklets to let users share content from other sites onto their platform. We are going to create a bookmarklet, in a similar way, to let users share images from other sites in our website.

We are going to use jQuery to build our bookmarklet. jQuery is a popular JavaScript framework that allows you to develop client-side functionality faster. You can read more about jQuery at its official website `http://jquery.com/`.

This is how your users will add a bookmarklet to their browser and use it:

1. The user drags a link from your site to his browser's bookmarks. The link contains JavaScript code in its `href` attribute. This code will be stored in the bookmark.

2. The user navigates to any website and clicks the bookmark. The JavaScript code of the bookmark is executed.

Since the JavaScript code will be stored as a bookmark, you will not be able to update it later. This is an important drawback, but you can solve it by implementing a simple launcher script that loads the actual JavaScript bookmarklet from a URL. Your users will save this launcher script as a bookmark and you will be able to update the code of the bookmarklet anytime. This is the approach we are going to take to build our bookmarklet. Let's start!

Create a new template under `images/templates/` and name it `bookmarklet_launcher.js`. This will be the launcher script. Add the following JavaScript code to this file:

```
(function(){
    if (window.myBookmarklet !== undefined){
        myBookmarklet();
    }
```

```
    else {
        document.body.appendChild(document.createElement('script')).
src='http://127.0.0.1:8000/static/js/bookmarklet.js?r='+Math.
floor(Math.random()*9999999999999999999);
    }
})();
```

This script discovers if the bookmarklet is already loaded by checking if the myBookmarklet variable is defined. By doing so, we avoid loading it again if the user clicks on the bookmarklet repeatedly. If myBookmarklet is not defined, we load another JavaScript file adding a <script> element to the document. The script tag loads the bookmarklet.js script using a random number as parameter to prevent loading the file from the browser's cache.

The actual bookmarklet code will reside in the bookmarklet.js static file. This will allow us to update our bookmarklet code without requiring our users to update the bookmark they previously added to their browser. Let's add the bookmarklet launcher to the dashboard pages, so that our users can copy it to their bookmarks.

Edit the account/dashboard.html template of the account application and make it look like the following:

```
{% extends "base.html" %}

{% block title %}Dashboard{% endblock %}

{% block content %}
  <h1>Dashboard</h1>

  {% with total_images_created=request.user.images_created.count %}
    <p>Welcome to your dashboard. You have bookmarked {{ total_images_
created }} image{{ total_images_created|pluralize }}.</p>
  {% endwith %}

  <p>Drag the following button to your bookmarks toolbar to bookmark
images from other websites → <a href="javascript:{% include
"bookmarklet_launcher.js" %}" class="button">Bookmark it</a><p>

  <p>You can also <a href="{% url "edit" %}">edit your profile</a> or
<a href="{% url "password_change" %}">change your password</a>.<p>
{% endblock %}
```

The dashboard displays now the total number of images bookmarked by the user. We use the {% with %} template tag to set a variable with the total number of images bookmarked by the current user. We also include a link with an href attribute that contains the bookmarklet launcher script. We are including this JavaScript code from the bookmarklet_launcher.js template.

Open http://127.0.0.1:8000/account/ in your browser. You should see the following page:

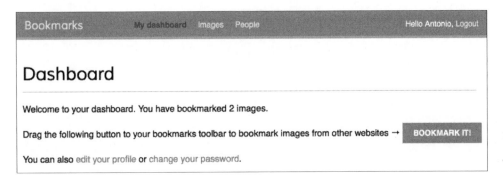

Drag the **Bookmark it!** link to the bookmarks toolbar of your browser.

Now create the following directories and files inside the images application directory:

- static/
- js/
- bookmarklet.js

You will find a static/css/ directory under the images application directory, in the code that comes along with this chapter. Copy the css/ directory into the static/ directory of your code. The css/bookmarklet.css file provides the styles for our JavaScript bookmarklet.

Edit the bookmarklet.js static file and add the following JavaScript code to it:

```
(function(){
  var jquery_version = '2.1.4';
  var site_url = 'http://127.0.0.1:8000/';
  var static_url = site_url + 'static/';
  var min_width = 100;
  var min_height = 100;

  function bookmarklet(msg) {
    // Here goes our bookmarklet code
  };
```

```
// Check if jQuery is loaded
if(typeof window.jQuery != 'undefined') {
  bookmarklet();
} else {
  // Check for conflicts
  var conflict = typeof window.$ != 'undefined';
  // Create the script and point to Google API
  var script = document.createElement('script');
  script.setAttribute('src',
    'http://ajax.googleapis.com/ajax/libs/jquery/' +
    jquery_version + '/jquery.min.js');
  // Add the script to the 'head' for processing
  document.getElementsByTagName('head')[0].appendChild(script);
  // Create a way to wait until script loading
  var attempts = 15;
  (function() {
    // Check again if jQuery is undefined
    if(typeof window.jQuery == 'undefined') {
      if(--attempts > 0) {
        // Calls himself in a few milliseconds
        window.setTimeout(arguments.callee, 250)
      } else {
        // Too much attempts to load, send error
        alert('An error ocurred while loading jQuery')
      }
    } else {
      bookmarklet();
    }
  })();
}
})()
```

This is the main jQuery loader script. It takes care of using jQuery if it's already loaded in the current website, or it loads jQuery from Google's CDN otherwise. When jQuery is loaded it executes the `bookmarklet()` function that will contain our bookmarklet code. We also set some variables at the top of the file:

- `jquery_version`: The jQuery version to load

- `site_url` and `static_url`: The base URL for our website and base URL for static files respectively

- `min_width` and `min_height`: minimum width and height in pixels for the images our bookmarklet will try to find in the site

Now let's implement the `bookmarklet` function. Edit the `bookmarklet()` function to make it look like this:

```
function bookmarklet(msg) {
  // load CSS
  var css = jQuery('<link>');
  css.attr({
    rel: 'stylesheet',
    type: 'text/css',
    href: static_url + 'css/bookmarklet.css?r=' + Math.floor(Math.
random()*9999999999999999999)
  });
  jQuery('head').append(css);

  // load HTML
  box_html = '<div id="bookmarklet"><a href="#" id="close">&times;</
a><h1>Select an image to bookmark:</h1><div class="images"></div></
div>';
  jQuery('body').append(box_html);

  // close event
  jQuery('#bookmarklet #close').click(function(){
    jQuery('#bookmarklet').remove();
  });
};
```

This code works as follows:

1.  We load the `bookmarklet.css` stylesheet using a random number as parameter to avoid the browser's cache.

2.  We add custom HTML to the document `<body>` element of the current website. This consists of a `<div>` element that will contain the images found on the current website.

3.  We add an event that removes our HTML from the document when the user clicks the close link of our HTML block. We use the `#bookmarklet #close` selector to find the HTML element with an ID named `close`, which has a parent element with an ID named `bookmarklet`. A jQuery selectors allow you to find HTML elements. A jQuery selector returns all elements found by the given CSS selector. You can find a list of jQuery selectors at `http://api.jquery.com/category/selectors/`.

After loading the CSS styles and the HTML code for the bookmarklet we need to find the images in the website. Add the following JavaScript code at the bottom of the bookmarklet() function:

```
// find images and display them
jQuery.each(jQuery('img[src$="jpg"]'), function(index, image) {
  if (jQuery(image).width() >= min_width && jQuery(image).height() >=
min_height)
  {
    image_url = jQuery(image).attr('src');
    jQuery('#bookmarklet .images').append('<a href="#"><img src="'+
image_url +'" /></a>');
  }
});
```

This code uses the img[src$="jpg"] selector to find all <img> HTML elements, whose src attribute finishes with a *jpg* string. This means that we are finding all JPG images displayed in the current website. We iterate over the results using the each() method of jQuery. We add to our <div class="images"> HTML container the images with a size larger than the one specified with the min_width and min_height variables.

The HTML container now includes the images that can be bookmarked. We want the user to click on the desired image and bookmark it. Add the following code at the bottom of the bookmarklet() function:

```
// when an image is selected open URL with it
jQuery('#bookmarklet .images a').click(function(e){
  selected_image = jQuery(this).children('img').attr('src');
  // hide bookmarklet
  jQuery('#bookmarklet').hide();
  // open new window to submit the image
  window.open(site_url +'images/create/?url='
              + encodeURIComponent(selected_image)
              + '&title='
              + encodeURIComponent(jQuery('title').text()),
              '_blank');
});
```

This code works as follows:

1. We attach a `click()` event to the images' link elements.

2. When a user clicks on an image we set a new variable called `selected_image` that contains the URL of the selected image.

3. We hide the bookmarklet and open a new browser window with the URL for bookmarking a new image in our site. We pass the `<title>` element of the website and the selected image URL as GET parameters.

Open a website of your own choice in your browser and click on your bookmarklet. You will see that a new white box appears on the the website, displaying all JPG images found with higher dimensions than 100 x 100 px. It should look like the following example:

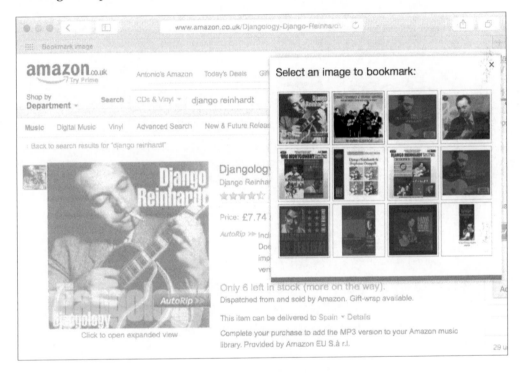

Since we are using the Django development server, and we are serving pages via HTTP, the bookmarklet will not work in websites served via HTTPS due to security restrictions of the browser.

If you click on an image, you will be redirected to the image create page, passing the title of the website and the URL of the selected image as GET parameters:

Congratulations! This is your first JavaScript bookmarklet and it is fully integrated into your Django project.

# Creating a detail view for images

We are going to create a simple detail view for displaying an image that has been saved into our site. Open the `views.py` file of the `images` application and add the following code to it:

```python
from django.shortcuts import get_object_or_404
from .models import Image
def image_detail(request, id, slug):
    image = get_object_or_404(Image, id=id, slug=slug)
    return render(request,
                  'images/image/detail.html',
                  {'section': 'images',
                   'image': image})
```

This is a simple view to display an image. Edit the `urls.py` file of the `images` application and add the following URL pattern:

```
url(r'^detail/(?P<id>\d+)/(?P<slug>[-\w]+)/$',
    views.image_detail, name='detail'),
```

Edit the `models.py` file of the images application and add the `get_absolute_url()` method to the `Image` model as follows:

```python
from django.core.urlresolvers import import reverse

class Image(models.Model):
    # ...
    def get_absolute_url(self):
        return reverse('images:detail', args=[self.id, self.slug])
```

Remember that the common pattern for providing canonical URLs for objects is to define a `get_absolute_url()` method in the model.

Finally, create a template inside the `/images/image/` template directory of the images application and name it `detail.html`. Add the following code to it:

```
{% extends "base.html" %}

{% block title %}{{ image.title }}{% endblock %}

{% block content %}
  <h1>{{ image.title }}</h1>
  <img src="{{ image.image.url }}" class="image-detail">
  {% with total_likes=image.users_like.count %}
    <div class="image-info">
      <div>
        <span class="count">
          {{ total_likes }} like{{ total_likes|pluralize }}
        </span>
      </div>
      {{ image.description|linebreaks }}
    </div>
    <div class="image-likes">
      {% for user in image.users_like.all %}
        <div>
          <img src="{{ user.profile.photo.url }}">
          <p>{{ user.first_name }}</p>
        </div>
      {% empty %}
        Nobody likes this image yet.
```

```
        {% endfor %}
      </div>
    {% endwith %}
  {% endblock %}
```

This is the template to display the detail of a bookmarked image. We make use of the {% with %} tag to store the result of the QuerySet counting all user likes in a new variable called `total_likes`. By doing so we avoid evaluating the same QuerySet twice. We also include the image description and we iterate over `image.users_like.all` to display all the users that like this image.

> Using the {% with %} template tag is useful to prevent Django from evaluating QuerySets multiple times.

Now bookmark a new image using the bookmarklet. You will be redirected to the image detail page after you posted the image. The page will include a success message as follows:

# Creating image thumbnails using sorl-thumbnail

We are displaying the original image in the detail page but dimensions for different images may vary a lot. Also, the original files for some images might be huge, and loading them might take too long time. The best way to display optimized images in a uniform way is to generate thumbnails. We are going to use a Django application called `sorl-thumbnail` for this purpose.

Open the terminal and install `sorl-thumbnail` using the following command:

**pip install sorl-thumbnail==12.3**

Edit the `settings.py` file of the bookmarks project and add `sorl.thumbnail` to the INSTALLED_APPS settings.

Then run the following command to sync the application with your database:

**python manage.py migrate**

You should see an output that includes the following line:

```
Creating table thumbnail_kvstore
```

The `sorl-thumbnail` application offers you different ways to define image thumbnails. The application provides a `{% thumbnail %}` template tag to generate thumbnails in templates and a custom `ImageField` if you want to define thumbnails in your models. We are going to use the template tag approach. Edit the `images/image/detail.html` template and replace the following line:

```
<img src="{{ image.image.url }}" class="image-detail">
```

With these lines:

```
{% load thumbnail %}
{% thumbnail image.image "300" as im %}
  <a href="{{ image.image.url }}">
    <img src="{{ im.url }}" class="image-detail">
  </a>
{% endthumbnail %}
```

Here, we define a thumbnail with fixed width of of 300 pixels. The first time a user loads this page, a thumbnail image will be created. The generated thumbnail will be served in the following requests. Start the development server with the `python manage.py runserver` command and access the image detail page for an existing image. The thumbnail will be generated and displayed on the site.

The `sorl-thumbnail` application offers several options to customize your thumbnails, including cropping algorithms and different effects that can be applied. If you have any difficulty generating thumbnails, you can add `THUMBNAIL_DEBUG` `= True` to your settings in order to obtain debug information. You can read the full documentation of the `sorl-thumbnail` application at `http://sorl-thumbnail.` `readthedocs.org/.`

# Adding AJAX actions with jQuery

Now we are going to add AJAX actions to our application. AJAX comes from Asynchronous JavaScript and XML. This term encompasses a group of techniques to make asynchronous HTTP requests. It consists in sending and retrieving data from the server asynchronously, without reloading the whole page. Despite the name, XML is not required. You can send or retrieve data in other formats such as JSON, HTML, or plain text.

We are going to add a link to the image detail page to let users click it to like an image. We will perform this action with an AJAX call to avoid reloading the whole page. First, we are going to create a view for users to like/unlike images. Edit the `views.py` file of the `images` application and add the following code to it:

```python
from django.http import JsonResponse
from django.views.decorators.http import require_POST

@login_required
@require_POST
def image_like(request):
    image_id = request.POST.get('id')
    action = request.POST.get('action')
    if image_id and action:
        try:
            image = Image.objects.get(id=image_id)
            if action == 'like':
                image.users_like.add(request.user)
            else:
                image.users_like.remove(request.user)
            return JsonResponse({'status':'ok'})
        except:
            pass
    return JsonResponse({'status':'ko'})
```

We are using two decorators for our view. The `login_required` decorator prevents users that are not logged in from accessing this view. The `require_GET` decorator returns an `HttpResponseNotAllowed` object (status code `405`) if the HTTP request is not done via GET. This way we only allow GET requests for this view. Django also provides a `require_POST` decorator to only allow POST requests and a `require_http_methods` decorator to which you can pass a list of allowed methods as an argument.

In this view we use two GET parameters:

- `image_id`: The ID of the image object on which the user is performing the action
- `action`: The action that the user wants to perform, which we assume to be a string with the value *like* or *unlike*

We use the manager provided by Django for the `users_like` many-to-many field of the `Image` model in order to add or remove objects from the relationship using the `add()` or `remove()` methods. Calling `add()` passing an object that is already present in the related object set does not duplicate it and thus, calling `remove()` passing an object that is not in the related object set does nothing. Another useful method of the many-to-many manager is `clear()`, which removes all objects from the related object set.

Finally, we use the `JsonResponse` class provided by Django, which returns an HTTP response with an `application/json` content type, converting the given object into a JSON output.

Edit the `urls.py` file of the `images` application and add the following URL pattern to it:

```
url(r'^like/$', views.image_like, name='like'),
```

# Loading j Query

We need to add the AJAX functionality to our image detail template. In order to use jQuery in our templates, we are going to include it in the `base.html` template of our project first. Edit the `base.html` template of the account application and include the following code before the closing `</body>` HTML tag:

```
<script src="https://ajax.googleapis.com/ajax/libs/jquery/2.1.4/
jquery.min.js"></script>
<script>
  $(document).ready(function(){
    {% block domready %}
    {% endblock %}
    });
</script>
```

We load the jQuery framework from Google, which hosts popular JavaScript frameworks in a high-speed reliable content delivery network. You can also download jQuery from `http://jquery.com/` and add it to the `static` directory of your application.

We add a `<script>` tag to include JavaScript code. `$(document).ready()` is a jQuery function that takes a handler that is executed when the **DOM** hierarchy has been fully constructed. DOM comes from Document Object Model. The DOM is created by the browser when a webpage is loaded, and it is constructed as a tree of objects. By including our code inside this function we make sure all HTML elements we are going to interact with are loaded in the DOM. Our code will be only executed once the DOM is ready.

Inside the document ready handler function, we include a Django template block called **domready**, in which templates that extend the base template will be able to include specific JavaScript.

Don't get confused with JavaScript code and Django template tags. Django template language is rendered in the server side outputting the final HTML document and JavaScript is executed in the client side. In some cases, it is useful to generate JavaScript code dynamically using Django.

 In the examples of this chapter we include JavaScript code in Django templates. The preferred way to include JavaScript code is by loading `.js` files, which are served as static files, especially when they are large scripts.

# Cross-Site Request Forgery in AJAX requests

You have learned about Cross-Site Request Forgery in *Chapter 2, Enhancing Your Blog With Advanced Features*. With the CSRF protection active, Django checks for a CSRF token in all POST requests. When you submit forms you can use the `{% csrf_token %}` template tag to send the token along with the form. However, it is a bit inconvenient for AJAX requests to pass the CSRF token as POST data in with every POST request. Therefore, Django allows you to set a custom `X-CSRFToken` header in your AJAX requests with the value of the CSRF token. This allows you to set up jQuery or any other JavaScript library, to automatically set the `X-CSRFToken` header in every request.

In order to include the token in all requests, you need to:

1.  Retrieve the CSRF token form the `csrftoken` cookie, which is set if CSRF protection is active.

2.  Send the token in the AJAX request using the `X-CSRFToken` header.

You can find more information about CSRF protection and AJAX at `https://docs.djangoproject.com/en/1.8/ref/csrf/#ajax`.

Edit the last code you included in your `base.html` template and make it look like the following:

```
<script src="https://ajax.googleapis.com/ajax/libs/jquery/2.1.4/
jquery.min.js"></script>
<script src=" http://cdn.jsdelivr.net/jquery.cookie/1.4.1/jquery.
cookie.min.js "></script>
<script>
  var csrftoken = $.cookie('csrftoken');
  function csrfSafeMethod(method) {
    // these HTTP methods do not require CSRF protection
    return (/^(GET|HEAD|OPTIONS|TRACE)$/.test(method));
  }
  $.ajaxSetup({
    beforeSend: function(xhr, settings) {
      if (!csrfSafeMethod(settings.type) && !this.crossDomain) {
        xhr.setRequestHeader("X-CSRFToken", csrftoken);
      }
    }
  });
  $(document).ready(function(){
    {% block domready %}
    {% endblock %}
  });
</script>
```

The code above is as follows:

1.  We load the jQuery Cookie plugin from a public CDN, so that we can interact with cookies.

2.  We read the value of the `csrftoken` cookie.

3.  We define the `csrfSafeMethod()` function to check whether an HTTP method is safe. Safe methods don't require CSRF protection. These are GET, HEAD, OPTIONS, and TRACE.

4. We setup jQuery AJAX requests using $.ajaxSetup(). Before each AJAX request is performed, we check if the request method is safe and the current request is not cross-domain. If the request is unsafe, we set the X-CSRFToken header with the value obtained from the cookie. This setup will apply to all AJAX requests performed with jQuery.

The CSRF token will be included in all AJAX request that use unsafe HTTP methods such as POST or PUT.

# Performing AJAX requests with jQuery

Edit the images/image/detail.html template of the images application and replace the following line:

```
{% with total_likes=image.users_like.count %}
```

With the following one:

```
{% with total_likes=image.users_like.count users_like=image.users_
like.all %}
```

Then modify the <div> element with the image-info class as follows:

```
<div class="image-info">
  <div>
    <span class="count">
      <span class="total">{{ total_likes }}</span>
      like{{ total_likes|pluralize }}
    </span>
    <a href="#" data-id="{{ image.id }}" data-action="{% if request.
user in users_like %}un{% endif %}like" class="like button">
      {% if request.user not in users_like %}
        Like
      {% else %}
        Unlike
      {% endif %}
    </a>
  </div>
  {{ image.description|linebreaks }}
</div>
```

First, we add another variable to the {% with %} template tag to store the results of the image.users_like.all query and avoid executing it twice. We display the total number of users that like this image and include a link to like/unlike the image: We check if the user is in the related object set of users_like to display either like or unlike based on the current relationship of the user and this image. We add the following attributes to the <a> HTML element:

- data-id: The ID of the image displayed.
- data-action: The action to run when the user clicks the link. This can be like or unlike.

We will send the value of both attributes in the AJAX request to the image_like view. When a user clicks the like/unlike link, we need to perform the following actions on the client side:

1. Call the AJAX view passing the image ID and the action parameters to it.
2. If the AJAX request is successful, update the data-action attribute of the <a> HTML element with the opposite action (like / unlike), and modify its display text accordingly.
3. Update the total number of likes that is displayed.

Add the domready block at the bottom of the images/image/detail.html template with the following JavaScript code:

```
{% block domready %}
  $('a.like').click(function(e){
    e.preventDefault();
    $.post('{% url "images:like" %}',
      {
        id: $(this).data('id'),
        action: $(this).data('action')
      },
      function(data){
        if (data['status'] == 'ok')
        {
          var previous_action = $('a.like').data('action');

          // toggle data-action
          $('a.like').data('action', previous_action == 'like' ?
'unlike' : 'like');
          // toggle link text
          $('a.like').text(previous_action == 'like' ? 'Unlike' :
'Like');
```

```
        // update total likes
        var previous_likes = parseInt($('span.count .total').
text());
        $('span.count .total').text(previous_action == 'like' ?
previous_likes + 1 : previous_likes - 1);
      }
    }
  );
});
{% endblock %}
```

This code works as follows:

1.  We use the $('a.like') jQuery selector to find all <a> elements of the HTML document with the class like.

2.  We define a handler function for the click event. This function will be executed every time the user clicks the like/unlike link.

3.  Inside the handler function we use e.preventDefault() to avoid the default behavior of the <a> element. This will prevent from the link taking us anywhere.

4.  We use $.post() to perform an asynchronous POST request to the server. jQuery also provides a $.get() method to perform GET requests and a low-level $.ajax() method.

5.  We use Django's {% url %} template tag to build the URL for the AJAX request.

6.  We build the POST parameters dictionary to send in the request. These are the ID and action parameters expected by our Django view. We retrieve these values from the <a> element's data-id and data-action attributes.

7.  We define a callback function that is executed when the HTTP response is received. It takes a data attribute that contains the content of the response.

8.  We access the status attribute of the data received and check if it equals to ok. If the returned data is as expected, we toggle the data-action attribute of the link and its text. This allows the user to undo his action.

9.  We increase or decrease the total likes count by one, depending on the action performed.

Open the image detail page in your browser for an image you have uploaded. You should be able to see the following initial likes count and the LIKE button as follows:

Click the **LIKE** button. You will see that the total likes count increases in one and the button text changes into **UNLIKE** like this:

When you click the **UNLIKE** button the action is performed, the button's text changes back to **LIKE** and the total count changes accordingly.

When programming JavaScript, especially when performing AJAX requests, it is recommended to use a tool such as Firebug for debugging. Firebug is a Firefox add-on that allows you to debug JavaScript and monitor CSS and HTML changes. You can download Firebug from `http://getfirebug.com/`. Other browsers such as Chrome or Safari also include developer tools to debug JavaScript. In those browsers you can right-click anywhere in the website and click on **Inspect element** to access the web developer tools.

# Creating custom decorators for your views

We are going to restrict our AJAX views to allow only requests generated via AJAX. The Django Request object provides an `is_ajax()` method that checks if the request is being made with `XMLHttpRequest`, which means it is an AJAX request. This value is set in the `HTTP_X_REQUESTED_WITH` HTTP header, which is included in AJAX requests by most JavaScript libraries.

We are going to create a decorator for checking the `HTTP_X_REQUESTED_WITH` header in our views. A decorator is a function that takes another function and extends the behavior of the latter without explicitly modifying it. If the concept of decorators is foreign to you, you might like to take a look at `https://www.python.org/dev/peps/pep-0318/` before you continue reading.

Since our decorator will be generic and could be applied to any view, we will create a `common` Python package in our project. Create the following directory and files inside the `bookmarks` project directory:

- `common/`
- `__init__.py`
- `decorators.py`

Edit the `decorators.py` file and add the following code to it:

```python
from django.http import HttpResponseBadRequest

def ajax_required(f):
    def wrap(request, *args, **kwargs):
        if not request.is_ajax():
            return HttpResponseBadRequest()
        return f(request, *args, **kwargs)
    wrap.__doc__=f.__doc__
    wrap.__name__=f.__name__
    return wrap
```

This is our custom `ajax_required` decorator. It defines a wrap function that returns an `HttpResponseBadRequest` object (HTTP 400 code) if the request is not AJAX. Otherwise, it returns the decorated function.

Now you can edit the `views.py` file of the `images` application and add this decorator to your `image_like` AJAX view as follows:

```python
from common.decorators import ajax_required

@ajax_required
@login_required
@require_POST
def image_like(request):
    # ...
```

If you try to access `http://127.0.0.1:8000/images/like/` directly with your browser, you will get an HTTP 400 response.

 Build custom decorators for your views if you find that you are repeating the same checks in multiple views.

# Adding AJAX pagination to your list views

We need to list all bookmarked images in our website. We are going to use AJAX pagination to build infinite scroll functionality. Infinite scroll is achieved by loading the next results automatically when the user scrolls to the bottom of the page.

We are going to implement an image list view that will handle both standard browser requests and AJAX requests including pagination. When the user initially loads the image list page, we display the first page of images. When he scrolls to the bottom of the page we load the following page of items via AJAX and append it to the bottom of the main page.

The same view will handle both standard and AJAX pagination. Edit the `views.py` file of the `images` application and add the following code to it:

```python
from django.http import HttpResponse
from django.core.paginator import Paginator, EmptyPage, \
                                    PageNotAnInteger


@login_required
def image_list(request):
    images = Image.objects.all()
    paginator = Paginator(images, 8)
    page = request.GET.get('page')
    try:
        images = paginator.page(page)
    except PageNotAnInteger:
        # If page is not an integer deliver the first page
        images = paginator.page(1)
    except EmptyPage:
        if request.is_ajax():
            # If the request is AJAX and the page is out of range
            # return an empty page
            return HttpResponse('')
        # If page is out of range deliver last page of results
        images = paginator.page(paginator.num_pages)
    if request.is_ajax():
        return render(request,
                      'images/image/list_ajax.html',
                      {'section': 'images', 'images': images})
    return render(request,
                  'images/image/list.html',
                  {'section': 'images', 'images': images})
```

In this view, we create a QuerySet to return all images from the database. Then we build a `Paginator` object to paginate the results retrieving eight images per page. We get an `EmptyPage` exception if the requested page is out of range. If this the case and the request is done via AJAX, we return an empty `HttpResponse` that will help us stop the AJAX pagination on the client side. We render the results to two different templates:

- For AJAX requests, we render the `list_ajax.html` template. This template will only contain the images of the requested page.

- For standard requests, we render the `list.html` template. This template will extend the `base.html` template to display the whole page and will include the `list_ajax.html` template to include the list of images.

Edit the `urls.py` file of the `images` application and add the following URL pattern to it:

```
url(r'^$', views.image_list, name='list'),
```

Finally, we need to create the templates mentioned above. Inside the `images/image/` template directory create a new template and name it `list_ajax.html`. Add the following code to it:

```
{% load thumbnail %}

{% for image in images %}
  <div class="image">
    <a href="{{ image.get_absolute_url }}">
      {% thumbnail image.image "300x300" crop="100%" as im %}
        <a href="{{ image.get_absolute_url }}">
          <img src="{{ im.url }}">
        </a>
      {% endthumbnail %}
    </a>
    <div class="info">
      <a href="{{ image.get_absolute_url }}" class="title">
        {{ image.title }}
      </a>
    </div>
  </div>
{% endfor %}
```

This template displays the list of images. We will use it to return results for AJAX requests. Create another template in the same directory and name it `list.html`. Add the following code to it:

```
{% extends "base.html" %}

{% block title %}Images bookmarked{% endblock %}

{% block content %}
  <h1>Images bookmarked</h1>
  <div id="image-list">
    {% include "images/image/list_ajax.html" %}
  </div>
{% endblock %}
```

The list template extends the `base.html` template. To avoid repeating code, we include the `list_ajax.html` template for displaying images. The `list.html` template will hold the JavaScript code for loading additional pages when scrolling to the bottom of the page.

Add the following code to the `list.html` template:

```
{% block domready %}
  var page = 1;
  var empty_page = false;
  var block_request = false;

  $(window).scroll(function() {
    var margin = $(document).height() - $(window).height() - 200;
    if ($(window).scrollTop() > margin && empty_page == false &&
block_request == false) {
      block_request = true;
      page += 1;
      $.get('?page=' + page, function(data) {
        if(data == '') {
          empty_page = true;
        }
        else {
          block_request = false;
          $('#image-list').append(data);
        }
      });
    }
  });
{% endblock %}
```

This code provides the infinite scroll functionality. We include the JavaScript code in the `domready` block that we defined in the `base.html` template. The code is as follows:

1. We define the following variables:
   - `page`: Stores the current page number.
   - `empty_page`: Allows us to know if the user is in the last page and retrieves an empty page. As soon as we get an empty page we will stop sending additional AJAX requests because we will assume there are no more results.
   - `block_request`: Prevents from sending additional requests while an AJAX request is in progress.

2. We use `$(window).scroll()` to capture the scroll event and we define a handler function for it.

3. We calculate the margin variable getting the difference between the total document height and the window height because that's the height of the remaining content for the user to scroll. We subtract a value of 200 from the result so that we load the next page when the user is closer than 200 pixels to the bottom of the page.

4. We only send an AJAX request if no other AJAX request is being done (`block_request` has to be `false`) and the user didn't got to the last page of results (`empty_page` is also `false`).

5. We set `block_request` to `true` to avoid that the scroll event triggers additional AJAX requests, and we increase the `page` counter by one, in order to retrieve the next page.

6. We perform an AJAX GET request using `$.get()` and we receive the HTML response back in a variable called `data`. There are two scenarios:
   - The response has no content: We got to the end of the results and there are no more pages to load. We set `empty_page` to true to prevent additional AJAX requests.
   - The response contains data: We append the data to the HTML element with the image-list id. The page content expands vertically appending results when the user approaches the bottom of the page.

Open `http://127.0.0.1:8000/images/` in your browser. You will see the list of images you have bookmarked so far. It should look similar to this:

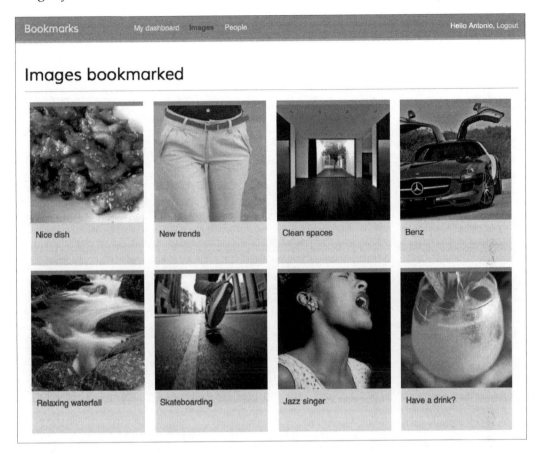

Scroll to the bottom of the page to load additional pages. Make sure that you have bookmarked more than eight images using the bookmarklet, because that's the number of images we are displaying per page. Remember that you can use Firebug or a similar tool to track the AJAX requests and debug your JavaScript code.

Finally, edit the `base.html` template of the `account` application and add the URL for the Images item of the main menu as follows:

```
<li {% if section == "images" %}class="selected"{% endif %}><a
href="{% url "images:list" %}">Images</a></li>
```

Now you can access the image list from the main menu.

# Summary

In this chapter, we have built a JavaScript bookmarklet to share images from other websites into our site. You have implemented AJAX views with jQuery and added AJAX pagination.

Next chapter will teach you how to build a follower system and an activity stream. You will work with generic relations, signals, and denormalization. You will also learn how to use Redis with Django.

# 6
# Tracking User Actions

In the previous chapter, you implemented AJAX views into your project using jQuery and built a JavaScript bookmarklet for sharing content from other websites in your platform.

In this chapter, you will learn how to build a follower system and create a user activity stream. You will discover how Django signals work and integrate Redis fast I/O storage into your project to store item views.

This chapter will cover the following points:

- Creating many-to-many relationships with an intermediary model
- Building AJAX views
- Creating an activity stream application
- Adding generic relations to models
- Optimizing QuerySets for related objects
- Using signals for denormalizing counts
- Storing item views in Redis

## Building a follower system

We will build a follower system into our project. Our users will be able to follow each other and track what other users share on the platform. The relationship between users is a many-to-many relationship, A user can follow multiple users and can be followed back by multiple users.

# Creating many-to-many relationships with an intermediary model

In previous chapters, you created many-to-many relationships by adding a `ManyToManyField` to one of the related models and letting Django create the database table for the relationship. This is suitable for most of the cases, but sometimes you might need to create an intermediate model for the relation. Creating an intermediary model is necessary when you want to store additional information for the relationship, for example the date when the relation was created or a field that describes the type of the relationship.

We will create an intermediary model for building relationships between users. There are two reasons why we want to use an intermediate model:

- We are using the `user` model provided by Django and we want to avoid altering it
- We want to store the time when the relation is created

Edit the `models.py` file of your `account` application and add the following code to it:

```
from django.contrib.auth.models import User

class Contact(models.Model):
    user_from = models.ForeignKey(User,
                                  related_name='rel_from_set')
    user_to = models.ForeignKey(User,
                                related_name='rel_to_set')
    created = models.DateTimeField(auto_now_add=True,
                                   db_index=True)

    class Meta:
        ordering = ('-created',)

    def __str__(self):
        return '{} follows {}'.format(self.user_from,
                                      self.user_to)
```

This is the `Contact` model we will use for user relationships. It contains the following fields:

- `user_from`: A `ForeignKey` for the user that creates the relationship
- `user_to`: A `ForeignKey` for the user being followed
- `created`: A `DateTimeField` field with `auto_now_add=True` to store the time when the relationship was created

A database index is automatically created on `ForeignKey` fields. We use `db_index=True` to create a database index for the `created` field. This will improve query performance when ordering QuerySets by this field.

Using the ORM, we could create a relationship for a user `user1` following another user `user2`, like this:

```
user1 = User.objects.get(id=1)
user2 = User.objects.get(id=2)
Contact.objects.create(user_from=user1, user_to=user2)
```

The related managers `rel_from_set` and `rel_to_set` will return a QuerySet for the `Contact` model. In order to access the end side of the relationship from the `User` model, it would be desirable that `User` contained a `ManyToManyField` as follows:

```
following = models.ManyToManyField('self',
                                    through=Contact,
                                    related_name='followers',
                                    symmetrical=False)
```

In this example, we tell Django to use our custom intermediary model for the relationship by adding `through=Contact` to the `ManyToManyField`. This is a many-to-many relationship from the `User` model to itself: We refer to `'self'` in the `ManyToManyField` field to create a relationship to the same model.

 When you need additional fields in a many-to-many relationship, create a custom model with a `ForeignKey` for each side of the relationship. Add a `ManyToManyField` in one of the related models and indicate Django to use your intermediary model by including it in the `through` parameter.

If the `User` model was part of our application, we could add the previous field to the model. However, we cannot alter the `User` class directly because it belongs to the `django.contrib.auth` application. We are going to take a slightly different approach, by adding this field dynamically to the `User` model. Edit the `models.py` file of the `account` application and add the following lines:

```
# Add following field to User dynamically
User.add_to_class('following',
                  models.ManyToManyField('self',
                                         through=Contact,
                                         related_name='followers',
                                         symmetrical=False))
```

In this code, we use the `add_to_class()` method of Django models to monkey-patch the `User` model. Be aware that using `add_to_class()` is not the recommended way for adding fields to models. However, we take advantage from using it in this case because of the following reasons:

- We simplify the way we retrieve related objects using the Django ORM with `user.followers.all()` and `user.following.all()`. We use the intermediary `Contact` model and avoid complex queries that would involve additional database joins, as it would have been if we had defined the relationship in our custom `Profile` model.

- The table for this many-to-many relationship will be created using the `Contact` model. Thus, the `ManyToManyField` added dynamically will not imply any database changes for the Django `User` model.

- We avoid creating a custom user model, keeping all the advantages of Django's built-in `User`.

Keep in mind that in most cases, it is preferable to add fields to the `Profile` model we created before, instead of monkey-patching the `User` model. Django also allows you to use custom user models. If you want to use your custom user model, take a look at the documentation at `https://docs.djangoproject.com/en/1.8/topics/auth/customizing/#specifying-a-custom-user-model`.

You can see that the relationship includes `symmetrical=False`. When you define a `ManyToManyField` to the model itself, Django forces the relationship to be symmetrical. In this case, we are setting `symmetrical=False` to define a non-symmetric relation. This is, if I follow you, it doesn't mean you automatically follow me.

> When you use an intermediate model for many-to-many relationships some of the related manager's methods are disabled, such as `add()`, `create()` or `remove()`. You need to create or delete instances of the intermediate model instead.

Run the following command to generate the initial migrations for the `account` application:

```
python manage.py makemigrations account
```

You will see the following output:

```
Migrations for 'account':
  0002_contact.py:
    - Create model Contact
```

Now run the following command to sync the application with the database:

```
python manage.py migrate account
```

You should see an output that includes the following line:

```
Applying account.0002_contact... OK
```

The `Contact` model is now synced to the database and we are able to create relationships between users . However, our site doesn't offer a way to browse through users or see a particular user profile yet. Let's build list and detail views for the `User` model.

# Creating list and detail views for user profiles

Open the `views.py` file of the `account` application and add the following code to it:

```python
from django.shortcuts import get_object_or_404
from django.contrib.auth.models import User

@login_required
def user_list(request):
    users = User.objects.filter(is_active=True)
    return render(request,
                  'account/user/list.html',
                  {'section': 'people',
                   'users': users})

@login_required
def user_detail(request, username):
    user = get_object_or_404(User,
                             username=username,
                             is_active=True)
    return render(request,
                  'account/user/detail.html',
                  {'section': 'people',
                   'user': user})
```

These are simple list and detail views for `User` objects. The `user_list` view gets all active users. The Django `User` model contains a flag `is_active` to designate whether the user account is considered active. We filter the query by `is_active=True` to return only active users. This view returns all results, but you can improve it by adding pagination the same way we did for the `image_list` view.

The `user_detail` view uses the `get_object_or_404()` shortcut to retrieve the active user with the given username. The view returns an HTTP 404 response if no active user with the given username is found.

Edit the `urls.py` file of the `account` application, and add an URL pattern for each view as follows:

```
urlpatterns = [
    # ...
    url(r'^users/$', views.user_list, name='user_list'),
    url(r'^users/(?P<username>[-\w]+)/$',
        views.user_detail,
        name='user_detail'),
]
```

We are going to use the `user_detail` URL pattern to generate the canonical URL for users. You have already defined a `get_absolute_url()` method in a model to return the canonical URL for each object. Another way to specify an URL for a model is by adding the `ABSOLUTE_URL_OVERRIDES` setting to your project.

Edit the `settings.py` file of your project and add the following code to it:

```
ABSOLUTE_URL_OVERRIDES = {
    'auth.user': lambda u: reverse_lazy('user_detail',
                                        args=[u.username])
}
```

Django adds a `get_absolute_url()` method dynamically to any models that appear in the `ABSOLUTE_URL_OVERRIDES` setting. This method returns the corresponding URL for the given model specified in the setting. We return the `user_detail` URL for the given user. Now you can use `get_absolute_url()` on a `User` instance to retrieve its corresponding URL. Open the Python shell with the command `python manage.py shell` and run the following code to test it:

```
>>> from django.contrib.auth.models import User
>>> user = User.objects.latest('id')
>>> str(user.get_absolute_url())
'/account/users/ellington/'
```

The returned URL is as expected. We need to create templates for the views we just built. Add the following directory and files to the `templates/account/` directory of the `account` application:

```
/user/
    detail.html
    list.html
```

Edit the `account/user/list.html` template and add the following code to it:

```
{% extends "base.html" %}
{% load thumbnail %}

{% block title %}People{% endblock %}

{% block content %}
  <h1>People</h1>
  <div id="people-list">
    {% for user in users %}
      <div class="user">
        <a href="{{ user.get_absolute_url }}">
          {% thumbnail user.profile.photo "180x180" crop="100%" as im
%}
            <img src="{{ im.url }}">
          {% endthumbnail %}
        </a>
        <div class="info">
          <a href="{{ user.get_absolute_url }}" class="title">
            {{ user.get_full_name }}
          </a>
        </div>
      </div>
    {% endfor %}
  </div>
{% endblock %}
```

This template allows us to list all the active users in the site. We iterate over the given users and use sorl-thumbnail's {% thumbnail %} template tag to generate profile image thumbnails.

Open the `base.html` template of your project and include the `user_list` URL in the `href` attribute of the following menu item:

```
<li {% if section == "people" %}class="selected"{% endif %}><a
href="{% url "user_list" %}">People</a></li>
```

Start the development server with the command `python manage.py runserver` and open `http://127.0.0.1:8000/account/users/` in your browser. You should see a list of users like the following one:

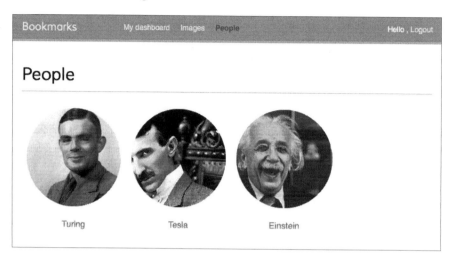

Edit `account/user/detail.html` template of the `account` application and add the following code to it:

```
{% extends "base.html" %}
{% load thumbnail %}

{% block title %}{{ user.get_full_name }}{% endblock %}

{% block content %}
  <h1>{{ user.get_full_name }}</h1>
  <div class="profile-info">
    {% thumbnail user.profile.photo "180x180" crop="100%" as im %}
      <img src="{{ im.url }}" class="user-detail">
    {% endthumbnail %}
  </div>
  {% with total_followers=user.followers.count %}
    <span class="count">
      <span class="total">{{ total_followers }}</span>
      follower{{ total_followers|pluralize }}
    </span>
    <a href="#" data-id="{{ user.id }}" data-action="{% if request.
user in user.followers.all %}un{% endif %}follow" class="follow
button">
        {% if request.user not in user.followers.all %}
```

```
        Follow
      {% else %}
        Unfollow
      {% endif %}
    </a>
    <div id="image-list" class="image-container">
      {% include "images/image/list_ajax.html" with images=user.
  images_created.all %}
    </div>
  {% endwith %}
{% endblock %}
```

In the detail template we display the user profile and we use the `{% thumbnail %}` template tag to display the profile image. We show the total number of followers and a link to `follow`/`unfollow` the user. We prevent users from following themselves by hiding this link if the user is watching their own profile. We are going to perform an AJAX request to follow/unfollow a particular user. We add `data-id` and `data-action` attributes to the `<a>` HTML element including the user ID and the initial action to perform when it's clicked, follow or unfollow, that depends on the user requesting the page being or not a follower of this user. We display the images bookmarked by the user with the `list_ajax.html` template.

Open your browser again and click on a user that has bookmarked some images. You will see a profile detail like the following one:

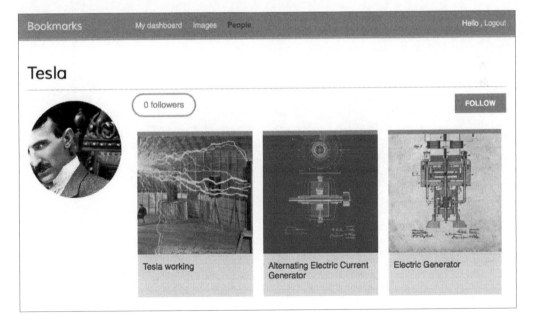

# Building an AJAX view to follow users

We will create a simple view to follow/unfollow a user using AJAX. Edit the
views.py file of the account application and add the following code to it:

```python
from django.http import JsonResponse
from django.views.decorators.http import require_POST
from common.decorators import ajax_required
from .models import Contact


@ajax_required
@require_POST
@login_required
def user_follow(request):
    user_id = request.POST.get('id')
    action = request.POST.get('action')
    if user_id and action:
        try:
            user = User.objects.get(id=user_id)
            if action == 'follow':
                Contact.objects.get_or_create(
                    user_from=request.user,
                    user_to=user)
            else:
                Contact.objects.filter(user_from=request.user,
                                       user_to=user).delete()
            return JsonResponse({'status':'ok'})
        except User.DoesNotExist:
            return JsonResponse({'status':'ko'})
    return JsonResponse({'status':'ko'})
```

The user_follow view is quite similar to the image_like view we created before.
Since we are using a custom intermediary model for the users' many-to-many
relationship, the default add() and remove() methods of the automatic manager
of ManyToManyField are not available. We use the intermediary Contact model
to create or delete user relationships.

Import the view you just created in the urls.py file of the account application and
add the following URL pattern to it:

```python
url(r'^users/follow/$', views.user_follow, name='user_follow'),
```

Make sure that you place this pattern before the `user_detail` URL pattern. Otherwise, any requests to `/users/follow/` will match the regular expression of the `user_detail` pattern and it will be executed instead. Remember that in every HTTP request Django checks the requested URL against each pattern in order of appearance and stops at the first match.

Edit the `user/detail.html` template of the `account application` and append the following code to it:

```
{% block domready %}
  $('a.follow').click(function(e){
    e.preventDefault();
    $.post('{% url "user_follow" %}',
      {
        id: $(this).data('id'),
        action: $(this).data('action')
      },
      function(data){
        if (data['status'] == 'ok') {
          var previous_action = $('a.follow').data('action');

          // toggle data-action
          $('a.follow').data('action',
            previous_action == 'follow' ? 'unfollow' : 'follow');
          // toggle link text
          $('a.follow').text(
            previous_action == 'follow' ? 'Unfollow' : 'Follow');

          // update total followers
          var previous_followers = parseInt(
            $('span.count .total').text());
          $('span.count .total').text(previous_action == 'follow' ?
previous_followers + 1 : previous_followers - 1);
        }
      }
    );
  });
{% endblock %}
```

This is the JavaScript code to perform the AJAX request to follow or unfollow a particular user and also toggle the follow/unfollow link. We use jQuery to perform the AJAX request and set both the `data-action` attribute and the text of the HTML `<a>` element based on its previous value. When the AJAX action is performed, we also update the count of total followers displayed on the page. Open the user detail page of an existing user and click the **Follow** link to try the functionality we just built.

# Building a generic activity stream application

Many social websites show an activity stream to their users, so that they can track what other users do in the platform. An activity stream is a list of recent activities performed by a user or a group of users. For example, Facebook's News Feed is an activity stream. Example actions can be User X bookmarked image Y or User X is now following user Y. We will build an activity stream application so that every user can see recent interactions of users he follows. To do so, we will need a model to save the actions performed by users on the website and simple way to add actions to the feed.

Create a new application named `actions` inside your project with the following command:

**django-admin startapp actions**

Add `'actions'` to INSTALLED_APPS in the `settings.py` file of your project to let Django know the new application is active:

```
INSTALLED_APPS = (
    # ...
    'actions',
)
```

Edit the `models.py` file of the `actions` application and add the following code to it:

```
from django.db import models
from django.contrib.auth.models import User

class Action(models.Model):
    user = models.ForeignKey(User,
                             related_name='actions',
                             db_index=True)
    verb = models.CharField(max_length=255)
    created = models.DateTimeField(auto_now_add=True,
                                   db_index=True)

    class Meta:
        ordering = ('-created',)
```

This is the `Action` model that will be used for storing user activities. The fields of this model are as follows:

- `user`: The user that performed the action. This is a `ForeignKey` to the Django `User` model.

- `verb`: The verb describing the action that the user has performed.

- `created`: The date and time when this action was created. We use `auto_now_add=True` to automatically set this to the current datetime when the object is saved for the first time in the database.

With this basic model, we can only store actions such as User X did something. We need an extra `ForeignKey` field in order to save actions that involve a `target` object, such as User X bookmarked image Y or User X is now following user Y. As you already know, a normal `ForeignKey` can only point to one other model. Instead, we need a way for the action's `target` object to be an instance of any existing model. This is where the Django contenttypes framework comes on the scene.

# Using the contenttypes framework

Django includes a contenttypes framework located at `django.contrib.contenttypes`. This application can track all models installed in your project and provides a generic interface to interact with your models.

The `'django.contrib.contenttypes'` is included in the INSTALLED_APPS setting by default when you create a new project using the `startproject` command. It is used by other `contrib` packages such as the authentication framework and the admin application.

The `contenttypes` application contains a `ContentType` model. Instances of this model represent the actual models of your application, and new instances of `ContentType` are automatically created when new models are installed in your project. The `ContentType` model has the following fields:

- `app_label`: The name of the application the model belongs to. This is automatically taken from the `app_label` attribute of the model `Meta` options. For example, our `Image` model belongs to the application `images`.

- `model`: The name of the model class.

- `name`: The human-readable name of the model. This is automatically taken from the `verbose_name` attribute of the model `Meta` options.

Let's take a look at how we can interact with `ContentType` objects. Open the Python console using the `python manage.py shell` command. You can get the `ContentType` object corresponding to a specific model by performing a query with the `app_label` and `model` attributes such as this:

```
>>> from django.contrib.contenttypes.models import ContentType
>>> image_type = ContentType.objects.get(app_label='images',
model='image')
>>> image_type
<ContentType: image>
```

You can also retrieve the model class back from a `ContentType` object by calling its `model_class()` method:

```
>>> image_type.model_class()
<class 'images.models.Image'>
```

It's also common to get the `ContentType` object for a particular model class as follows:

```
>>> from images.models import Image
>>> ContentType.objects.get_for_model(Image)
<ContentType: image>
```

These are just some examples of using contenttypes. Django offers more ways to work with them. You can find the official documentation about the contenttypes framework at `https://docs.djangoproject.com/en/1.8/ref/contrib/contenttypes/`.

# Adding generic relations to your models

In generic relations `ContentType` objects play the role of pointing to the model used for the relationship. You will need three fields to setup a generic relation in a model:

- A `ForeignKey` field to `ContentType`. This will tell us the model for the relationship.
- A field to store the primary key of the related object. This will usually be a `PositiveIntegerField` to match Django automatic primary key fields.
- A field to define and manage the generic relation using the two previous fields. The contenttypes framework offers a `GenericForeignKey` field for this purpose.

Edit the `models.py` file of the `actions` application and make it look like this:

```python
from django.db import models
from django.contrib.auth.models import User
from django.contrib.contenttypes.models import ContentType
from django.contrib.contenttypes.fields import GenericForeignKey


class Action(models.Model):
    user = models.ForeignKey(User,
                             related_name='actions',
                             db_index=True)
    verb = models.CharField(max_length=255)

    target_ct = models.ForeignKey(ContentType,
                                  blank=True,
                                  null=True,
                                  related_name='target_obj')
    target_id = models.PositiveIntegerField(null=True,
                                            blank=True,
                                            db_index=True)
    target = GenericForeignKey('target_ct', 'target_id')
    created = models.DateTimeField(auto_now_add=True,
                                   db_index=True)

    class Meta:
        ordering = ('-created',)
```

We have added the following fields to the `Action` model:

- `target_ct`: A `ForeignKey` field to the `ContentType` model.
- `target_id`: A `PositiveIntegerField` for storing the primary key of the related object.
- `target`: A `GenericForeignKey` field to the related object based on the combination of the two previous fields.

Django does not create any field in the database for `GenericForeignKey` fields. The only fields that are mapped to database fields are `target_ct` and `target_id`. Both fields have `blank=True` and `null=True` attributes so that a `target` object is not required when saving `Action` objects.

 You can make your applications more flexible by using generic relationships instead of foreign-keys when it makes sense to have a generic relation.

Run the following command to create initial migrations for this application:

```
python manage.py makemigrations actions
```

You should see the following output:

```
Migrations for 'actions':
  0001_initial.py:
    - Create model Action
```

Then, run the next command to sync the application with the database:

```
python manage.py migrate
```

The output of the command should indicate that the new migrations have been applied as follows:

```
Applying actions.0001_initial... OK
```

Let's add the `Action` model to the administration site. Edit the `admin.py` file of the actions application and add the following code to it:

```python
from django.contrib import admin
from .models import Action

class ActionAdmin(admin.ModelAdmin):
    list_display = ('user', 'verb', 'target', 'created')
    list_filter = ('created',)
    search_fields = ('verb',)

admin.site.register(Action, ActionAdmin)
```

You just registered the `Action` model in the administration site. Run the command `python manage.py runserver` to initialize the development server and open `http://127.0.0.1:8000/admin/actions/action/add/` in your browser. You should see the page for creating a new `Action` object as follows:

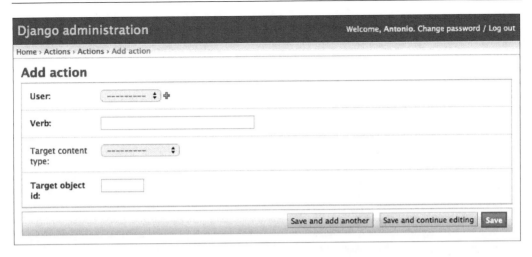

As you can see, only the `target_ct` and `target_id` fields that are mapped to actual database fields are shown, and the `GenericForeignKey` field does not appear here. The `target_ct` allows you to select any of the registered models of your Django project. You can restrict the contenttypes to choose from to a limited set of models by using the `limit_choices_to` attribute in the `target_ct` field: The `limit_choices_to` attribute allows you to restrict the content of `ForeignKey` fields to a specific set of values.

Create a new file inside the `actions` application directory and name it `utils.py`. We will define a shortcut function that will allow us to create new `Action` objects in a simple way. Edit the new file and add the following code to it:

```python
from django.contrib.contenttypes.models import ContentType
from .models import Action

def create_action(user, verb, target=None):
    action = Action(user=user, verb=verb, target=target)
    action.save()
```

The `create_action()` function allows us to create actions that optionally include a `target` object. We can use this function anywhere in our code to add new actions to the activity stream.

# Avoiding duplicate actions in the activity stream

Sometimes your users might perform an action multiple times. They might click several times on like/unlike buttons or perform the same action multiple times in a short period of time. This will make you end up storing and displaying duplicated actions. In order to avoid this we will improve the create_action() function to avoid most of the duplicates.

Edit the utils.py file of the actions application and make it look like the following:

```python
import datetime
from django.utils import timezone
from django.contrib.contenttypes.models import ContentType
from .models import Action

def create_action(user, verb, target=None):
    # check for any similar action made in the last minute
    now = timezone.now()
    last_minute = now - datetime.timedelta(seconds=60)
    similar_actions = Action.objects.filter(user_id=user.id,
                                            verb= verb,
                                            timestamp__gte=last_minute)
    if target:
        target_ct = ContentType.objects.get_for_model(target)
        similar_actions = similar_actions.filter(
                                            target_ct=target_ct,
                                            target_id=target.id)
    if not similar_actions:
        # no existing actions found
        action = Action(user=user, verb=verb, target=target)
        action.save()
        return True
    return False
```

We have changed the create_action() function to avoid saving duplicate actions and return a boolean to tell if the action was saved or not. This is how we avoid duplicates:

- First, we get the current time using the timezone.now() method provided by Django. This method does the same as datetime.datetime.now() but returns a timezone-aware object. Django provides a setting called USE_TZ to enable or disable timezone support. The default settings.py file created using the startproject command includes USE_TZ=True.

- We use the `last_minute` variable to store the datetime one minute ago and we retrieve any identical actions performed by the user since then.

- We create an `Action` object if no identical action already exists in the last minute. We return `True` if an `Action` object was created, `False` otherwise.

# Adding user actions to the activity stream

It's time to add some actions to our views to build the activity stream for our users. We are going to store an action for each of the following interactions:

- A user bookmarks an image
- A user likes/unlikes an image
- A user creates an account
- A user follows/unfollows another user

Edit the `views.py` file of the `images` application and add the following import:

```
from actions.utils import create_action
```

In the `image_create` view, add `create_action()` after saving the image like this:

```
new_item.save()
create_action(request.user, 'bookmarked image', new_item)
```

In the `image_like` view, add `create_action()` after adding the user to the `users_like` relationship as follows:

```
image.users_like.add(request.user)
create_action(request.user, 'likes', image)
```

Now edit the `views.py` file of the `account` application and add the following import:

```
from actions.utils import create_action
```

In the `register` view, add `create_action()` after creating the `Profile` object as follows:

```
new_user.save()
profile = Profile.objects.create(user=new_user)
create_action(new_user, 'has created an account')
```

In the `user_follow` view add `create_action()` like this:

```
Contact.objects.get_or_create(user_from=request.user,
                               user_to=user)
create_action(request.user, 'is following', user)
```

As you can see, thanks to our `Action` model and our helper function, it's very easy to save new actions to the activity stream.

# Displaying the activity stream

Finally, we need a way to display the activity stream for each user. We are going to include it in the user's dashboard. Edit the `views.py` file of the account application. Import the `Action` model and modify the dashboard view as follows:

```
from actions.models import Action

@login_required
def dashboard(request):
    # Display all actions by default
    actions = Action.objects.exclude(user=request.user)
    following_ids = request.user.following.values_list('id',
                                                        flat=True)
    if following_ids:
        # If user is following others, retrieve only their actions
        actions = actions.filter(user_id__in=following_ids)
    actions = actions[:10]

    return render(request,
                  'account/dashboard.html',
                  {'section': 'dashboard',
                   'actions': actions})
```

In this view, we retrieve all actions from the database, excluding the ones performed by the current user. If the user is not following anybody yet, we display the latest actions performed by other users on the platform. This is the default behavior when the user is not following any other users yet. If the user is following other users, we restrict the query to only display actions performed by the users he follows. Finally, we limit the result to the first 10 actions returned. We are not using `order_by()` here because we are relying on the default ordering we provided in the `Meta` options of the `Action` model. Recent actions will come first, since we have set `ordering = ('-created',)` in the `Action` model.

# Optimizing QuerySets that involve related objects

Every time you retrieve an `Action` object, you will probably access its related `User` object, and probably the user's related `Profile` object too. The Django ORM offers a simple way to retrieve related objects at once, avoiding additional queries to the database.

## Using select_related

Django offers a QuerySet method called `select_related()` that allows you to retrieve related objects for one-to-many relationships. This translates to a single, more complex QuerySet, but you avoid additional queries when accessing the related objects. The `select_related` method is for `ForeignKey` and `OneToOne` fields. It works by performing a SQL `JOIN` and including the fields of the related object in the `SELECT` statement.

To take advantage of `select_related()`, edit the following line of the previous code:

```
actions = actions.filter(user_id__in=following_ids)
```

And add `select_related` on the fields that you will use:

```
actions = actions.filter(user_id__in=following_ids)\
                .select_related('user', 'user__profile')
```

We are using `user__profile` to join the profile table too in one single SQL query. If you call `select_related()` without passing any arguments to it, it will retrieve objects from all `ForeignKey` relationships. Always limit `select_related()` to the relationships that will be accessed afterwards.

 Using `select_related()` carefully can vastly improve execution time.

## Using prefetch_related

As you see, `select_related()` will help you boost performance for retrieving related objects in one-to-many relationships. However, `select_related()` cannot work for many-to-many or many-to-one relationships (`ManyToMany` or reverse `ForeignKey` fields). Django offers a different QuerySet method called `prefetch_related` that works for many-to-many and many-to-one relations in addition to the relations supported by `select_related()`. The `prefetch_related()` method performs a separate lookup for each relationship and joins the results using Python. This method also supports prefetching of `GenericRelation` and `GenericForeignKey`.

Complete your query by adding `prefetch_related()` to it for the target `GenericForeignKey` field as follows:

```
actions = actions.filter(user_id__in=following_ids)\
                .select_related('user', 'user__profile')\
                .prefetch_related('target')
```

This query is now optimized for retrieving the user actions including related objects.

# Creating templates for actions

We are going to create the template to display a particular `Action` object. Create a new directory inside the actions application directory and name it templates. Add the following file structure to it:

```
actions/
    action/
        detail.html
```

Edit the `actions/action/detail.html` template file and add the following lines to it:

```
{% load thumbnail %}

{% with user=action.user profile=action.user.profile %}
<div class="action">
  <div class="images">
    {% if profile.photo %}
      {% thumbnail user.profile.photo "80x80" crop="100%" as im %}
        <a href="{{ user.get_absolute_url }}">
          <img src="{{ im.url }}" alt="{{ user.get_full_name }}"
class="item-img">
        </a>
      {% endthumbnail %}
      {% endif %}

    {% if action.target %}
      {% with target=action.target %}
        {% if target.image %}
          {% thumbnail target.image "80x80" crop="100%" as im %}
            <a href="{{ target.get_absolute_url }}">
              <img src="{{ im.url }}" class="item-img">
            </a>
          {% endthumbnail %}
        {% endif %}
```

```
        {% endwith %}
         {% endif %}
    </div>
    <div class="info">
      <p>
        <span class="date">{{ action.created|timesince }} ago</span>
        <br />
        <a href="{{ user.get_absolute_url }}">
          {{ user.first_name }}
        </a>
        {{ action.verb }}
        {% if action.target %}
          {% with target=action.target %}
            <a href="{{ target.get_absolute_url }}">{{ target }}</a>
          {% endwith %}
        {% endif %}
      </p>
    </div>
  </div>
{% endwith %}
```

This is the template to display an Action object. First, we use the {% with %} template tag to retrieve the user performing the action and their profile. Then, we display the image of the target object if the Action object has a related target object. Finally, we display the link to the user that performed the action, the verb and the target object, if any.

Now, edit the account/dashboard.html template and append the following code to the bottom of the content block:

```
<h2>What's happening</h2>
<div id="action-list">
  {% for action in actions %}
    {% include "actions/action/detail.html" %}
  {% endfor %}
</div>
```

Open `http://127.0.0.1:8000/account/` in your browser. Log in with an existing user and perform several actions so that they get stored in the database. Then, log in using another user, follow the previous user, and take a look at the generated action stream in the dashboard page. It should look like the following:

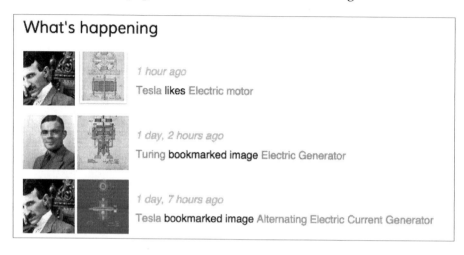

We just created a complete activity stream for our users and we can easily add new user actions to it. You can also add infinite scroll functionality to the activity stream by implementing the same AJAX paginator we used for the `image_list` view.

# Using signals for denormalizing counts

There are some cases when you would like to denormalize your data. Denormalization is making data redundant in a way that it optimizes read performance. You have to be careful about denormalization and only start using it when you really need it. The biggest issue you will find with denormalization is it's difficult to keep your denormalized data updated.

We will see an example of how to improve our queries by denormalizing counts. The drawback is that we have to keep the redundant data updated. We are going to denormalize data from our `Image` model and use Django signals to keep the data updated.

# Working with signals

Django comes with a signal dispatcher that allows `receiver` functions to get notified when certain actions occur. Signals are very useful when you need your code to do something every time something else happens. You can also create your own signals so that others can get notified when an event happens.

Django provides several signals for models located at `django.db.models.signals`. Some of these signals are:

- `pre_save` and `post_save`: Sent before or after calling the `save()` method of a model

- `pre_delete` and `post_delete`: Sent before or after calling the `delete()` method of a model or QuerySet

- `m2m_changed`: Sent when a `ManyToManyField` on a model is changed

These are just a subset of the signals provided by Django. You can find the list of all built-in signals at `https://docs.djangoproject.com/en/1.8/ref/signals/`.

Let's say you want to retrieve images by popularity. You can use the Django aggregation functions to retrieve images ordered by then number of users who like them. Remember you used Django aggregation functions in *Chapter 3, Extending Your Blog Application*. The following code will retrieve images by their number of likes:

```
from django.db.models import Count
from images.models import Image

images_by_popularity = Image.objects.annotate(
    total_likes=Count('users_like')).order_by('-total_likes')
```

However, ordering images by counting their total `likes` is more expensive in terms of performance than ordering them by a field which stores total counts. You can add a field to the `Image` model to denormalize the total number of `likes` to boost performance in queries that involve this field. How to keep this field updated?

Edit the `models.py` file of the `images` application and add the following field to the `Image` model:

```
total_likes = models.PositiveIntegerField(db_index=True,
                                           default=0)
```

The `total_likes` field will allow us to store the total count of users that like each image. Denormalizing counts is useful when you want to filter or order QuerySets by them.

There are several ways to improve performance that you have to take into account before denormalizing fields. Consider database indexes, query optimization and caching before starting to denormalize your data.

Run the following command to create the migrations for adding the new field to the database table:

**python manage.py makemigrations images**

You should see the following output:

```
Migrations for 'images':
  0002_image_total_likes.py:
    - Add field total_likes to image
```

Then, run the following command to apply the migration:

**python manage.py migrate images**

The output should include the following line:

```
Applying images.0002_image_total_likes... OK
```

We are going to attach a `receiver` function to the `m2m_changed` signal. Create a new file inside the `images` application directory and name it `signals.py`. Add the following code to it:

```python
from django.db.models.signals import m2m_changed
from django.dispatch import receiver
from .models import Image

@receiver(m2m_changed, sender=Image.users_like.through)
def users_like_changed(sender, instance, **kwargs):
    instance.total_likes = instance.users_like.count()
    instance.save()
```

First, we register the `users_like_changed` function as a `receiver` function using the `receiver()` decorator and we attach it to the `m2m_changed` signal. We connect the function to `Image.users_like.through` so that the function is only called if the `m2m_changed` signal has been launched by this sender. There is an alternate method for registering a `receiver` function, which consists of using the `connect()` method of the `Signal` object.

Django signals are synchronous and blocking. Don't confuse signals with asynchronous tasks. However, you can combine both to launch asynchronous tasks when your code gets notified by a signal.

You have to connect your receiver function to a signal, so that it gets called every time the signal is sent. The recommended method for registering your signals is by importing them in the `ready()` method of your application configuration class. Django provides an application registry that allows you to configure and introspect your applications.

# Defining application configuration classes

Django allows you to specify configuration classes for your applications. To provide a custom configuration for your application, create a custom class that inherits the `AppConfig` class located in `django.apps`. The application configuration class allows you to store metadata and configuration for the application and provides introspection.

You can find more information about application configuration at `https://docs.djangoproject.com/en/1.8/ref/applications/`.

In order to register your signal `receiver` functions, when you are using the `receiver()` decorator you just need to import the signals module of your application inside the `ready()` method of the `AppConfig` class. This method is called as soon as the application registry is fully populated. Any other initializations for your application should be also included inside this method.

Create a new file inside the `images` application directory and name it `apps.py`. Add the following code to it:

```python
from django.apps import AppConfig

class ImagesConfig(AppConfig):
    name = 'images'
    verbose_name = 'Image bookmarks'

    def ready(self):
        # import signal handlers
        import images.signals
```

The name attribute defines the full Python path to the application. The verbose_name attribute sets the human-readable name for this application. It's displayed in the administration site. The ready() method is where we import the signals for this application.

Now we need to tell Django where our application configuration resides. Edit the __init__.py file located inside the images application directory and add the following line to it:

```
default_app_config = 'images.apps.ImagesConfig'
```

Open your browser to view an image detail page and click on the **like** button. Go back to the administration site and take a look at the total_likes attribute. You should see that the total_likes attribute is updated like in the following example:

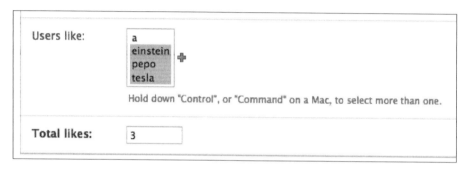

Now you can use the total_likes attribute to order images by popularity or display the value anywhere, avoiding complex queries to calculate it. The following query to get images ordered by their like count:

```
images_by_popularity = Image.objects.annotate(
    likes=Count('users_like')).order_by('-likes')
```

Can now become like this:

```
images_by_popularity = Image.objects.order_by('-total_likes')
```

This results in a much less expensive SQL query. This is just an example about how to use Django signals.

Use signals with caution, since they make difficult to know the control flow. In many cases you can avoid using signals if you know which receivers need to be notified.

You will need to set initial counts to match the current status of the database. Open the shell with the command `python manage.py shell` and run the following code:

```
from images.models import Image
for image in Image.objects.all():
    image.total_likes = image.users_like.count()
    image.save()
```

The likes count for each image is now updated.

# Using Redis for storing item views

Redis is and advanced key-value database that allows you to save different types of data and is extremely fast on I/O operations. Redis stores everything in memory, but the data can be persisted by dumping the dataset to disk every once in a while or by adding each command to a log. Redis is very versatile compared to other key-value stores: It provides a set of powerful commands and supports diverse data structures such as strings, hashes, lists, sets, ordered sets, and even bitmaps or HyperLogLogs.

While SQL is best suitable for schema-defined persistent data storage, Redis offers numerous advantages when dealing with rapidly changing data, volatile storage, or when a quick cache is needed. Let's see how Redis can be used for building new functionality into our project.

## Installing Redis

Download the latest Redis version from `http://redis.io/download.` Unzip the `tar.gz` file, enter the `redis` directory and compile Redis using the `make` command as follows:

```
cd redis-3.0.4
make
```

After installing it use the following shell command to initialize the Redis server:

```
src/redis-server
```

You should see an output that ends with the following lines:

```
# Server started, Redis version 3.0.4
* DB loaded from disk: 0.001 seconds
* The server is now ready to accept connections on port 6379
```

By default, Redis runs on port 6379, but you can also specify a custom port using the --port flag, for example redis-server --port 6655. When your server is ready, you can open the Redis client in another shell using the following command:

```
src/redis-cli
```

You should see the Redis client shell like the following:

```
127.0.0.1:6379>
```

The Redis client allows you to execute Redis commands directly from the shell. Let's try some commands. Enter the SET command in the Redis shell to store a value in a key:

```
127.0.0.1:6379> SET name "Peter"
OK
```

The previous command creates a name key with the string value "Peter" in the Redis database. The OK output indicates that the key has been saved successfully. Then, retrieve the value using the GET command as follows:

```
127.0.0.1:6379> GET name
"Peter"
```

You can also check if a key exists by using the EXISTS command. This command returns 1 if the given key exists, 0 otherwise:

```
127.0.0.1:6379> EXISTS name
(integer) 1
```

You can set the time for a key to expire using the EXPIRE command, which allows you to set time to live in seconds. Another option is using the EXPIREAT command that expects a Unix timestamp. Key expiration is useful to use Redis as a cache or to store volatile data:

```
127.0.0.1:6379> GET name
"Peter"
127.0.0.1:6379> EXPIRE name 2
(integer) 1
```

Wait for 2 seconds and try to get the same key again:

```
127.0.0.1:6379> GET name
(nil)
```

The (nil) response is a null response and means no key has been found. You can also delete any key using the DEL command as follows:

```
127.0.0.1:6379> SET total 1
OK
127.0.0.1:6379> DEL total
(integer) 1
127.0.0.1:6379> GET total
(nil)
```

These are just basic commands for key operations. Redis includes a large set of commands for other data types such as strings, hashes, sets, ordered sets, and so on. You can take a look at all Redis commands at http://redis.io/commands and all Redis data types at http://redis.io/topics/data-types.

# Using Redis with Python

We need Python bindings for Redis. Install redis-py via pip using the command:

```
pip install redis==2.10.3
```

You can find the redis-py docs at http://redis-py.readthedocs.org/.

The redis-py offers two classes for interacting with Redis: StrictRedis and Redis. Both offer the same functionality. The StrictRedis class attempts to adhere to the official Redis command syntax. The Redis class extends StrictRedis overriding some methods to provide backwards compatibility. We are going to use the StrictRedis class since it follows the Redis command syntax. Open the Python shell and execute the following code:

```
>>> import redis
>>> r = redis.StrictRedis(host='localhost', port=6379, db=0)
```

This code creates a connection with the Redis database. In Redis, databases are identified by an integer index instead of a database name. By default, a client is connected to database 0. The number of available Redis databases is set to 16, but you can change this in the redis.conf file.

Now set a key using the Python shell:

```
>>> r.set('foo', 'bar')
True
```

The command returns `True` indicating that the key has been successfully created. Now you can retrieve the key using the `get()` command:

```
>>> r.get('foo')
'bar'
```

As you can see, the methods of `StrictRedis` follow the Redis command syntax.

Let's integrate Redis into our project. Edit the `settings.py` file of the bookmarks project and add the following settings to it:

```
REDIS_HOST = 'localhost'
REDIS_PORT = 6379
REDIS_DB = 0
```

These are the settings for the Redis server and the database that we will use for our project.

## Storing item views in Redis

Let's store the total number of times an image has been viewed. If we did this using the Django ORM, it would involve an SQL UPDATE statement every time an image is displayed. Using Redis instead, we just need to increment a counter stored in memory, resulting in much better performance.

Edit the `views.py` file of the `images` application and add the following code to it:

```
import redis
from django.conf import settings

# connect to redis
r = redis.StrictRedis(host=settings.REDIS_HOST,
                      port=settings.REDIS_PORT,
                      db=settings.REDIS_DB)
```

Here we establish the Redis connection in order to use it in our views. Edit the `image_detail` view and make it look as follows:

```
def image_detail(request, id, slug):
    image = get_object_or_404(Image, id=id, slug=slug)
    # increment total image views by 1
    total_views = r.incr('image:{}:views'.format(image.id))
    return render(request,
                  'images/image/detail.html',
                  {'section': 'images',
                   'image': image,
                   'total_views': total_views})
```

In this view, we use the INCR command that increments the value of a key by 1 and sets the value to 0 before performing the operation if the key does not exist. The incr() method returns the value of the key after performing the operation and we store it in the total_views variable. We build the Redis key using a notation like object-type:id:field (for example image:33:id).

> The convention for naming Redis keys is to use a colon sign as separator for creating namespaced keys. By doing so, the key names are specially verbose and related keys share part of the same schema in their names.

Edit the image/detail.html template and add the following code to it after the existing <span class="count"> element:

```
<span class="count">
  <span class="total">{{ total_views }}</span>
  view{{ total_views|pluralize }}
</span>
```

Now open an image detail page in your browser and load it several times. You will see that each time the view is executed the total views displayed are incremented by 1. See the following example:

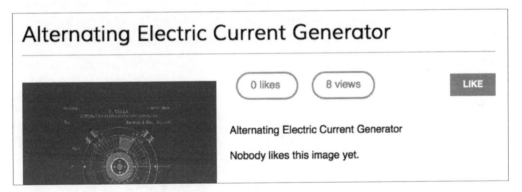

You have successfully integrated Redis into your project to store item counts.

# Storing a ranking in Redis

Let's built some more functionality with Redis. We are going to create a ranking of the most viewed images in our platform. For building this ranking we will use Redis sorted sets. A sorted set is a non-repeating collection of strings in which every member is associated with a score. Items are sorted by their score.

Edit the `views.py` file of the `images` application and make the `image_detail` view look as follows:

```
def image_detail(request, id, slug):
    image = get_object_or_404(Image, id=id, slug=slug)
    # increment total image views by 1
    total_views = r.incr('image:{}:views'.format(image.id))
    # increment image ranking by 1
    r.zincrby('image_ranking', image.id, 1)
    return render(request,
                  'images/image/detail.html',
                  {'section': 'images',
                   'image': image,
                   'total_views': total_views})
```

We use the `zincrby()` command to store image views in a sorted set with the key `image:ranking`. We are storing the image `id`, and a score of 1 that will be added to the total score of this element in the sorted set. This will allow us to keep track of all image views globally and have a sorted set ordered by the total number of views.

Now create a new view to display the ranking of the most viewed images. Add the following code to the `views.py` file:

```
@login_required
def image_ranking(request):
    # get image ranking dictionary
    image_ranking = r.zrange('image_ranking', 0, -1,
                             desc=True)[:10]
    image_ranking_ids = [int(id) for id in image_ranking]
    # get most viewed images
    most_viewed = list(Image.objects.filter(
                            id__in=image_ranking_ids))
    most_viewed.sort(key=lambda x: image_ranking_ids.index(x.id))
    return render(request,
                  'images/image/ranking.html',
                  {'section': 'images',
                   'most_viewed': most_viewed})
```

This is the `image_ranking` view. We use the `zrange()` command to obtain the elements in the sorted set. This command expects a custom range by lowest and highest score. By using `0` as lowest and `-1` as highest score we are telling Redis to return all elements in the sorted set. We also specify `desc=True` to retrieve the elements ordered by descending score. Finally, we slice the results using `[:10]` to get the first 10 elements with highest scores. We build a list of returned image IDs and we store it in the `image_ranking_ids` variable as a list of integers. We retrieve the `Image` objects for those IDs and force the query to be executed by using the `list()` function. It is important to force the QuerySet execution because next we use the `sort()` list method on it (at this point we need a list of objects instead of a queryset). We sort the `Image` objects by their index of appearance in the image ranking. Now we can use the `most_viewed` list in our template to display the 10 most viewed `images`.

Create a new `image/ranking.html` template file and add the following code to it:

```
{% extends "base.html" %}

{% block title %}Images ranking{% endblock %}

{% block content %}
  <h1>Images ranking</h1>
  <ol>
    {% for image in most_viewed %}
      <li>
        <a href="{{ image.get_absolute_url }}">
          {{ image.title }}
        </a>
      </li>
    {% endfor %}
  </ol>
{% endblock %}
```

The template is pretty straightforward, as we just iterate over the `Image` objects contained in the `most_viewed` list.

Finally create an URL pattern for the new view. Edit the `urls.py` file of the images application and add the following pattern to it:

```
url(r'^ranking/$', views.image_ranking, name='create'),
```

Open `http://127.0.0.1:8000/images/ranking/` in your browser. You should be able to see an image ranking as follows:

# Next steps with Redis

Redis is not a replacement for your SQL database but a fast in-memory storage that is more suitable for certain tasks. Add it to your stack and use it when you really feel it's needed. The following are some scenarios in which Redis suits pretty well:

- **Counting**: As you have seen, it is very easy to manage counters with Redis. You can use `incr()` and `incrby()` for counting stuff.
- **Storing latest items**: You can add items to the start/end of a list using `lpush()` and `rpush()`. Remove and return first/last element using `lpop()` / `rpop()`. You can trim the list length using `ltrim()` to maintain its length.
- **Queues**: In addition to push and pop commands, Redis offers blocking queue commands.
- **Caching**: Using `expire()` and `expireat()` allows you to use Redis as a cache. You can also find third-party Redis cache backends for Django.
- **Pub/Sub**: Redis provides commands for subscribing/unsubscribing and sending messages to channels.
- **Rankings and leaderboards**: Redis sorted sets with scores make it very easy to create leaderboards.
- **Real-time tracking**: Redis fast I/O makes it perfect for real-time scenarios.

# Summary

In this chapter, you have built a follower system and a user activity stream. You have learned how Django signals work and you have integrated Redis into your project.

In the next chapter, you will learn how to build an on-line shop. You will create a product catalog and build a shopping cart using sessions. You will also learn how to launch asynchronous tasks with Celery.

# 7
# Building an Online Shop

In the previous chapter, you created a follower system and built a user activity stream. You also learned how Django signals work and integrated Redis into your project to count image views. In this chapter, you will learn how to build a basic online shop. You will create a catalog of products and implement a shopping cart using Django sessions. You will also learn how to create custom context processors and launch asynchronous tasks using Celery.

In this chapter, you will learn to:

- Create a product catalog
- Build a shopping cart using Django sessions
- Manage customer orders
- Send asynchronous notifications to customers using Celery

## Creating an online shop project

We are going to start with a new Django project to build an online shop. Our users will be able to browse through a product catalog and add products to a shopping cart. Finally, they will be able to checkout the cart and place an order. This chapter will cover the following functionalities of an online shop:

- Creating the product catalog models, adding them to the administration site, and building the basic views to display the catalog
- Building a shopping cart system using Django sessions to allow users to keep selected products while they browse the site
- Creating the form and functionality to place orders
- Sending an asynchronous email confirmation to users when they place an order

First, create a virtual environment for your new project and activate it with the following commands:

```
mkdir env
virtualenv env/myshop
source env/myshop/bin/activate
```

Install Django in your virtual environment with the following command:

```
pip install Django==1.8.6
```

Start a new project called `myshop` with an application called `shop` by opening a shell and running the following commands:

```
django-admin startproject myshop
cd myshop/
django-admin startapp shop
```

Edit the `settings.py` file of your project and add your application to the `INSTALLED_APPS` setting as follows:

```
INSTALLED_APPS = (
    # ...
    'shop',
)
```

Your application is now active for this project. Let's define the models for the product catalog.

# Creating product catalog models

The catalog of our shop will consist of products that are organized into different categories. Each product will have a name, optional description, optional image, a price, and an available stock. Edit the `models.py` file of the `shop` application that you just created and add the following code:

```
from django.db import models

class Category(models.Model):
    name = models.CharField(max_length=200,
                            db_index=True)
    slug = models.SlugField(max_length=200,
                            db_index=True,
                            unique=True)
```

```
    class Meta:
        ordering = ('name',)
        verbose_name = 'category'
        verbose_name_plural = 'categories'

    def __str__(self):
        return self.name

class Product(models.Model):
    category = models.ForeignKey(Category,
                                 related_name='products')
    name = models.CharField(max_length=200, db_index=True)
    slug = models.SlugField(max_length=200, db_index=True)
    image = models.ImageField(upload_to='products/%Y/%m/%d',
                              blank=True)
    description = models.TextField(blank=True)
    price = models.DecimalField(max_digits=10, decimal_places=2)
    stock = models.PositiveIntegerField()
    available = models.BooleanField(default=True)
    created = models.DateTimeField(auto_now_add=True)
    updated = models.DateTimeField(auto_now=True)

    class Meta:
        ordering = ('name',)
        index_together = (('id', 'slug'),)

    def __str__(self):
        return self.name
```

These are our `Category` and `Product` models. The `Category` model consists of a `name` field and a `slug` unique field. The `Product` model fields are as follows:

- `category`: This is `ForeignKey` to the `Category` model. This is a many-to-one relationship: A product belongs to one category and a category contains multiple products.

- `name`: This is the name of the product.

- `slug`: This is the slug for this product to build beautiful URLs.

- `image`: This is an optional product image.

- `description`: This is an optional description of the product.

- price: This is DecimalField. This field uses Python's decimal.Decimal type to store a fixed-precision decimal number. The maximum number of digits (including the decimal places) is set using the max_digits attribute and decimal places with the decimal_places attribute.

- stock: This is PositiveIntegerField to store the stock of this product.

- available: This is a boolean that indicates whether the product is available or not. This allows us to enable/disable the product in the catalog.

- created: This field stores when the object was created.

- updated: This field stores when the object was last updated.

For the price field, we use DecimalField instead of FloatField to avoid rounding issues.

 Always use DecimalField to store monetary amounts. FloatField uses Python's float type internally, whereas DecimalField uses Python's Decimal type. By using the Decimal type, you will avoid the float rounding issues.

In the Meta class of the Product model, we use the index_together meta option to specify an index for the id and slug fields together. We define this index, because we plan to query products by both, id and slug. Both fields are indexed together to improve performances for queries that utilize the two fields.

Since we are going to deal with images in our models, open the shell and install Pillow with the following command:

```
pip install Pillow==2.9.0
```

Now, run the next command to create initial migrations for your project:

```
python manage.py makemigrations
```

You will see the following output:

```
Migrations for 'shop':
  0001_initial.py:
    - Create model Category
    - Create model Product
    - Alter index_together for product (1 constraint(s))
```

Run the next command to sync the database:

```
python manage.py migrate
```

You will see an output that includes the following line:

```
Applying shop.0001_initial... OK
```

The database is now synced with your models.

# Registering catalog models in the admin site

Let's add our models to the administration site so that we can easily manage categories and products. Edit the admin.py file of the shop application and add the following code to it:

```python
from django.contrib import admin
from .models import Category, Product

class CategoryAdmin(admin.ModelAdmin):
    list_display = ['name', 'slug']
    prepopulated_fields = {'slug': ('name',)}
admin.site.register(Category, CategoryAdmin)

class ProductAdmin(admin.ModelAdmin):
    list_display = ['name', 'slug', 'price', 'stock',
                    'available', 'created', 'updated']
    list_filter = ['available', 'created', 'updated']
    list_editable = ['price', 'stock', 'available']
    prepopulated_fields = {'slug': ('name',)}
admin.site.register(Product, ProductAdmin)
```

Remember that we use the prepopulated_fields attribute to specify fields where the value is automatically set using the value of other fields. As you have seen before, this is convenient for generating slugs. We use the list_editable attribute in the ProductAdmin class to set the fields that can be edited from the list display page of the administration site. This will allow you to edit multiple rows at once. Any field in list_editable must also be listed in the list_display attribute, since only the fields displayed can be edited.

Now, create a superuser for your site using the following command:

```
python manage.py createsuperuser
```

Start the development server with the command `python manage.py runserver`. Open `http://127.0.0.1:8000/admin/shop/product/add/` in your browser and log in with the user that you just created. Add a new category and product using the administration interface. The product change list page of the administration page will then look like this:

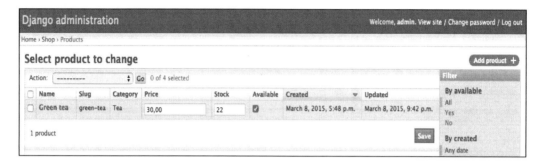

# Building catalog views

In order to display the product catalog, we need to create a view to list all the products or filter products by a given category. Edit the `views.py` file of the `shop` application and add the following code to it:

```python
from django.shortcuts import render, get_object_or_404
from .models import Category, Product

def product_list(request, category_slug=None):
    category = None
    categories = Category.objects.all()
    products = Product.objects.filter(available=True)
    if category_slug:
        category = get_object_or_404(Category, slug=category_slug)
        products = products.filter(category=category)
    return render(request,
                  'shop/product/list.html',
                  {'category': category,
                   'categories': categories,
                   'products': products})
```

We will filter the QuerySet with `available=True` to retrieve only available products. We will use an optional `category_slug` parameter to optionally filter products by a given category.

We also need a view to retrieve and display a single product. Add the following view to the `views.py` file:

```
def product_detail(request, id, slug):
    product = get_object_or_404(Product,
                                id=id,
                                slug=slug,
                                available=True)
    return render(request,
                  'shop/product/detail.html',
                  {'product': product})
```

The `product_detail` view expects the `id` and `slug` parameters in order to retrieve the `Product` instance. We can get this instance by just the ID since it's a unique attribute. However, we include the slug in the URL to build SEO-friendly URLs for products.

After building the product list and detail views, we have to define URL patterns for them. Create a new file inside the `shop` application directory and name it `urls.py`. Add the following code to it:

```
from django.conf.urls import url
from . import views

urlpatterns = [
    url(r'^$', views.product_list, name='product_list'),
    url(r'^(?P<category_slug>[-\w]+)/$',
        views.product_list,
        name='product_list_by_category'),
    url(r'^(?P<id>\d+)/(?P<slug>[-\w]+)/$',
        views.product_detail,
        name='product_detail'),
]
```

These are the URL patterns for our product catalog. We have defined two different URL patterns for the `product_list` view: a pattern named `product_list`, which calls the `product_list` view without any parameters; and a pattern named `product_list_by_category`, which provides a `category_slug` parameter to the view for filtering products by a given category. We added a pattern for the `product_detail` view, which passes the `id` and `slug` parameters to the view in order to retrieve a specific product.

Edit the urls.py file of the myshop project to make it look like this:

```
from django.conf.urls import include, url
from django.contrib import admin

urlpatterns = [
    url(r'^admin/', include(admin.site.urls)),
    url(r'^', include('shop.urls', namespace='shop')),
]
```

In the main URLs patterns of the project, we will include URLs for the shop application under a custom namespace named 'shop'.

Now, edit the models.py file of the shop application, import the reverse() function, and add a get_absolute_url() method to the Category and Product models as follows:

```
from django.core.urlresolvers import reverse
# ...
class Category(models.Model):
    # ...
    def get_absolute_url(self):
        return reverse('shop:product_list_by_category',
                        args=[self.slug])

class Product(models.Model):
    # ...
    def get_absolute_url(self):
        return reverse('shop:product_detail',
                        args=[self.id, self.slug])
```

As you already know, get_absolute_url() is the convention to retrieve URL for a given object. Here, we will use the URLs patterns that we just defined in the urls.py file.

# Creating catalog templates

Now, we need to create templates for the product list and detail views. Create the following directory and file structure inside the shop application directory:

```
templates/
    shop/
        base.html
        product/
            list.html
            detail.html
```

We need to define a base template, and then extend it in the product list and detail templates. Edit the `shop/base.html` template and add the following code to it:

```
{% load static %}
<!DOCTYPE html>
<html>
<head>
  <meta charset="utf-8" />
  <title>{% block title %}My shop{% endblock %}</title>
  <link href="{% static "css/base.css" %}" rel="stylesheet">
</head>
<body>
  <div id="header">
    <a href="/" class="logo">My shop</a>
  </div>
  <div id="subheader">
    <div class="cart">
      Your cart is empty.
    </div>
  </div>
  <div id="content">
    {% block content %}
    {% endblock %}
  </div>
</body>
</html>
```

This is the base template that we will use for our shop. In order to include the required CSS styles and images that are used by the templates, you will need to copy the static files that come along with this chapter, located in the `static/` directory of the `shop` application. Copy them to the same location of your project.

Edit the `shop/product/list.html` template and add the following code to it:

```
{% extends "shop/base.html" %}
{% load static %}

{% block title %}
  {% if category %}{{ category.name }}{% else %}Products{% endif %}
{% endblock %}

{% block content %}
  <div id="sidebar">
    <h3>Categories</h3>
    <ul>
```

```
    <li {% if not category %}class="selected"{% endif %}>
      <a href="{% url "shop:product_list" %}">All</a>
    </li>
    {% for c in categories %}
      <li {% if category.slug == c.slug %}class="selected"{% endif
%}>
        <a href="{{ c.get_absolute_url }}">{{ c.name }}</a>
      </li>
    {% endfor %}
  </ul>
</div>
<div id="main" class="product-list">
  <h1>{% if category %}{{ category.name }}{% else %}Products{% endif
%}</h1>
    {% for product in products %}
      <div class="item">
        <a href="{{ product.get_absolute_url }}">
          <img src="{% if product.image %}{{ product.image.url }}{%
else %}{% static "img/no_image.png" %}{% endif %}">
        </a>
        <a href="{{ product.get_absolute_url }}">{{ product.name }}</
a><br>
          ${{ product.price }}
      </div>
    {% endfor %}
  </div>
{% endblock %}
```

This is the product list template. It extends the shop/base.html template and
uses the categories context variable to display all the categories in a sidebar and
products to display the products of the current page. The same template is used for
both: listing all available products and listing products filtered by a category. Since
the image field of the Product model can be blank, we need to provide a default
image for the products that don't have an image. The image is located in our static
files directory with the relative path img/no_image.png.

Since we are using ImageField to store product images, we need the development
server to serve uploaded image files. Edit the settings.py file of myshop and add
the following settings:

```
MEDIA_URL = '/media/'
MEDIA_ROOT = os.path.join(BASE_DIR, 'media/')
```

MEDIA_URL is the base URL that serves media files uploaded by users. MEDIA_ROOT is the local path where these files reside, which we build dynamically prepending the BASE_DIR variable.

For Django to serve the uploaded media files using the development server, edit the urls.py file of myshop and add make it look like this:

```
from django.conf import settings
from django.conf.urls.static import static

urlpatterns = [
    # ...
]
if settings.DEBUG:
    urlpatterns += static(settings.MEDIA_URL,
                          document_root=settings.MEDIA_ROOT)
```

Remember that we only serve static files this way during the development. In a production environment, you should never serve static files with Django.

Add a couple of products to your shop using the administration site and open http://127.0.0.1:8000/ in your browser. You will see the product list page, which looks like this:

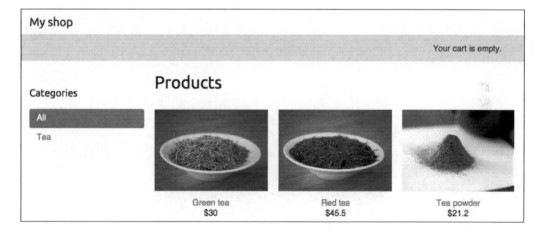

If you create a product using the administration site and don't upload any images, the default no_image.png image will be displayed:

Let's edit the product detail template. Edit the shop/product/detail.html template and add the following code to it:

```
{% extends "shop/base.html" %}
{% load static %}

{% block title %}
  {% if category %}{{ category.title }}{% else %}Products{% endif %}
{% endblock %}

{% block content %}
  <div class="product-detail">
    <img src="{% if product.image %}{{ product.image.url }}{% else %}
{% static "img/no_image.png" %}{% endif %}">
    <h1>{{ product.name }}</h1>
    <h2><a href="{{ product.category.get_absolute_url }}">{{ product.
category }}</a></h2>
    <p class="price">${{ product.price }}</p>
      {{ product.description|linebreaks }}
  </div>
{% endblock %}
```

We call the `get_absolute_url()` method on the related category object to display the available products that belong to the same category. Now, open `http://127.0.0.1:8000/` in your browser and click on any product to see the product detail page. It will look as follows:

We have now created a basic product catalog.

# Building a shopping cart

After building the product catalog, the next step is to create a shopping cart that will allow users to select the products that they want to purchase. A shopping cart allows users to select the products they want and store them temporarily while they browse the site, until they eventually place an order. The cart has to be persisted in the session so that the cart items are kept during the user's visit.

We will use Django's session framework to persist the cart. The cart will be kept in the session until it finishes or the user checks out of the cart. We will also need to build additional Django models for the cart and its items.

# Using Django sessions

Django provides a session framework that supports anonymous and user sessions. The session framework allows you to store arbitrary data for each visitor. Session data is stored on the server side, and cookies contain the session ID, unless you use the cookie-based session engine. The session middleware manages sending and receiving cookies. The default session engine stores session data in the database, but as you will see next, you can choose between different session engines.

To use sessions, you have to make sure that the MIDDLEWARE_CLASSES setting of your project contains 'django.contrib.sessions.middleware.SessionMiddleware'. This middleware manages sessions and is added by default when you create a new project using the startproject command.

The session middleware makes the current session available in the request object. You can access the current session using request.session, by utilizing it similar to a Python dictionary to store and retrieve session data. The session dictionary accepts any Python object by default that can be serialized into JSON. You can set a variable in the session like this:

```
request.session['foo'] = 'bar'
```

Retrieve a session key:

```
request.session.get('foo')
```

Delete a key you stored in the session:

```
del request.session['foo']
```

As you saw, we just treated request.session like a standard Python dictionary.

> When users log into the site, their anonymous session is lost and a new session is created for the authenticated users. If you store items in an anonymous session that you need to keep after users log in, you will have to copy the old session data into the new session.

# Session settings

There are several settings you can use to configure sessions for your project. The most important is SESSION_ENGINE. This setting allows you to set the place where sessions are stored. By default, Django stores sessions in the database using the Session model of the django.contrib.sessions application.

Django offers the following options for storing session data:

- **Database sessions**: Session data is stored in the database. This is the default session engine.

- **File-based sessions**: Session data is stored in the file system.

- **Cached sessions**: Session data is stored in a cache backend. You can specify cache backends using the CACHES setting. Storing session data in a cache system offers best performance.

- **Cached database sessions**: Session data is stored in a write-through cache and database. Reads only use the database if the data is not already in the cache.

- **Cookie-based sessions**: Session data is stored in the cookies that are sent to the browser.

 For better performance, use a cache-based session engine. Django supports Memcached and there are other third-party cache backends for Redis and other cache systems.

You can customize sessions with other settings. Here are some of the important session related settings:

- SESSION_COOKIE_AGE: This is the duration of session cookies in seconds. The default value is 1209600 (2 weeks).

- SESSION_COOKIE_DOMAIN: This domain is used for session cookies. Set this to .mydomain.com to enable cross-domain cookies.

- SESSION_COOKIE_SECURE: This is a boolean indicating that the cookie should only be sent if the connection is an HTTPS connection.

- SESSION_EXPIRE_AT_BROWSER_CLOSE: This is a boolean indicating that the session has to expire when the browser is closed.

- SESSION_SAVE_EVERY_REQUEST: This is a boolean that, if True, will save the session to the database on every request. The session expiration is also updated each time.

You can see all the session settings at https://docs.djangoproject.com/en/1.8/ref/settings/#sessions.

# Session expiration

You can choose to use browser-length sessions or persistent sessions using the SESSION_EXPIRE_AT_BROWSER_CLOSE setting. This is set to False by default, forcing the session duration to the value stored in the SESSION_COOKIE_AGE setting. If you set SESSION_EXPIRE_AT_BROWSER_CLOSE to True, the session will expire when the user closes the browser, and the SESSION_COOKIE_AGE setting will not have any effect.

You can use the set_expiry() method of request.session to overwrite the duration of the current session.

# Storing shopping carts in sessions

We need to create a simple structure that can be serialized to JSON for storing cart items in a session. The cart has to include the following data for each item contained in it:

- id of a Product instance
- The quantity selected for this product
- The unit price for this product

Since product prices may vary, we take the approach of storing the product's price along with the product itself when it's added to the cart. By doing so, we keep the same price that users saw when they added the item to the cart, even if the product's price is changed afterward.

Now, you have to manage creating carts and associate them with sessions. The shopping cart has to work as follows:

- When a cart is needed, we check if a custom session key is set. If no cart is set in the session, we create a new cart and save it in the cart session key.
- For successive requests, we perform the same check and get the cart items from the cart session key. We retrieve the cart items from the session and their related Product objects from the database.

Edit the settings.py file of your project and add the following setting to it:

```
CART_SESSION_ID = 'cart'
```

This is the key that we are going to use to store the cart in the user session. Since Django sessions are per-visitor, we can use the same cart session key for all sessions.

Let's create an application for managing shopping carts. Open the terminal and create a new application, running the following command from the project directory:

```
python manage.py startapp cart
```

Then, edit the settings.py file of your project and add 'cart' to the INSTALLED_APPS setting as follows:

```
INSTALLED_APPS = (
    # ...
    'shop',
    'cart',
)
```

Create a new file inside the cart application directory and name it cart.py. Add the following code to it:

```
from decimal import Decimal
from django.conf import settings
from shop.models import Product


class Cart(object):

    def __init__(self, request):
        """
        Initialize the cart.
        """
        self.session = request.session
        cart = self.session.get(settings.CART_SESSION_ID)
        if not cart:
            # save an empty cart in the session
            cart = self.session[settings.CART_SESSION_ID] = {}
        self.cart = cart
```

This is the Cart class that will allow us to manage the shopping cart. We require the cart to be initialized with a request object. We store the current session using self.session = request.session to make it accessible to the other methods of the Cart class. First, we try to get the cart from the current session using self.session.get(settings.CART_SESSION_ID). If no cart is present in the session, we set an empty cart just by setting an empty dictionary in the session. We expect our cart dictionary to use product IDs as keys and a dictionary with quantity and price as value for each key. By doing so, we can guarantee that a product is not added more than once in the cart; we can also simplify the way to access any cart item data.

Let's create a method to add products to the cart or update their quantity. Add the following `add()` and `save()` methods to the `Cart` class:

```python
def add(self, product, quantity=1, update_quantity=False):
    """
    Add a product to the cart or update its quantity.
    """
    product_id = str(product.id)
    if product_id not in self.cart:
        self.cart[product_id] = {'quantity': 0,
                                 'price': str(product.price)}
    if update_quantity:
        self.cart[product_id]['quantity'] = quantity
    else:
        self.cart[product_id]['quantity'] += quantity
    self.save()

def save(self):
    # update the session cart
    self.session[settings.CART_SESSION_ID] = self.cart
    # mark the session as "modified" to make sure it is saved
    self.session.modified = True
```

The `add()` method takes the following parameters:

- `product`: The `Product` instance to add or update in the cart.
- `quantity`: An optional integer for product quantity. This defaults to 1.
- `update_quantity`: This is a boolean that indicates whether the quantity needs to be updated with the given quantity (`True`), or the new quantity has to be added to the existing quantity (`False`).

We use the product id as a key in the cart contents dictionary. We convert the product id into a string because Django uses JSON to serialize session data, and JSON only allows string key names. The product id is the key and the value that we persist is a dictionary with `quantity` and `price` for the product. The product's price is converted from `Decimal` into `string` in order to serialize it. Finally, we call the `save()` method to save the cart in the session.

The `save()` method saves all the changes to the cart in the session and marks the session as modified using `session.modified = True`. This tells Django that the session has changed and needs to be saved.

We also need a method for removing products from the cart. Add the following method to the `Cart` class:

```
def remove(self, product):
    """
    Remove a product from the cart.
    """
    product_id = str(product.id)
    if product_id in self.cart:
        del self.cart[product_id]
        self.save()
```

The `remove()` method removes a given product from the cart dictionary and calls the `save()` method to update the cart in the session.

We will have to iterate through the items contained in the cart and access the related `Product` instances. To do so, you can define an `__iter__()` method in your class. Add the following method to the `Cart` class:

```
def __iter__(self):
    """
    Iterate over the items in the cart and get the products
    from the database.
    """
    product_ids = self.cart.keys()
    # get the product objects and add them to the cart
    products = Product.objects.filter(id__in=product_ids)
    for product in products:
        self.cart[str(product.id)]['product'] = product

    for item in self.cart.values():
        item['price'] = Decimal(item['price'])
        item['total_price'] = item['price'] * item['quantity']
        yield item
```

In the `__iter__()` method, we retrieve the `Product` instances that are present in the cart to include them in the cart items. Finally, we iterate over the cart items converting the item's `price` back into `Decimal` and add a `total_price` attribute to each item. Now, we can easily iterate over the items in the cart.

We also need a way to return the number of total items in the cart. When the `len()` function is executed on an object, Python calls its `__len__()` method to retrieve its length. We are going to define a custom `__len__()` method to return the total number of items stored in the cart. Add the following `__len__()` method to the `Cart` class:

```python
def __len__(self):
    """
    Count all items in the cart.
    """
    return sum(item['quantity'] for item in self.cart.values())
```

We return the sum of the quantities of all the cart items.

Add the following method to calculate the total cost for the items in the cart:

```python
def get_total_price(self):
    return sum(Decimal(item['price']) * item['quantity'] for item in
self.cart.values())
```

And finally, add a method to clear the cart session:

```python
def clear(self):
    # remove cart from session
    del self.session[settings.CART_SESSION_ID]
        self.session.modified = True
```

Our `Cart` class is now ready to manage shopping carts.

# Creating shopping cart views

Now that we have a `Cart` class to manage the cart, we need to create the views to add, update, or remove items from it. We need to create the following views:

- A view to add or update items in a cart, which can handle current and new quantities
- A view to remove items from the cart
- A view to display cart items and totals

# Adding items to the cart

In order to add items to the cart, we need a form that allows the user to select a quantity. Create a `forms.py` file inside the `cart` application directory and add the following code to it:

```python
from django import forms

PRODUCT_QUANTITY_CHOICES = [(i, str(i)) for i in range(1, 21)]

class CartAddProductForm(forms.Form):
    quantity = forms.TypedChoiceField(
                            choices=PRODUCT_QUANTITY_CHOICES,
                            coerce=int)
    update = forms.BooleanField(required=False,
                            initial=False,
                            widget=forms.HiddenInput)
```

We will use this form to add products to the cart. Our `CartAddProductForm` class contains the following two fields:

- `quantity`: This allows the user to select a quantity between 1-20. We use a `TypedChoiceField` field with `coerce=int` to convert the input into an integer.

- `update`: This allows you to indicate whether the quantity has to be added to any existing quantity in the cart for this product (`False`), or if the existing quantity has to be updated with the given quantity (`True`). We use a `HiddenInput` widget for this field, since we don't want to display it to the user.

Let's create a view for adding items to the cart. Edit the `views.py` file of the `cart` application and add the following code to it:

```python
from django.shortcuts import render, redirect, get_object_or_404
from django.views.decorators.http import require_POST
from shop.models import Product
from .cart import Cart
from .forms import CartAddProductForm

@require_POST
def cart_add(request, product_id):
    cart = Cart(request)
    product = get_object_or_404(Product, id=product_id)
    form = CartAddProductForm(request.POST)
```

```
    if form.is_valid():
        cd = form.cleaned_data
        cart.add(product=product,
                    quantity=cd['quantity'],
                    update_quantity=cd['update'])
    return redirect('cart:cart_detail')
```

This is the view for adding products to the cart or updating quantities for existing products. We use the `require_POST` decorator to allow only POST requests, since this view is going to change data. The view receives the product `ID` as parameter. We retrieve the `Product` instance with the given ID and validate `CartAddProductForm`. If the form is valid, we will either add or update the product in the cart. The view redirects to the `cart_detail` URL that will display the contents of the cart. We are going to create the `cart_detail` view shortly.

We also need a view to remove items from the cart. Add the following code to the `views.py` file of the `cart` application:

```
def cart_remove(request, product_id):
    cart = Cart(request)
    product = get_object_or_404(Product, id=product_id)
    cart.remove(product)
    return redirect('cart:cart_detail')
```

The `cart_remove` view receives the product id as parameter. We retrieve the `Product` instance with the given id and remove the product from the cart. Then, we redirect the user to the `cart_detail` URL.

Finally, we need a view to display the cart and its items. Add the following view to the `views.py` file:

```
def cart_detail(request):
    cart = Cart(request)
    return render(request, 'cart/detail.html', {'cart': cart})
```

The `cart_detail` view gets the current cart to display it.

We have created views to add items to the cart, update quantities, remove items from the cart, and display the cart. Let's add URL patterns for these views. Create a new file inside the `cart` application directory and name it `urls.py`. Add the following URLs to it:

```
from django.conf.urls import url
from . import views

urlpatterns = [
    url(r'^$', views.cart_detail, name='cart_detail'),
```

```
    url(r'^add/(?P<product_id>\d+)/$',
        views.cart_add,
        name='cart_add'),
    url(r'^remove/(?P<product_id>\d+)/$',
        views.cart_remove,
        name='cart_remove'),
]
```

Edit the main urls.py file of myshop and add the following URL pattern to include the cart URLs:

```
urlpatterns = [
    url(r'^admin/', include(admin.site.urls)),
    url(r'^cart/', include('cart.urls', namespace='cart')),
    url(r'^', include('shop.urls', namespace='shop')),
]
```

Make sure that you include this URL pattern before the shop.urls pattern, since it's more restrictive than the latter.

# Building a template to display the cart

The cart_add and cart_remove views don't render any templates, but we need to create a template for the cart_detail view to display cart items and totals.

Create the following file structure inside the cart application directory:

```
templates/
    cart/
        detail.html
```

Edit the cart/detail.html template and add the following code to it:

```
{% extends "shop/base.html" %}
{% load static %}

{% block title %}
  Your shopping cart
{% endblock %}

{% block content %}
  <h1>Your shopping cart</h1>
  <table class="cart">
    <thead>
      <tr>
        <th>Image</th>
```

```
            <th>Product</th>
            <th>Quantity</th>
            <th>Remove</th>
            <th>Unit price</th>
            <th>Price</th>
        </tr>
    </thead>
    <tbody>
      {% for item in cart %}
        {% with product=item.product %}
          <tr>
            <td>
              <a href="{{ product.get_absolute_url }}">
                <img src="{% if product.image %}{{ product.image.url
}}{% else %}{% static "img/no_image.png" %}{% endif %}">
              </a>
            </td>
            <td>{{ product.name }}</td>
            <td>{{ item.quantity }}</td>
            <td><a href="{% url "cart:cart_remove" product.id
%}">Remove</a></td>
            <td class="num">${{ item.price }}</td>
            <td class="num">${{ item.total_price }}</td>
          </tr>
        {% endwith %}
      {% endfor %}
      <tr class="total">
        <td>Total</td>
        <td colspan="4"></td>
        <td class="num">${{ cart.get_total_price }}</td>
      </tr>
    </tbody>
  </table>
  <p class="text-right">
    <a href="{% url "shop:product_list" %}" class="button
light">Continue shopping</a>
    <a href="#" class="button">Checkout</a>
  </p>
{% endblock %}
```

This is the template that is used to display the cart contents. It contains a table with the items stored in the current cart. We allow users to change the quantity for the selected products using a form that is posted to the cart_add view. We also allow users to remove items from the cart by providing a **Remove** link for each of them.

# Adding products to the cart

Now, we need to add an **Add to cart** button to the product detail page. Edit the `views.py` file of the `shop` application, and add `CartAddProductForm` to the `product_detail` view like this:

```python
from cart.forms import CartAddProductForm

def product_detail(request, id, slug):
    product = get_object_or_404(Product, id=id,
                                         slug=slug,
                                         available=True)
    cart_product_form = CartAddProductForm()
    return render(request,
                    'shop/product/detail.html',
                    {'product': product,
                     'cart_product_form': cart_product_form})
```

Edit the `shop/product/detail.html` template of the `shop` application, and add the following form the product's price like this:

```html
<p class="price">${{ product.price }}</p>
<form action="{% url "cart:cart_add" product.id %}" method="post">
  {{ cart_product_form }}
  {% csrf_token %}
  <input type="submit" value="Add to cart">
</form>
```

Make sure the development server is running with the command `python manage.py runserver`. Now, open `http://127.0.0.1:8000/` in your browser and navigate to a product detail page. It now contains a form to choose a quantity before adding the product to the cart. The page will look like this:

Choose a quantity and click on the **Add to cart** button. The form is submitted to the `cart_add` view via POST. The view adds the product to the cart in the session, including its current price and the selected quantity. Then, it redirects the user to the cart detail page, which will look like the following screenshot:

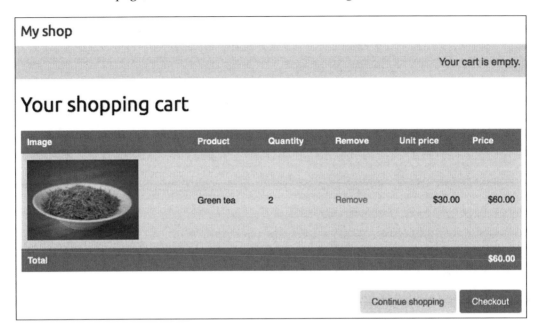

## Updating product quantities in the cart

When users see the cart, they might want to change product quantities before placing an order. We are going to allow users to change quantities from the cart detail page.

Edit the `views.py` file of the `cart` application and change the `cart_detail` view to this:

```python
def cart_detail(request):
    cart = Cart(request)
    for item in cart:
        item['update_quantity_form'] = CartAddProductForm(
                            initial={'quantity': item['quantity'],
                            'update': True})
    return render(request, 'cart/detail.html', {'cart': cart})
```

We create an instance of `CartAddProductForm` for each item in the cart to allow changing product quantities. We initialize the form with the current item quantity and set the `update` field to `True` so that when we submit the form to the `cart_add` view, the current quantity is replaced with the new one.

Now, edit the `cart/detail.html` template of the `cart` application and find following line:

```
<td>{{ item.quantity }}</td>
```

Replace the previous line with the following code:

```
<td>
  <form action="{% url "cart:cart_add" product.id %}" method="post">
    {{ item.update_quantity_form.quantity }}
    {{ item.update_quantity_form.update }}
    <input type="submit" value="Update">
    {% csrf_token %}
  </form>
</td>
```

Open `http://127.0.0.1:8000/cart/` in your browser. You will see a form to edit the quantity for each cart item, shown as follows:

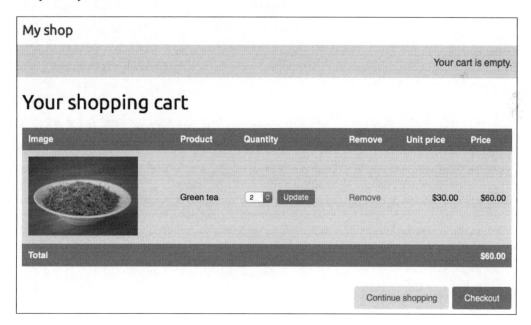

Change the quantity of an item and click on the **Update** button to test the new functionality.

# Creating a context processor for the current cart

You might have noticed that we are still showing the message **Your cart is empty** in the header of the site. When we start adding items to the cart, we will see the total number of items in the cart and the total cost instead. Since this is something that should be displayed in all the pages, we will build a context processor to include the current cart in the request context, regardless of the view that has been processed.

## Context processors

A context processor is a Python function that takes the `request` object as an argument and returns a dictionary that gets added to the request context. They come in handy when you need to make something available to all templates.

By default, when you create a new project using the `startproject` command, your project will contain the following template context processors, in the `context_processors` option inside the `TEMPLATES` setting:

- `django.template.context_processors.debug`: This sets the Boolean `debug` and `sql_queries` variables in the context representing the list of SQL queries executed in the request

- `django.template.context_processors.request`: This sets the `request` variable in the context

- `django.contrib.auth.context_processors.auth`: This sets the user variable in the request

- `django.contrib.messages.context_processors.messages`: This sets a `messages` variable in the context containing all messages that have been sent using the messages framework.

Django also enables `django.template.context_processors.csrf` to avoid cross-site request forgery attacks. This context processor is not present in the settings, but it is always enabled and cannot be turned off for security reasons.

You can see the list of all built-in context processors at `https://docs.djangoproject.com/en/1.8/ref/templates/api/#built-in-template-context-processors`.

# Setting the cart into the request context

Let's create a context processor to set the current cart into the request context for templates. We will be able to access this cart in any template.

Create a new file into the `cart` application directory and name it `context_processors.py`. Context processors can reside anywhere in your code, but creating them here will keep your code well organized. Add the following code to the file:

```
from .cart import Cart

def cart(request):
    return {'cart': Cart(request)}
```

As you can see, a context processor is a function that receives the `request` object as parameter, and returns a dictionary of objects that will be available to all the templates rendered using `RequestContext`. In our context processor, we instantiate the cart using the `request` object and make it available for the templates as a variable named `cart`.

Edit the `settings.py` file of your project and add `'cart.context_processors.cart'` to the `context_processors` option inside the TEMPLATES setting. The setting will look as follows after the change:

```
TEMPLATES = [
    {
        'BACKEND': 'django.template.backends.django.DjangoTemplates',
        'DIRS': [],
        'APP_DIRS': True,
        'OPTIONS': {
            'context_processors': [
                'django.template.context_processors.debug',
                'django.template.context_processors.request',
                'django.contrib.auth.context_processors.auth',
                'django.contrib.messages.context_processors.messages',
                'cart.context_processors.cart',
            ],
        },
    },
]
```

Your context processor will now be executed every time a template is rendered using Django's `RequestContext`. The `cart` variable will be set in the context for your templates.

Context processors are executed in all the requests that use `RequestContext`. You might want to create a custom template tag instead of a context processor, if you are going to access the database.

Now, edit the `shop/base.html` template of the `shop` application and find the:

```
<div class="cart">
  Your cart is empty.
</div>
```

Replace the previous lines with the following code:

```
<div class="cart">
  {% with total_items=cart|length %}
    {% if cart|length > 0 %}
      Your cart:
      <a href="{% url "cart:cart_detail" %}">
        {{ total_items }} item{{ total_items|pluralize }},
        ${{ cart.get_total_price }}
      </a>
    {% else %}
      Your cart is empty.
    {% endif %}
  {% endwith %}
</div>
```

Reload your server using the command `python manage.py runserver`. Open `http://127.0.0.1:8000/` in your browser and add some products to the cart. In the header of the website, you can see the total number of items in the current and the total cost like this:

| My shop | |
|---|---|
| | Your cart: 2 items, $60.00 |

# Registering customer orders

When a shopping cart is checked out, you need to save an order into the database. Orders will contain information about customers and the products they are buying.

Create a new application for managing customer orders using the following command:

```
python manage.py startapp orders
```

Edit the `settings.py` file of your project and add `'orders'` to the `INSTALLED_APPS` setting as follows:

```
INSTALLED_APPS = (
    # ...
    'orders',
)
```

You have activated the new application.

# Creating order models

You will need a model to store the order details, and a second model to store items bought, including their price and quantity. Edit the `models.py` file of the `orders` application and add the following code to it:

```
from django.db import models
from shop.models import Product

class Order(models.Model):
    first_name = models.CharField(max_length=50)
    last_name = models.CharField(max_length=50)
    email = models.EmailField()
    address = models.CharField(max_length=250)
    postal_code = models.CharField(max_length=20)
    city = models.CharField(max_length=100)
    created = models.DateTimeField(auto_now_add=True)
    updated = models.DateTimeField(auto_now=True)
    paid = models.BooleanField(default=False)

    class Meta:
        ordering = ('-created',)

    def __str__(self):
        return 'Order {}'.format(self.id)

    def get_total_cost(self):
        return sum(item.get_cost() for item in self.items.all())


class OrderItem(models.Model):
    order = models.ForeignKey(Order, related_name='items')
    product = models.ForeignKey(Product,
                                related_name='order_items')
```

```
        price = models.DecimalField(max_digits=10, decimal_places=2)
        quantity = models.PositiveIntegerField(default=1)

        def __str__(self):
            return '{}'.format(self.id)

        def get_cost(self):
            return self.price * self.quantity
```

The `Order` model contains several fields for customer information and a `paid` boolean field, which defaults to `False`. Later on, we are going to use this field to differentiate between paid and unpaid orders. We also define a `get_total_cost()` method to obtain the total cost of the items bought in this order.

The `OrderItem` model allows us to store the product, quantity, and price paid for each item. We include `get_cost()` to return the cost of the item.

Run the next command to create initial migrations for the `orders` application:

**python manage.py makemigrations**

You will see the following output:

```
    Migrations for 'orders':
      0001_initial.py:
        - Create model Order
        - Create model OrderItem
```

Run the following command to apply the new migration:

**python manage.py migrate**

Your order models are now synced to the database.

# Including order models in an administration site

Let's add the order models to the administration site. Edit the `admin.py` file of the `orders` application to make it look like this:

```
    from django.contrib import admin
    from .models import Order, OrderItem

    class OrderItemInline(admin.TabularInline):
        model = OrderItem
        raw_id_fields = ['product']
```

```
class OrderAdmin(admin.ModelAdmin):
    list_display = ['id', 'first_name', 'last_name', 'email',
                    'address', 'postal_code', 'city', 'paid',
                    'created', 'updated']
    list_filter = ['paid', 'created', 'updated']
    inlines = [OrderItemInline]

admin.site.register(Order, OrderAdmin)
```

We use a `ModelInline` for the `OrderItem` model to include it as an *inline* in the `OrderAdmin` class. An inline allows you to include a model for appearing on the same edit page as the parent model.

Run the development server with the command `python manage.py runserver`, and then open `http://127.0.0.1:8000/admin/orders/order/add/` in your browser. You will see the following page:

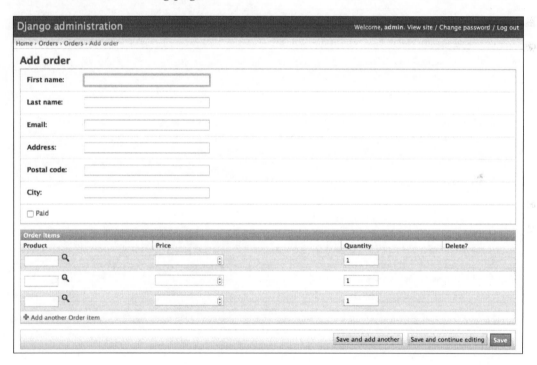

# Creating customer orders

We need to use the order models that we just created to persist the items contained in the shopping cart when the user finally wishes to place an order. The functionality for creating a new order will work as follows:

1. We present users an order form to fill in their data.

2. We create a new `Order` instance with the data entered by users, and then we create an associated `OrderItem` instance for each item in the cart.

3. We clear all the cart contents and redirect users to a success page.

First, we need a form to enter order details. Create a new file inside the `orders` application directory and name it `forms.py`. Add the following code to it:

```python
from django import forms
from .models import Order

class OrderCreateForm(forms.ModelForm):
    class Meta:
        model = Order
        fields = ['first_name', 'last_name', 'email', 'address',
                  'postal_code', 'city']
```

This is the form that we are going to use for creating new `Order` objects. Now, we need a view to handle the form and create a new order. Edit the `views.py` file of the `orders` application and add the following code to it:

```python
from django.shortcuts import render
from .models import OrderItem
from .forms import OrderCreateForm
from cart.cart import Cart

def order_create(request):
    cart = Cart(request)
    if request.method == 'POST':
        form = OrderCreateForm(request.POST)
        if form.is_valid():
            order = form.save()
            for item in cart:
                OrderItem.objects.create(order=order,
                                         product=item['product'],
                                         price=item['price'],
                                         quantity=item['quantity'])
            # clear the cart
            cart.clear()
```

```
        return render(request,
                        'orders/order/created.html',
                        {'order': order})
    else:
        form = OrderCreateForm()
    return render(request,
                    'orders/order/create.html',
                    {'cart': cart, 'form': form})
```

In the `order_create` view, we will obtain the current cart from the session with `cart = Cart(request)`. Depending on the request method, we will perform the following tasks:

- **The GET request**: This instantiates the `OrderCreateForm` form and renders the template `orders/order/create.html`.

- **The POST request**: This validates the data that get posted. If the data is valid, we will use `order = form.save()` to create a new `Order` instance. We will then save it to the database, and then store it in the `order` variable. After creating the `order`, we will iterate over the cart items and create `OrderItem` for each of them. Finally, we will clear the cart contents.

Now, create a new file inside the `orders` application directory and name it `urls.py`. Add the following code to it:

```
from django.conf.urls import url
from . import views

urlpatterns = [
    url(r'^create/$',
        views.order_create,
        name='order_create'),
]
```

This is the URL pattern for the `order_create` view. Edit the `urls.py` file of myshop and include the following pattern. Remember to place it before the `shop.urls` pattern:

```
url(r'^orders/', include('orders.urls', namespace='orders')),
```

Edit the `cart/detail.html` template of the `cart` application and replace this line:

```
<a href="#" class="button">Checkout</a>
```

Replace this with the following ones:

```
<a href="{% url "orders:order_create" %}" class="button">
    Checkout
</a>
```

Users can now navigate from the cart detail page to the order form. We still need to define templates for placing orders. Create the following file structure inside the `orders` application directory:

```
templates/
    orders/
        order/
            create.html
            created.html
```

Edit the `orders/order/create.html` template and include the following code:

```
{% extends "shop/base.html" %}

{% block title %}
  Checkout
{% endblock %}

{% block content %}
  <h1>Checkout</h1>

  <div class="order-info">
    <h3>Your order</h3>
    <ul>
      {% for item in cart %}
        <li>
          {{ item.quantity }}x {{ item.product.name }}
          <span>${{ item.total_price }}</span>
        </li>
      {% endfor %}
    </ul>
    <p>Total: ${{ cart.get_total_price }}</p>
  </div>

  <form action="." method="post" class="order-form">
    {{ form.as_p }}
    <p><input type="submit" value="Place order"></p>
    {% csrf_token %}
  </form>
{% endblock %}
```

This template displays the cart items including totals and the form to place an order.

Edit the `orders/order/created.html` template and add the following code:

```
{% extends "shop/base.html" %}

{% block title %}
  Thank you
{% endblock %}

{% block content %}
  <h1>Thank you</h1>
  <p>Your order has been successfully completed. Your order number is
<strong>{{ order.id }}</strong>.</p>
{% endblock %}
```

This is the template that we render when the order is successfully created. Start the web development server to track new files. Open `http://127.0.0.1:8000/` in your browser, add a couple of products to the cart, and continue to checkout the page. You will see a page like the following one:

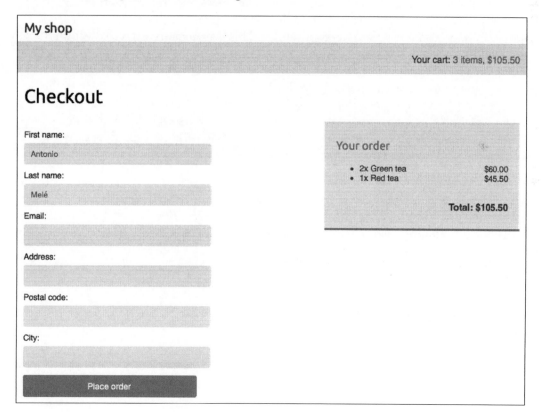

Fill in the form with the valid data and click on **Place order** button. The order will be created and you will see a success page like this:

| My shop | |
|---|---|
| | Your cart: 3 items, $105.50 |
| **Thank you** | |
| Your order has been successfully completed. Your order number is **1**. | |

# Launching asynchronous tasks with Celery

Everything you execute in a view will affect response time. In many situations you might want to return a response to the user as quickly as possible and let the server execute some process asynchronously. This is especially relevant for time-consuming processes or processes subject to failure, which might need a retry policy. For example, a video sharing platform allows users to upload videos but requires a long time to transcode uploaded videos. The site might return a response to the user, telling him the transcoding will start soon, and start transcoding the video asynchronously. Another example is sending e-mails to users. If your site sends e-mail notifications from a view, the SMTP connection might fail or slow down the response. Launching asynchronous tasks is essential to avoid blocking execution.

Celery is a distributed task queue that can process vast amounts of messages. It does real-time processing, but also supports task scheduling. Using Celery, not only can you create asynchronous tasks easily and let them be executed by workers as soon as possible, but you can also schedule them to run at a specific time.

You can find the Celery documentation at http://celery.readthedocs.org/en/latest/.

## Installing Celery

Let's install Celery and integrate it into our project. Install Celery via pip using the following command:

```
pip install celery==3.1.18
```

Celery requires a message broker in order to handle requests from an external source. The broker takes care of sending messages to Celery workers, which process tasks as they receive them. Let's install a message broker.

# Installing RabbitMQ

There are several options to choose as a message broker for Celery, including key-value stores such as Redis or an actual message system such as RabbitMQ. We will configure Celery with RabbitMQ, since it's a recommended message worker for Celery.

If you are using Linux, you can install RabbitMQ from the shell using the following command:

```
apt-get install rabbitmq
```

If you need to install RabbitMQ on Mac OS X or Windows, you can find standalone versions at https://www.rabbitmq.com/download.html.

After installing it, launch RabbitMQ using the following command from the shell:

```
rabbitmq-server
```

You will see an output that ends with the following line:

```
Starting broker... completed with 10 plugins.
```

RabbitMQ is running and ready to receive messages.

# Adding Celery to your project

You have to provide a configuration for the Celery instance. Create a new file next to the settings.py file of myshop and name it celery.py. This file will contain the Celery configuration for your project. Add the following code to it:

```
import os
from celery import Celery
from django.conf import settings

# set the default Django settings module for the 'celery' program.
os.environ.setdefault('DJANGO_SETTINGS_MODULE', 'myshop.settings')

app = Celery('myshop')

app.config_from_object('django.conf:settings')
app.autodiscover_tasks(lambda: settings.INSTALLED_APPS)
```

In this code we set the DJANGO_SETTINGS_MODULE variable for the Celery command-line program. Then we create an instance of our application with app = Celery('myshop'). We load any custom configuration from our project settings using the config_from_object() method. Finally we tell Celery to auto-discover asynchronous tasks for the applications listed in the INSTALLED_APPS setting. Celery will look for a tasks.py file in each application directory to load asynchronous tasks defined in it.

You need to import the celery module in the __init__.py file of your project to make sure it is loaded when Django starts. Edit the myshop/__init__.py file and add the following code to it:

```
# import celery
from .celery import app as celery_app
```

Now, you can start programming asynchronous tasks for your applications.

 The CELERY_ALWAYS_EAGER setting allows you to execute tasks locally in a synchronous way instead of sending them to the queue. This is useful for running unit tests or the project in your local environment without running Celery.

# Adding asynchronous tasks to your application

We are going to create an asynchronous task to send an email notification to our users when they place an order.

The convention is to include asynchronous tasks for your application in a tasks module within your application directory. Create a new file inside the orders application and name it tasks.py. This is the place where Celery will look for asynchronous tasks. Add the following code to it:

```
from celery import task
from django.core.mail import send_mail
from .models import Order

@task
def order_created(order_id):
    """
    Task to send an e-mail notification when an order is
    successfully created.
    """
```

```
order = Order.objects.get(id=order_id)
subject = 'Order nr. {}'.format(order.id)
message = 'Dear {},\n\nYou have successfully placed an order.\
            Your order id is {}.'.format(order.first_name,
                                          order.id)
mail_sent = send_mail(subject,
                      message,
                      'admin@myshop.com',
                      [order.email])
return mail_sent
```

We define the order_created task by using the task decorator. As you can see, a Celery task is just a Python function decorated with task. Our task function receives an order_id parameter. It's always recommended to pass only IDS to task functions and lookup objects when the task is executed. We use the send_mail() function provided by Django to send an email notification to the user that placed the order. If you don't want to set up email settings, you can tell Django to write emails to the console by adding the following setting to the settings.py file:

```
EMAIL_BACKEND = 'django.core.mail.backends.console.EmailBackend'
```

>
> Use asynchronous tasks not only for time-consuming processes, but also for other processes that are subject to failure, which do not take so much time to be executed, but which are subject to connection failures or require a retry policy.

Now we have to add the task to our order_create view. Open the views.py file of the orders application and import the task as follows:

```
from .tasks import order_created
```

Then, call the order_created asynchronous task after clearing the cart as follows:

```
# clear the cart
cart.clear()
# launch asynchronous task
order_created.delay(order.id)
```

We call the delay() method of the task to execute it asynchronously. The task will be added to the queue and will be executed by a worker as soon as possible.

Open another shell and start the celery worker, using the following command:

```
celery -A myshop worker -l info
```

The Celery worker is now running and ready to process tasks. Make sure the Django development server is also running. Open `http://127.0.0.1:8000/` in your browser, add some products to your shopping cart, and complete an order. In the shell, you started the Celery worker and you will see an output similar to this one:

```
[2015-09-14 19:43:47,526: INFO/MainProcess] Received task: orders.
tasks.order_created[933e383c-095e-4cbd-b909-70c07e6a2ddf]
[2015-09-14 19:43:50,851: INFO/MainProcess] Task orders.tasks.
order_created[933e383c-095e-4cbd-b909-70c07e6a2ddf] succeeded in
3.318835098994896s: 1
```

The task has been executed and you will receive an email notification for your order.

# Monitoring Celery

You might want to monitor the asynchronous tasks that are executed. Flower is a web-based tool for monitoring Celery. You can install Flower using the command `pip install flower`

Once installed, you can launch Flower running the following command from your project directory:

```
celery -A myshop flower
```

Open `http://localhost:5555/dashboard` in your browser. You will be able to see the active Celery workers and asynchronous tasks' statistics:

You can find documentation for Flower at `http://flower.readthedocs.org/en/latest/`.

# Summary

In this chapter, you created a basic shop application. You created a product catalog and built a shopping cart using sessions. You implemented a custom context processor to make the cart available to your templates and created a form for placing orders. You also learned how to launch asynchronous tasks with Celery.

In the next chapter, you will learn to integrate a payment gateway into your shop, add custom actions to the administration site, export data as CSV, and generate PDF files dynamically.

# 8

# Managing Payments
# and Orders

In the previous chapter, you created a basic on-line shop with a product catalog and ordering system. You also learned how to launch asynchronous tasks with Celery. In this chapter, you will learn how to integrate a payment gateway into your site. You will also extend the administration site to manage orders and export them to different formats.

In this chapter, we will cover how to:

- Integrate a payment gateway into your project
- Manage payment notifications
- Export orders to CSV files
- Create custom views for the administration site
- Generate PDF invoices dynamically

## Integrating a payment gateway

A payment gateway allows you to process payments online. Using a payment gateway, you can manage customer's orders and delegate payment processing through a reliable, secure third party. This means you don't have to worry about storing credit cards in your own system.

There are many payment gateway providers to choose from. We are going to integrate PayPal, which is one of the most popular payment gateways.

PayPal offers several methods to integrate its gateway into your site. The standard integration consists of a **Buy now** button, which you probably have seen on other websites. The button redirects buyers to PayPal to process the payment. We are going to integrate PayPal Payments Standard including a custom **Buy now** button in our site. PayPal will process the payment and will send a notification to our server indicating the payment status.

# Creating a PayPal account

You need to have a PayPal Business account to integrate the payment gateway into your site. If you don't own a PayPal account yet, sign up at `https://www.paypal.com/signup/account`. Make sure that you choose a **Business Account** and sign up to the PayPal Payments Standard solution, as shown in the following screenshot:

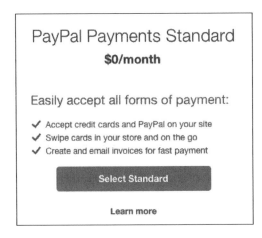

Fill in your details in the sign up form and complete the sign up process. PayPal will send you an e-mail to verify your account.

# Installing django-paypal

Django-paypal is a third-party Django application that simplifies integrating PayPal into Django projects. We are going to use it to integrate the PayPal Payments Standard solution in our shop. You can find django-paypal's documentation at `http://django-paypal.readthedocs.org/`.

Install `django-paypal` from the shell with the following command:

```
pip install django-paypal==0.2.5
```

Edit the `settings.py` file of your project and add `'paypal.standard.ipn'` to the `INSTALLED_APPS` setting as follows:

```
INSTALLED_APPS = (
    #  ...
    'paypal.standard.ipn',
)
```

This is the application provided by django-paypal to integrate PayPal Payments Standard with **Instant Payment Notification (IPN)**. We are going to handle payment notifications later.

Add the following settings to the `settings.py` file of `myshop` to configure django-paypal:

```
# django-paypal settings
PAYPAL_RECEIVER_EMAIL = 'mypaypalemail@myshop.com'
PAYPAL_TEST = True
```

These settings are as follows:

- `PAYPAL_RECEIVER_EMAIL`: The e-mail of your PayPal account. Replace `mypaypalemail@myshop.com` with the e-mail you used to create your PayPal account.

- `PAYPAL_TEST`: A boolean indicating whether the PayPal's sandbox environment should be used to process payments. The sandbox allows you to test your PayPal integration before moving to a production environment.

Open the shell and run the following command to sync models of django-paypal with the database:

```
python manage.py migrate
```

You should see an output that ends in a similar way to this:

```
Running migrations:
  Rendering model states... DONE
  Applying ipn.0001_initial... OK
  Applying ipn.0002_paypalipn_mp_id... OK
  Applying ipn.0003_auto_20141117_1647... OK
```

The models of `django-paypal` are now synced with the database. You also need to add the URL patterns of `django-paypal` to your project. Edit the main `urls.py` file located in the `myshop` directory and add the following URL pattern. Remember to place it before the `shop.urls` pattern to avoid wrong pattern match:

```
url(r'^paypal/', include('paypal.standard.ipn.urls')),
```

Let's add the payment gateway to the checkout process.

# Adding the payment gateway

The checkout process should work as follows:

1. Users add items to their shopping cart.
2. Users check out their shopping cart.
3. Users are redirected to PayPal for payment.
4. PayPal sends a payment notification to our site.
5. PayPal redirects users back to our website.

Create a new application in your project using the following command:

```
python manage.py startapp payment
```

We are going to use this application to manage the checkout process and user payments.

Edit the `settings.py` file of your project and add `'payment'` to the `INSTALLED_APPS` setting as follows:

```
INSTALLED_APPS = (
    # ...
    'paypal.standard.ipn',
    'payment',
)
```

The `payment` application is now active in the project. Edit the `views.py` file of the `orders` application and make sure to include the following imports:

```
from django.shortcuts import render, redirect
from django.core.urlresolvers import reverse
```

Replace the following lines of the `order_create` view:

```
# launch asynchronous task
order_created.delay(order.id)
return render(request, 'orders/order/created.html', locals())
```

...with the following ones:

```
# launch asynchronous task
order_created.delay(order.id) # set the order in the session
request.session['order_id'] = order.id # redirect to the payment
return redirect(reverse('payment:process'))
```

After successfully creating an order, we set the order ID in the current session using the `order_id` session key. Then, we redirect the user to the `payment:process` URL, which we are going to create next.

Edit the `views.py` file of the `payment` application and add the following code to it:

```
from decimal import Decimal
from django.conf import settings
from django.core.urlresolvers import reverse
from django.shortcuts import render, get_object_or_404
from paypal.standard.forms import PayPalPaymentsForm
from orders.models import Order

def payment_process(request):
    order_id = request.session.get('order_id')
    order = get_object_or_404(Order, id=order_id)
    host = request.get_host()

    paypal_dict = {
        'business': settings.PAYPAL_RECEIVER_EMAIL,
        'amount': '%.2f' % order.get_total_cost().quantize(
                                           Decimal('.01')),
        'item_name': 'Order {}'.format(order.id),
        'invoice': str(order.id),
        'currency_code': 'USD',
        'notify_url': 'http://{}{}'.format(host,
                                      reverse('paypal-ipn')),
        'return_url': 'http://{}{}'.format(host,
                                      reverse('payment:done')),
        'cancel_return': 'http://{}{}'.format(host,
                                    reverse('payment:canceled')),
    }
    form = PayPalPaymentsForm(initial=paypal_dict)
    return render(request,
                  'payment/process.html',
                  {'order': order, 'form':form})
```

In the `payment_process` view, we generate a custom PayPal's **Buy now** button to pay an order. First, we get the current order from the `order_id` session key, which was set before by the `order_create` view. We get the `Order` object for the given ID and build a new `PayPalPaymentsForm` including the following fields:

- `business`: The PayPal merchant account to process the payment. We use the e-mail account defined in the `PAYPAL_RECEIVER_EMAIL` setting here.

- `amount`: The total amount to charge the customer.

- `item_name`: The name of the item being sold. We use the order ID, since the order may contain multiple products.

- `invoice`: The invoice ID. This id has to be unique for each payment. We use the order ID.

- `currency_code`: The currency for this payment. We set this to USD for U.S. Dollar. Use the same currency as the one set in your PayPal account (EUR for Euro).

- `notify_url`: The URL PayPal will send IPN requests to. We use the `paypal-ipn` URL provided by `django-paypal`. The view associated to this URL handles payment notifications and stores them in the database.

- `return_url`: The URL to redirect the user after the payment is successful. We use the URL `payment:done`, which we have to create next.

- `cancel_return`: The URL to redirect the user if the payment was canceled or there was some other issue. We use the URL `payment:canceled`, which we also have to create next.

The `PayPalPaymentsForm` will be rendered as a standard form with hidden fields, and the user will only see the **Buy now** button. When users click the button, the form will be submitted to PayPal via POST.

Let's create simple views for PayPal to redirect users when the payment has been successful, or when it has been canceled for some reason. Add the following code to the same `views.py` file:

```
from django.views.decorators.csrf import csrf_exempt

@csrf_exempt
def payment_done(request):
    return render(request, 'payment/done.html')


@csrf_exempt
def payment_canceled(request):
    return render(request, 'payment/canceled.html')
```

We use the `csrf_exempt` decorator to avoid Django expecting a CSRF token, since PayPal can redirect the user to any of these views via POST. Create a new file inside the `payment` application directory and name it `urls.py`. Add the following code to it:

```python
from django.conf.urls import url
from . import views

urlpatterns = [
    url(r'^process/$', views.payment_process, name='process'),
    url(r'^done/$', views.payment_done, name='done'),
    url(r'^canceled/$', views.payment_canceled, name='canceled'),
]
```

These are the URLs for the payment workflow. We have included the following URL patterns:

- `process`: For the view that generates the PayPal form for the **Buy now** button
- `done`: For PayPal to redirect the user when the payment is successful
- `canceled`: For PayPal to redirect the user when the payment is canceled

Edit the main `urls.py` file of the `myshop` project and include the URL patterns for the `payment` application:

```python
url(r'^payment/', include('payment.urls', namespace='payment')),
```

Remember to place it before the `shop.urls` pattern to avoid wrong pattern match.

Create the following file structure inside the `payment` application directory:

```
templates/
    payment/
        process.html
        done.html
        canceled.html
```

Edit the `payment/process.html` template and add the following code to it:

```html
{% extends "shop/base.html" %}

{% block title %}Pay using PayPal{% endblock %}

{% block content %}
  <h1>Pay using PayPal</h1>
  {{ form.render }}
{% endblock %}
```

This is the template that renders `PayPalPaymentsForm` and displays the **Buy now** button.

Edit the `payment/done.html` template and add the following code to it:

```
{% extends "shop/base.html" %}

{% block content %}
  <h1>Your payment was successful</h1>
  <p>Your payment has been successfully received.</p>
{% endblock %}
```

This is the template for the page that the user is redirected to after a successful payment.

Edit the `payment/canceled.html` template and add the following code to it:

```
{% extends "shop/base.html" %}

{% block content %}
  <h1>Your payment has not been processed</h1>
  <p>There was a problem processing your payment.</p>
{% endblock %}
```

This is the template for the page that the user is redirected to when there is some issue processing the payment or if the user canceled the payment.

Let's try the complete payment process.

# Using PayPal's Sandbox

Open `http://developer.paypal.com` in your browser and log in with your PayPal business account. Click the **Dashboard** menu item, and on the left menu click the **Accounts** option under **Sandbox**. You should see the list of your sandbox test accounts as follows:

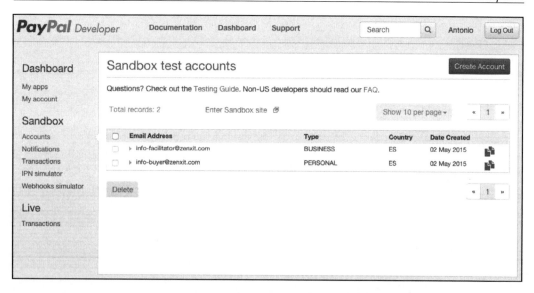

Initially, you will see a business and a personal test account automatically created by PayPal. You can create new sandbox test accounts with the **Create Account** button.

Click the **Personal Account** in the list to expand it, and then click the **Profile** link. You will see information about the test account including e-mail and profile information as follows:

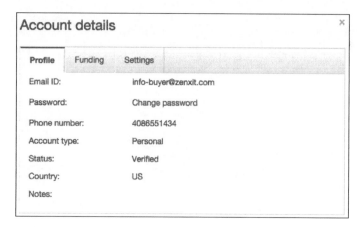

In the **Funding** tab, you will find bank account, credit card data, and PayPal credit balance.

The test accounts can be used to do payments in your website using the sandbox environment. Navigate to the **Profile** tab and click the **Change password** link. Create a custom password for this test account.

Open the shell and start the development server with the command `python manage.py runserver`. Open `http://127.0.0.1:8000/` in your browser, add some products to the shopping cart, and fill in the checkout form. When you click the **Place order** button, the order will be persisted to the database, the order ID will be saved in the current session, and you will be redirected to the payment process page. This page retrieves the order from the session and renders the PayPal form displaying a **Buy Now** button, like this:

You can take a look at the HTML source code to see the generated form fields.

Click the **Buy Now** button. You will be redirected to PayPal, and you should see the following page:

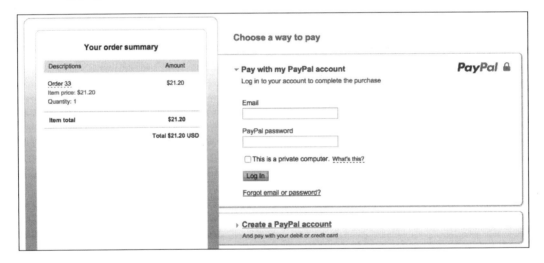

Enter the buyer test account e-mail and password and click the **Log In** button. You will be redirected to the following page:

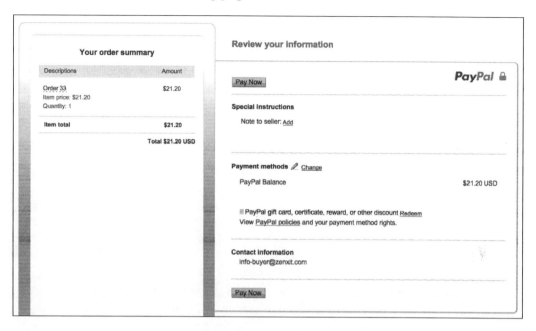

Now, click the **Pay Now** button. Finally, you will see a confirmation page that includes your transaction ID. The page should look like this:

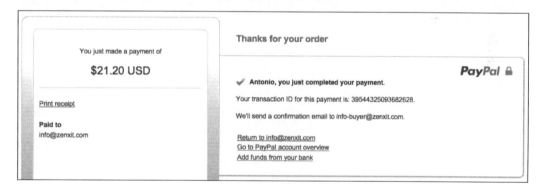

Click the **Return to e-mail@domain.com** button. You will be redirected to the URL you have specified in the `return_url` field of `PayPalPaymentsForm`. That is the URL for the `payment_done` view. The page will look like this:

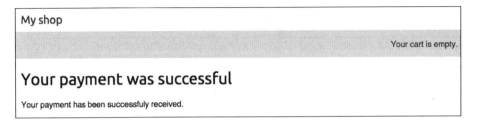

The payment has been successful. However, PayPal is unable to send a payment status notification to our application, since we are running our project on our local host with the IP `127.0.0.1` that is not publicly accessible. We are going to learn how to make our site accessible form the Internet and be able to receive IPN notifications.

# Getting payment notifications

IPN is a method offered by most payment gateways to track purchases real-time. A notification is instantly sent to your server when the gateway processes a payment. This notification contains all payment details, including the status and a signature of the payment, which can be used to confirm the origin of the notification. This notification is sent as a separate HTTP request to your server. In the case of connectivity issues, PayPal will make multiple attempts to notify your site.

The `django-paypal` application comes with two different signals for IPNs. These signals are:

- `valid_ipn_received`: Triggered when the IPN message received from PayPal is correct and is not a duplicate of an existing message in the database

- `invalid_ipn_received`: This signal is triggered when the IPN received from PayPal contains invalid data or is not well formed

We are going to create a custom receiver function and connect it to the `valid_ipn_received` signal to confirm payments.

Create a new file inside the `payment` application directory and name it `signals.py`. Add the following code to it:

```
from django.shortcuts import get_object_or_404
from paypal.standard.models import ST_PP_COMPLETED
from paypal.standard.ipn.signals import valid_ipn_received
from orders.models import Order
```

```
def payment_notification(sender, **kwargs):
    ipn_obj = sender
    if ipn_obj.payment_status == ST_PP_COMPLETED:
        # payment was successful
        order = get_object_or_404(Order, id=ipn_obj.invoice)
        # mark the order as paid
        order.paid = True
        order.save()


valid_ipn_received.connect(payment_notification)
```

We connect the `payment_notification` receiver function to the `valid_ipn_received` signal provided by `django-paypal`. The receiver function works as follows:

1. We receive the sender object, which is an instance of the `PayPalIPN` model defined in `paypal.standard.ipn.models`.

2. We check the `payment_status` attribute to make sure it equals the completed status of `django-paypal`. This status indicates that the payment was successfully processed.

3. Then we use the `get_object_or_404()` shortcut function to get the order whose ID matches the `invoice` parameter we provided for PayPal.

4. We mark the order as paid by setting its `paid` attribute to `True` and saving the `Order` object to the database.

You have to make sure that your signals module is loaded so that the receiver function is called when the `valid_ipn_received` signal is triggered. The best practice is to load your signals when the application containing them is loaded. This can be done by defining a custom application configuration, which will be explained in the next section.

# Configuring our application

You learned about application configuration in *Chapter 6, Tracking User Actions*. We are going to define a custom configuration for our `payment application` in order to load our signal receiver functions.

Create a new file inside the `payment application` directory and name it `apps.py`. Add the following code to it:

```
from django.apps import AppConfig


class PaymentConfig(AppConfig):
    name = 'payment'
```

```
        verbose_name = 'Payment'

    def ready(self):
        # import signal handlers
        import payment.signals
```

In this code, we define a custom `AppConfig` class for the `payment` application. The `name` parameter is the name of the application and `verbose_name` contains the human-readable format. We import the signals module in the `ready()` method to make sure they are loaded when the application is initialized.

Edit the `__init__.py` file of the `payment` application and add the following line to it:

```
    default_app_config = 'payment.apps.PaymentConfig'
```

This will make Django to automatically load your custom application configuration class. You can find further information about application configuration at `https://docs.djangoproject.com/en/1.8/ref/applications/`.

# Testing payment notifications

Since we are working in a local environment, we need to make sure that our site is available to PayPal. There are several applications that allow you to make your development environment available on the Internet. We are going to use Ngrok, which is one of the most popular ones.

Download Ngrok for your operating system from `https://ngrok.com/` and run it from the shell using the following command:

```
./ngrok http 8000
```

With this command, you are telling Ngrok to create a tunnel to your local host on port `8000` and assign an Internet accessible hostname for it. You should see an output similar to this one:

```
Tunnel Status          online
Version                2.0.17/2.0.17
Web Interface          http://127.0.0.1:4040
Forwarding             http://1a1b50f2.ngrok.io -> localhost:8000
Forwarding             https://1a1b50f2.ngrok.io -> localhost:8000

Connnections           ttl     opn     rt1     rt5     p50     p90
                       0       0       0.00    0.00    0.00    0.00
```

Ngrok tells us that our site, running locally at localhost on port `8000` using Django's development server, is made available on the Internet through the URLs `http://1a1b50f2.ngrok.io` and `https://1a1b50f2.ngrok.io` for the HTTP and HTTPS protocols respectively. Ngrok also provides a URL to access a web interface that displays information about requests sent to the server.

Open the URL provided by Ngrok with your browser; for example, `http://1a1b50f2.ngrok.io`. Add some products to the shopping cart, place an order, and pay using your PayPal test account. This time, PayPal will be able to reach the URL that is generated for the `notify_url` field of `PayPalPaymentsForm` in the `payment_process` view. If you take a look at the rendered form, you will see that the HTML form field looks like this:

```
<input id="id_notify_url" name="notify_url" type="hidden"
value="http://1a1b50f2.ngrok.io/paypal/">
```

After finishing the payment process, open `http://127.0.0.1:8000/admin/ipn/paypalipn/` in your browser. You should see an IPN object for the last payment with status **Completed**. This object contains all the information of the payment, which is sent by PayPal to the URL you provided for IPN notifications. The IPN admin list display page should look like this:

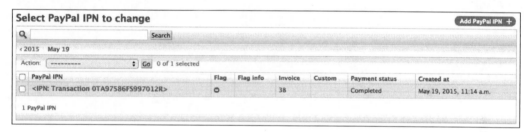

You can also launch IPNs using the PayPal's IPN simulator located at `https://developer.paypal.com/developer/ipnSimulator/`. The simulator allows you to specify the fields and the type of notification to send.

In addition to PayPal Payments Standard, PayPal offers Website Payments Pro, which is a subscription service that allows you to accept payments on your site without redirecting the user to PayPal. You can find information about how to integrate Website Payments Pro at `http://django-paypal.readthedocs.org/en/v0.2.5/pro/index.html`.

# Exporting orders to CSV files

Sometimes, you might want to export the information contained in a model to a file so that you can import it in any other system. One of the most widely used formats to export/import data is **Comma-Separated Values (CSV)**. A CSV file is a plain text file consisting of a number of records. There is usually one record per line, and some delimiter character, usually a literal comma, separates the record fields. We are going to customize the administration site to be able to export orders to CSV files.

## Adding custom actions to the administration site

Django offers you a wide range of options to customize the administration site. We are going to modify the object list view to include a custom admin action.

An admin action works as follows: A user selects objects from the admin's object list page with checkboxes, then selects an action to perform on all of the selected items, and executes the action. The following screenshot shows where actions are located in the administration site:

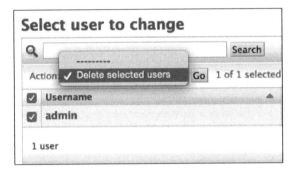

 Create custom admin actions to allow staff users to apply actions to multiple elements at once.

You can create a custom action by writing a regular function that receives the following parameters:

- The current `ModelAdmin` being displayed
- The current request object as an `HttpRequest` instance
- A QuerySet for the the the objects selected by the user

This function will be executed when the action is triggered from the administration site.

We are going to create a custom admin action to download a list of orders as a CSV file. Edit the admin.py file of the orders application and add the following code before the OrderAdmin class:

```
import csv
import datetime
from django.http import HttpResponse

def export_to_csv(modeladmin, request, queryset):
    opts = modeladmin.model._meta
    response = HttpResponse(content_type='text/csv')
    response['Content-Disposition'] = 'attachment; \
        filename={}.csv'.format(opts.verbose_name)
    writer = csv.writer(response)

    fields = [field for field in opts.get_fields() if not field.many_
to_many and not field.one_to_many]
    # Write a first row with header information
    writer.writerow([field.verbose_name for field in fields])
    # Write data rows
    for obj in queryset:
        data_row = []
        for field in fields:
            value = getattr(obj, field.name)
            if isinstance(value, datetime.datetime):
                value = value.strftime('%d/%m/%Y')
            data_row.append(value)
        writer.writerow(data_row)
    return response
export_to_csv.short_description = 'Export to CSV'
```

In this code, we perform the following tasks:

1. We create an instance of HttpResponse including a custom text/csv content type to tell the browser that the response has to be treated as a CSV file. We also add a Content-Disposition header to indicate that the HTTP response contains an attached file.

2. We create a CSV writer object that will write on the response object.

3. We get the model fields dynamically using the get_fields() method of the model _meta options. We exclude many-to-many and one-to-many relationships.

4. We write a header row including the field names.

5. We iterate over the given QuerySet and write a row for each object returned by the QuerySet. We take care of formatting `datetime` objects because the output value for CSV has to be a string.

6. We customize the display name for the action in the template by setting a `short_description` attribute to the function.

We have created a generic admin action that can be added to any `ModelAdmin` class.

Finally, add the new `export_to_csv` admin action to the `OrderAdmin` class as follows:

```
class OrderAdmin(admin.ModelAdmin):
    # ...
    actions = [export_to_csv]
```

Open `http://127.0.0.1:8000/admin/orders/order/` in your browser. The resulting admin action should look like this:

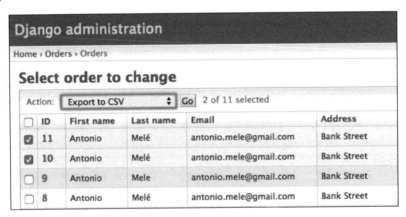

Select some orders and choose the **Export to CSV** action from the select box, then click the **Go** button. Your browser will download the generated CSV file named `order.csv`. Open the downloaded file using a text editor. You should see contents with the following format, including a header row and a row for each `Order` object you selected:

```
ID,first name,last name,email,address,postal
code,city,created,updated,paid
3,Antonio,Melé,antonio.mele@gmail.com,Bank Street 33,WS J11,London,25/
05/2015,25/05/2015,False

...
```

As you can see, creating admin actions is pretty straightforward.

# Extending the admin site with custom views

Sometimes you may want to customize the administration site beyond what is possible through configuration of `ModelAdmin`, creation of admin actions, and overriding admin templates. If this is the case, you need to create a custom admin view. With a custom view, you can build any functionality you need. You just have to make sure that only staff users can access your view and that you maintain the admin look and feel by making your template extend an admin template.

Let's create a custom view to display information about an order. Edit the `views.py` file of the `orders` application and add the following code to it:

```
from django.contrib.admin.views.decorators import staff_member_
required
from django.shortcuts import get_object_or_404
from .models import Order

@staff_member_required
def admin_order_detail(request, order_id):
    order = get_object_or_404(Order, id=order_id)
    return render(request,
                  'admin/orders/order/detail.html',
                  {'order': order})
```

The `staff_member_required` decorator checks that both `is_active` and `is_staff` fields of the user requesting the page are set to `True`. In this view, we get the `Order` object with the given id and render a template to display the order.

Now, edit the `urls.py` file of the `orders` application and add the following URL pattern to it:

```
url(r'^admin/order/(?P<order_id>\d+)/$',
    views.admin_order_detail,
    name='admin_order_detail'),
```

Create the following file structure inside the `templates/` directory of the `orders` application:

```
admin/
    orders/
        order/
            detail.html
```

Edit the `detail.html` template and add the following contents to it:

```
{% extends "admin/base_site.html" %}
{% load static %}

{% block extrastyle %}
  <link rel="stylesheet" type="text/css" href="{% static "css/admin.
css" %}" />
{% endblock %}

{% block title %}
  Order {{ order.id }} {{ block.super }}
{% endblock %}

{% block breadcrumbs %}
  <div class="breadcrumbs">
    <a href="{% url "admin:index" %}">Home</a> &rsaquo;
    <a href="{% url "admin:orders_order_changelist" %}">Orders</a>
    &rsaquo;
    <a href="{% url "admin:orders_order_change" order.id %}">Order {{
order.id }}</a>
    &rsaquo; Detail
  </div>
{% endblock %}

{% block content %}
<h1>Order {{ order.id }}</h1>
<ul class="object-tools">
  <li>
    <a href="#" onclick="window.print();">Print order</a>
  </li>
</ul>
<table>
  <tr>
    <th>Created</th>
    <td>{{ order.created }}</td>
  </tr>
  <tr>
    <th>Customer</th>
    <td>{{ order.first_name }} {{ order.last_name }}</td>
  </tr>
  <tr>
    <th>E-mail</th>
    <td><a href="mailto:{{ order.email }}">{{ order.email }}</a></td>
  </tr>
  <tr>
```

```
      <th>Address</th>
      <td>{{ order.address }}, {{ order.postal_code }} {{ order.city
}}</td>
    </tr>
    <tr>
      <th>Total amount</th>
      <td>${{ order.get_total_cost }}</td>
    </tr>
    <tr>
      <th>Status</th>
      <td>{% if order.paid %}Paid{% else %}Pending payment{% endif %}</
td>
    </tr>
</table>

<div class="module">
  <div class="tabular inline-related last-related">
    <table>
      <h2>Items bought</h2>
      <thead>
        <tr>
          <th>Product</th>
          <th>Price</th>
          <th>Quantity</th>
          <th>Total</th>
        </tr>
      </thead>
      <tbody>
        {% for item in order.items.all %}
          <tr class="row{% cycle "1" "2" %}">
            <td>{{ item.product.name }}</td>
            <td class="num">${{ item.price }}</td>
            <td class="num">{{ item.quantity }}</td>
            <td class="num">${{ item.get_cost }}</td>
          </tr>
        {% endfor %}
        <tr class="total">
          <td colspan="3">Total</td>
          <td class="num">${{ order.get_total_cost }}</td>
        </tr>
      </tbody>
    </table>
  </div>
</div>
{% endblock %}
```

This is the template to display an order detail in the administration site. This template extends the `admin/base_site.html` template of Django's administration site that contains the main HTML structure and CSS styles of the admin. We load the custom static file `css/admin.css`.

In order to use static files, you need to get them from the code that came with this chapter. Copy the static files located in the `static/` directory of `orders` `application` and add them to the same location in your project.

We use the blocks defined in the parent template to include our own content. We display information about the order and the items bought.

When you want to extend an admin template, you need to know its structure and identify existing blocks. You can find all admin templates at `https://github.com/django/django/tree/1.8.6/django/contrib/admin/templates/admin`.

You can also override an admin template if you need so. To override an admin template, copy it into your `templates` directory keeping the same relative path and filename. Django's administration site will use your custom template instead of the default one.

Finally, let's add a link to each `Order` object in the list display page of the administration site. Edit the `admin.py` file of the `orders` application and add the following code to it, above the `OrderAdmin` class:

```
from django.core.urlresolvers import import reverse

def order_detail(obj):
    return '<a href="{}">View</a>'.format(
        reverse('orders:admin_order_detail', args=[obj.id]))
order_detail.allow_tags = True
```

This is a function that takes an `Order` object as argument and returns an HTML link for the `admin_order_detail` URL. Django escapes HTML output by default. We have to set the `allow_tags` attribute of this callable to `True` to avoid auto-escaping.

 Set the `allow_tags` attribute to `True` to avoid HTML-escaping in any `Model` method, `ModelAdmin` method, or any other callable. When you use `allow_tags`, make sure to escape input that has come from the user to avoid cross-site scripting.

Then, edit the `OrderAdmin` class to display the link:

```
class OrderAdmin(admin.ModelAdmin):
    list_display = ['id',
                    'first_name',
                    # ...
                    'updated',
                    order_detail]
```

Open `http://127.0.0.1:8000/admin/orders/order/` in your browser. Each row now includes a **View** link as follows:

| City | Paid | Created | | Updated | Order detail |
|---|---|---|---|---|---|
| Madrid | ⊖ | May 19, 2015, 3:16 p.m. | ▽ | May 19, 2015, 3:16 p.m. | View |

Click the **View** link of any order to load the custom order detail page. You should see a page like the following one:

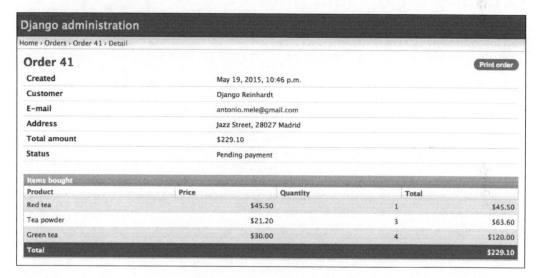

# Generating PDF invoices dynamically

Now that we have a complete checkout and payment system, we can generate a PDF invoice for each order. There are several Python libraries to generate PDF files. One popular library to generate PDFs with Python code is Reportlab. You can find information about how to output PDF files with Reportlab at `https://docs.djangoproject.com/en/1.8/howto/outputting-pdf/`.

In most cases, you will have to add custom styles and formatting to your PDF files. You will find it more convenient to render an HTML template and convert it into a PDF file, keeping Python away from the presentation layer. We are going to follow this approach and use a module to generate PDF files with Django. We will use WeasyPrint, which is a Python library that can generate PDF files from HTML templates.

# Installing WeasyPrint

First, install WeasyPrint's dependencies for your OS, which you will find at `http://weasyprint.org/docs/install/#platforms`.

Then, install WeasyPrint via `pip` using the following command:

```
pip install WeasyPrint==0.24
```

# Creating a PDF template

We need an HTML document as input for WeasyPrint. We are going to create an HTML template, render it using Django, and pass it to WeasyPrint to generate the PDF file.

Create a new template file inside the `templates/orders/order/` directory of the `orders` application and name it `pdf.html`. Add the following code to it:

```html
<html>
<body>
  <h1>My Shop</h1>
  <p>
    Invoice no. {{ order.id }}</br>
    <span class="secondary">
      {{ order.created|date:"M d, Y" }}
    </span>
  </p>

  <h3>Bill to</h3>
  <p>
    {{ order.first_name }} {{ order.last_name }}<br>
    {{ order.email }}<br>
    {{ order.address }}<br>
    {{ order.postal_code }}, {{ order.city }}
  </p>
```

```
<h3>Items bought</h3>
<table>
  <thead>
    <tr>
      <th>Product</th>
      <th>Price</th>
      <th>Quantity</th>
      <th>Cost</th>
    </tr>
  </thead>
  <tbody>
    {% for item in order.items.all %}
      <tr class="row{% cycle "1" "2" %}">
        <td>{{ item.product.name }}</td>
        <td class="num">${{ item.price }}</td>
        <td class="num">{{ item.quantity }}</td>
        <td class="num">${{ item.get_cost }}</td>
      </tr>
    {% endfor %}
    <tr class="total">
      <td colspan="3">Total</td>
      <td class="num">${{ order.get_total_cost }}</td>
    </tr>
  </tbody>
</table>

<span class="{% if order.paid %}paid{% else %}pending{% endif %}">
  {% if order.paid %}Paid{% else %}Pending payment{% endif %}
</span>
</body>
</html>
```

This is the template for the PDF invoice. In this template, we display all order details and an HTML `<table>` element including the products. We also include a message to display if the order has been paid or the payment is still pending.

# Rendering PDF files

We are going to create a view to generate PDF invoices for existing orders using the administration site. Edit the `views.py` file inside the `orders` application directory and add the following code to it:

```python
from django.conf import settings
from django.http import HttpResponse
from django.template.loader import render_to_string
import weasyprint

@staff_member_required
def admin_order_pdf(request, order_id):
    order = get_object_or_404(Order, id=order_id)
    html = render_to_string('orders/order/pdf.html',
                            {'order': order})
    response = HttpResponse(content_type='application/pdf')
    response['Content-Disposition'] = 'filename=\
        "order_{}.pdf"'.format(order.id)
    weasyprint.HTML(string=html).write_pdf(response,
        stylesheets=[weasyprint.CSS(
            settings.STATIC_ROOT + 'css/pdf.css')])
    return response
```

This is the view to generate a PDF invoice for an order. We use the `staff_member_required` decorator to make sure only staff users can access this view. We get the `Order` object with the given ID and we use the `render_to_string()` function provided by Django to render `orders/order/pdf.html`. The rendered HTML is saved in the `html` variable. Then, we generate a new `HttpResponse` object specifying the `application/pdf` content type and including the `Content-Disposition` header to specify the file name. We use WeasyPrint to generate a PDF file from the rendered HTML code and write the file to the `HttpResponse` object. We use the static file `css/pdf.css` to add CSS styles to the generated PDF file. We load it from the local path by using the `STATIC_ROOT` setting. Finally, we return the generated response.

Since we need to use the `STATIC_ROOT` setting, we have to add it to our project. This is the project's path for static files to reside. Edit the `settings.py` file of the `myshop` project and add the following setting:

```python
STATIC_ROOT = os.path.join(BASE_DIR, 'static/')
```

Then, run the command `python manage.py collectstatic`. You should see an output that ends as follows:

```
You have requested to collect static files at the destination
location as specified in your settings:

    code/myshop/static

This will overwrite existing files!
Are you sure you want to do this?
```

Write yes and press *Enter*. You should get a message indicating that the static files have been copied to the STATIC_ROOT directory.

The collectstatic command copies all static files from your applications into the directory defined in the STATIC_ROOT setting. This allows each application to provide its own static files using a static/ directory that contains them. You can also provide additional static files sources in the STATICFILES_DIRS setting. All of the directories specified in the STATICFILES_DIRS list will also be copied to the STATIC_ROOT directory when collectstatic is executed.

Edit the urls.py file inside the orders application directory and add the following URL pattern to it:

```
url(r'^admin/order/(?P<order_id>\d+)/pdf/$',
    views.admin_order_pdf,
    name='admin_order_pdf'),
```

Now, we can edit the admin list display page for the Order model to add a link to the PDF file for each result. Edit the admin.py file inside the orders application and add the following code above the OrderAdmin class:

```
def order_pdf(obj):
    return '<a href="{}">PDF</a>'.format(
        reverse('orders:admin_order_pdf', args=[obj.id]))
order_pdf.allow_tags = True
order_pdf.short_description = 'PDF bill'
```

Add order_pdf to the list_display attribute of the OrderAdmin class as follows:

```
class OrderAdmin(admin.ModelAdmin):
    list_display = ['id',
                    # ...
                    order_detail,
                    order_pdf]
```

If you specify a `short_description` attribute for your callable, Django will use it for the name of the column.

Open `http://127.0.0.1:8000/admin/orders/order/` in your browser. Each row should now include a PDF link like this:

| City | Paid | Created | | Updated | Order detail | PDF bill |
|------|------|---------|---|---------|--------------|----------|
| Madrid | ⊖ | May 19, 2015, 10:46 p.m. | ▽ | May 19, 2015, 10:46 p.m. | View | PDF |

Click the **PDF** link for any order. You should see a generated PDF file like the following one for orders that have not been paid yet:

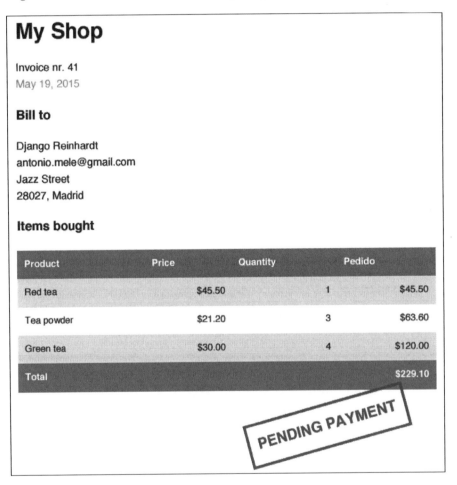

# My Shop

Invoice nr. 41

May 19, 2015

## Bill to

Django Reinhardt
antonio.mele@gmail.com
Jazz Street
28027, Madrid

## Items bought

| Product | Price | Quantity | Pedido |
|---------|-------|----------|--------|
| Red tea | $45.50 | 1 | $45.50 |
| Tea powder | $21.20 | 3 | $63.60 |
| Green tea | $30.00 | 4 | $120.00 |
| Total | | | $229.10 |

PENDING PAYMENT

For paid orders, you will see the following PDF file:

| Items bought | | | |
|---|---|---|---|
| Product | Price | Quantity | Pedido |
| Red tea | $45.50 | 1 | $45.50 |
| Tea powder | $21.20 | 3 | $63.60 |
| Green tea | $30.00 | 4 | $120.00 |
| Total | | | $229.10 |

PAID

# Sending PDF files by e-mail

Let's send an e-mail to our customers including the generated PDF invoice when a payment is received. Edit the `signals.py` file of the `payment` application and add the following imports:

```
from django.template.loader import render_to_string
from django.core.mail import EmailMessage
from django.conf import settings
import weasyprint
from io import BytesIO
```

Then add the following code after the `order.save()` line, with the same indentation level:

```
# create invoice e-mail
subject = 'My Shop - Invoice no. {}'.format(order.id)
message = 'Please, find attached the invoice for your recent
purchase.'
email = EmailMessage(subject,
                     message,
                     'admin@myshop.com',
                     [order.email])

# generate PDF
html = render_to_string('orders/order/pdf.html', {'order': order})
out = BytesIO()
```

```
stylesheets=[weasyprint.CSS(settings.STATIC_ROOT + 'css/pdf.css')]
weasyprint.HTML(string=html).write_pdf(out,
                                       stylesheets=stylesheets)
# attach PDF file
email.attach('order_{}.pdf'.format(order.id),
             out.getvalue(),
             'application/pdf')
# send e-mail
email.send()
```

In this signal, we use the `EmailMessage` class provided by Django to create an e-mail object. Then we render the template into the `html` variable. We generate the PDF file from the rendered template, and we output it to a `BytesIO` instance, which is a in-memory bytes buffer. Then we attach the generated PDF file to the `EmailMessage` object using its `attach()` method, including the contents of the `out` buffer.

Remember to set up your SMTP settings in the `settings.py` file of the project to send e-mails. You can refer to *Chapter 2, Enhancing Your Blog with Advanced Features* to see a working example for an SMTP configuration.

Now you can open the URL for your application provided by Ngrok and complete a new payment process in order to receive the PDF invoice into your e-mail.

# Summary

In this chapter, you integrated a payment gateway into your project. You customized the Django administration site and learned how to generate CSV and PDF files dynamically.

The next chapter will give you an insight into internationalization and localization for Django projects. You will also create a coupon system and build a product recommendation engine.

# 9
# Extending Your Shop

In the previous chapter, you learned how to integrate a payment gateway into your shop. You managed payment notifications and you learned how to generate CSV and PDF files. In this chapter, you will add a coupon system to your shop. You will learn how internationalization and localization work, and you will build a recommendation engine.

This chapter will cover the following points:

- Creating a coupon system to apply discounts
- Adding internationalization to your project
- Using Rosetta to manage translations
- Translating models using django-parler
- Building a product recommendation engine

## Creating a coupon system

Many online shops give out coupons to customers that can be redeemed for discounts on their purchases. An online coupon usually consists of a code that is given to users, which is valid for a specific time frame. The code can be redeemed one or multiple times.

We are going to create a coupon system for our shop. Our coupons will be valid for clients that enter the coupon in a specific time frame. The coupons will not have any limitation on the number of times they can be redeemed, and they will be applied to the total amount of the shopping cart. For this functionality, we will need to create a model to store the coupon code, a valid time frame, and the discount to apply.

Create a new application inside the myshop project using the following command:

```
python manage.py startapp coupons
```

Edit the settings.py file of myshop and add the application to the INSTALLED_APPS setting as follows:

```
INSTALLED_APPS = (
    # ...
    'coupons',
)
```

The new application is now active in our Django project.

# Building the coupon models

Let's start by creating the Coupon model. Edit the models.py file of the coupons application and add the following code to it:

```
from django.db import models
from django.core.validators import MinValueValidator, \
                                   MaxValueValidator


class Coupon(models.Model):
    code = models.CharField(max_length=50,
                              unique=True)
    valid_from = models.DateTimeField()
    valid_to = models.DateTimeField()
    discount = models.IntegerField(
                 validators=[MinValueValidator(0),
                             MaxValueValidator(100)])
    active = models.BooleanField()

    def __str__(self):
        return self.code
```

This is the model we are going to use to store coupons. The Coupon model contains the following fields:

- code: The code that users have to enter in order to apply the coupon to their purchase.

- valid_from: The datetime value that indicates when the coupon becomes valid.

- `valid_to`: The datetime value that indicates when the coupon becomes invalid.

- `discount`: The discount rate to apply (this is a percentage, so it takes values from 0 to 100). We use validators for this field to limit the minimum and maximum accepted values.

- `active`: A boolean that indicates whether the coupon is active.

Run the following command to generate the initial migration for the coupons application:

**python manage.py makemigrations**

The output should include the following lines:

```
Migrations for 'coupons':
  0001_initial.py:
    - Create model Coupon
```

Then we execute the next command to apply migrations:

**python manage.py migrate**

You should see an output that includes the following line:

```
Applying coupons.0001_initial... OK
```

The migrations are now applied in the database. Let's add the Coupon model to the administration site. Edit the admin.py file of the coupons application and add the following code to it:

```
from django.contrib import admin
from .models import Coupon

class CouponAdmin(admin.ModelAdmin):
    list_display = ['code', 'valid_from', 'valid_to',
                    'discount', 'active']
    list_filter = ['active', 'valid_from', 'valid_to']
    search_fields = ['code']
admin.site.register(Coupon, CouponAdmin)
```

The Coupon model is now registered in the administration site. Ensure your local server is running with the command python manage.py runserver. Open http://127.0.0.1:8000/admin/coupons/coupon/add/ in your browser. You should see the following form:

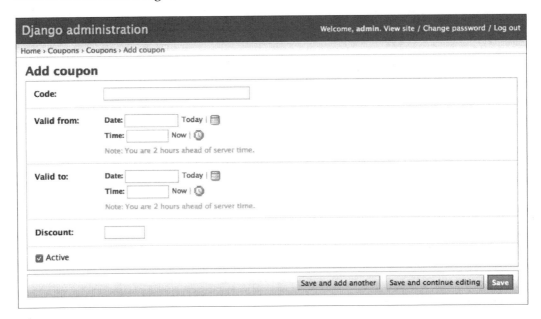

Fill in the form to create a new coupon that is valid for the current date, make sure you check the **Active** checkbox, and click the **Save** button.

# Applying a coupon to the shopping cart

We can store new coupons and make queries to retrieve existing coupons. Now we need a way for customers to apply coupons to their purchases. Take a moment to think about how this functionality would work. The way to apply a coupon would be as follows:

1. The user adds products to the shopping cart.

2. The user can enter a coupon code in a form displayed in the shopping cart detail page.

3. When a user enters a coupon code and submits the form, we look for an existing coupon with the given code that is currently valid. We have to check that the coupon's code matches the one entered by the user, the active attribute is True, and the current datetime is between the valid_from and valid_to values.

4.  If a coupon is found, we save it in the user's session and display the cart including the discount applied to it and the updated total amount.

5.  When the user places an order, we save the coupon to the given order.

Create a new file inside the `coupons` application directory and name it `forms.py`. Add the following code to it:

```
from django import forms

class CouponApplyForm(forms.Form):
    code = forms.CharField()
```

This is the form we are going to use for the user to enter a coupon code. Edit the `views.py` file inside the `coupons` application and add the following code to it:

```
from django.shortcuts import render, redirect
from django.utils import timezone
from django.views.decorators.http import require_POST
from .models import Coupon
from .forms import CouponApplyForm


@require_POST
def coupon_apply(request):
    now = timezone.now()
    form = CouponApplyForm(request.POST)
    if form.is_valid():
        code = form.cleaned_data['code']
        try:
            coupon = Coupon.objects.get(code__iexact=code,
                                        valid_from__lte=now,
                                        valid_to__gte=now,
                                        active=True)
            request.session['coupon_id'] = coupon.id
        except Coupon.DoesNotExist:
            request.session['coupon_id'] = None
    return redirect('cart:cart_detail')
```

The `coupon_apply` view validates the coupon and stores it in the user's session. We apply the `require_POST` decorator to this view to restrict it to POST requests. In the view, we perform the following tasks:

1.  We instantiate the `CouponApplyForm` form using the posted data and we check that the form is valid.

2. If the form is valid, we get the `code` entered by the user from the form's `cleaned_data` dictionary. We try to retrieve the `Coupon` object with the given code. We use the `iexact` field lookup to perform a case-insensitive exact match. The coupon has to be currently active (`active=True`) and valid for the current datetime. We use Django's `timezone.now()` function to get the current time-zone-aware datetime and we compare it with the `valid_from` and `valid_to` fields performing `lte` (less than or equal to) and `gte` (greater than or equal to) field lookups respectively.

3. We store the coupon `id` in the user's session.

4. We redirect the user to the `cart_detail` URL to display the cart with the coupon applied.

We need a URL pattern for the `coupon_apply` view. Create a new file inside the coupons application directory and name it `urls.py`. Add the following code to it:

```
from django.conf.urls import url
from . import views

urlpatterns = [
    url(r'^apply/$', views.coupon_apply, name='apply'),
]
```

Then, edit the main `urls.py` of the myshop project and include the coupons URL patterns as follows:

```
url(r'^coupons/', include('coupons.urls', namespace='coupons')),
```

Remember to place this pattern before the `shop.urls` pattern.

Now edit the `cart.py` file of the `cart` application. Include the following import:

```
from coupons.models import Coupon
```

Add the following code to the end of the `__init__()` method of the `Cart` class to initialize the coupon from the current session:

```
# store current applied coupon
self.coupon_id = self.session.get('coupon_id')
```

In this code, we try to get the `coupon_id` session key from the current session and store its value in the `Cart` object. Add the following methods to the `Cart` object:

```
@property
def coupon(self):
    if self.coupon_id:
```

```
            return Coupon.objects.get(id=self.coupon_id)
        return None

    def get_discount(self):
        if self.coupon:
            return (self.coupon.discount / Decimal('100')) \
                * self.get_total_price()
        return Decimal('0')

    def get_total_price_after_discount(self):
        return self.get_total_price() - self.get_discount()
```

These methods are as follows:

- coupon(): We define this method as a `property`. If the cart contains a coupon_id function, the `Coupon` object with the given `id` is returned.

- get_discount(): If the cart contains a `coupon`, we retrieve its discount rate and return the amount to be deducted from the total amount of the cart.

- get_total_price_after_discount(): We return the total amount of the cart after deducting the amount returned by the get_discount() method.

The `Cart` class is now prepared to handle a coupon applied to the current session and apply the corresponding discount.

Let's include the coupon system in the cart detail view. Edit the `views.py` file of the `cart` application and add the following import at the top of the file:

```
from coupons.forms import CouponApplyForm
```

Further down, edit the `cart_detail` view and add the new form to it as follows:

```
def cart_detail(request):
    cart = Cart(request)
    for item in cart:
        item['update_quantity_form'] = CartAddProductForm(
                            initial={'quantity': item['quantity'],
                            'update': True})
    coupon_apply_form = CouponApplyForm()

    return render(request,
                    'cart/detail.html',
                    {'cart': cart,
                    'coupon_apply_form': coupon_apply_form})
```

Edit the `cart/detail.html` template of the `cart` application and find the following lines:

```
<tr class="total">
  <td>Total</td>
  <td colspan="4"></td>
  <td class="num">${{ cart.get_total_price }}</td>
</tr>
```

Replace them with the following ones:

```
{% if cart.coupon %}
  <tr class="subtotal">
    <td>Subtotal</td>
    <td colspan="4"></td>
    <td class="num">${{ cart.get_total_price }}</td>
  </tr>
  <tr>
    <td>
      "{{ cart.coupon.code }}" coupon
      ({{ cart.coupon.discount }}% off)
    </td>
    <td colspan="4"></td>
    <td class="num neg">
      - ${{ cart.get_discount|floatformat:"2" }}
    </td>
  </tr>
{% endif %}
<tr class="total">
  <td>Total</td>
  <td colspan="4"></td>
  <td class="num">
    ${{ cart.get_total_price_after_discount|floatformat:"2" }}
  </td>
</tr>
```

This is the code to display an optional coupon and its discount rate. If the cart contains a coupon, we display a first row including the total amount of the cart as the **Subtotal**. Then we use a second row to display the current coupon applied to the cart. Finally, we display the total price including any discount by calling the `get_total_price_after_discount()` method of the `cart` object.

In the same file, include the following code after the `</table>` HTML tag:

```
<p>Apply a coupon:</p>
<form action="{% url "coupons:apply" %}" method="post">
  {{ coupon_apply_form }}
  <input type="submit" value="Apply">
  {% csrf_token %}
</form>
```

This will display the form to enter a coupon code and apply it to the current cart.

Open `http://127.0.0.1:8000/` in your browser, add a product to the cart, and apply the coupon you created by entering its code in the form. You should see that the cart displays the coupon discount as follows:

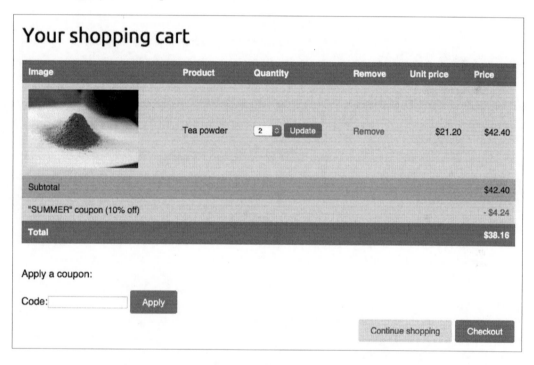

Let's add the coupon to the next step of the purchase process. Edit the `orders/order/create.html` template of the orders application and find the following lines:

```
<ul>
  {% for item in cart %}
    <li>
      {{ item.quantity }}x {{ item.product.name }}
      <span>${{ item.total_price }}</span>
```

```
        </li>
    {% endfor %}
</ul>
```

Replace them with the following code:

```
<ul>
    {% for item in cart %}
        <li>
            {{ item.quantity }}x {{ item.product.name }}
            <span>${{ item.total_price }}</span>
        </li>
    {% endfor %}
    {% if cart.coupon %}
        <li>
            "{{ cart.coupon.code }}" ({{ cart.coupon.discount }}% off)
            <span>- ${{ cart.get_discount|floatformat:"2" }}</span>
        </li>
    {% endif %}
</ul>
```

The order summary should now include the applied coupon, if there is any. Now find the following line:

```
<p>Total: ${{ cart.get_total_price }}</p>
```

Replace it with the following one:

```
<p>Total: ${{ cart.get_total_price_after_discount|floatformat:"2" }}</p>
```

By doing so, the total price will be also calculated by applying the discount of the coupon.

Open http://127.0.0.1:8000/orders/create/ in your browser. You should see that the order summary includes the applied coupon as follows:

Your order

- 1x Tea powder $21.20
- 1x Red tea $45.50
- SUMMER" (10% off) - $6.67

Total: $60.03

Users can now apply coupons to their shopping cart. However, we still need to store coupon information in the order that is created when users check out the cart.

# Applying coupons to orders

We are going to store the coupon that was applied for each order. First, we need to modify the Order model to store the related Coupon object, if there is any.

Edit the models.py file of the orders application and add the following imports to it:

```
from decimal import Decimal
from django.core.validators import MinValueValidator, \
                                   MaxValueValidator
from coupons.models import Coupon
```

Then, add the following fields to the Order model:

```
coupon = models.ForeignKey(Coupon,
                           related_name='orders',
                           null=True,
                           blank=True)
discount = models.IntegerField(default=0,
                               validators=[MinValueValidator(0),
                                           MaxValueValidator(100)])
```

These fields will allow us to store an optional coupon applied to the order and the discount applied by the coupon. The discount is stored in the related Coupon object, but we include it in the Order model to preserve it if the coupon is modified or deleted.

Since the Order model has changed, we need to create a migration. Run the following command from the command line:

**python manage.py makemigrations**

You should see an output like this:

```
Migrations for 'orders':
  0002_auto_20150606_1735.py:
    - Add field coupon to order
    - Add field discount to order
```

Apply the new migration with the next command:

**python manage.py migrate orders**

You should get the confirmation that the new migration has been applied. The `Order` model field changes are now synced with the database.

Go back to the `models.py` file and change the `get_total_cost()` method of the `Order` model as follows:

```
def get_total_cost(self):
    total_cost = sum(item.get_cost() for item in self.items.all())
    return total_cost - total_cost * \
        (self.discount / Decimal('100'))
```

The `get_total_cost()` method of the `Order` model will now take into account the applied discount, if there is any.

Edit the `views.py` file of the `orders` application and modify the `order_create` view to save the related coupon and its discount when creating a new order. Find the following line:

```
order = form.save()
```

Replace it with the following ones:

```
order = form.save(commit=False)
if cart.coupon:
    order.coupon = cart.coupon
    order.discount = cart.coupon.discount
order.save()
```

In the new code, we create an `Order` object using the `save()` method of the `OrderCreateForm` form. We avoid saving it to the database yet by using `commit=False`. If the cart contains a coupon, we store the related coupon and the discount that was applied. Then we save the `order` object to the database.

Make sure the development server is running with the command `python manage.py runserver`. Run Ngrok from the shell using the following command:

```
./ngrok http 8000
```

Open the URL provided by Ngrok in your browser and complete a purchase using the coupon you created. When you finish a successful purchase, you can go to `http://127.0.0.1:8000/admin/orders/order/` and check that the order object contains the coupon and the applied discount as follows:

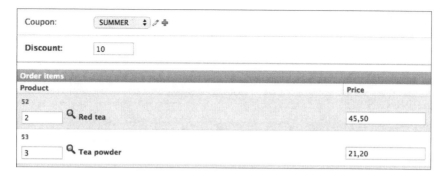

You can also modify the admin order detail template and the order PDF bill to display the applied coupon in the same manner we did for the cart.

Next, we are going to add internationalization to our project.

# Adding internationalization and localization

Django offers full internationalization and localization support. It allows you to translate your application into multiple languages and it handles locale-specific formatting for dates, times, numbers, and time zones. Let's clarify the difference between internationalization and localization. **Internationalization** (frequently abbreviated to **i18n**) is the process of adapting software for the potential use of different languages and locales, so that it isn't hard-wired to a specific language or locale. **Localization** (abbreviated to **l10n**) is the process of actually translating the software and adapting it to a particular locale. Django itself is translated into more than 50 languages using its internationalization framework.

## Internationalization with Django

The internationalization framework allows you to easily mark strings for translation both in Python code and in your templates. It relies on the GNU gettext toolset to generate and manage message files. A **message file** is a plain text file that represents a language. It contains a part, or all, translation strings found in your application and their respective translations for a single language. Message files have the `.po` extension.

Once the translation is done, message files are compiled to offer rapid access to translated strings. The compiled translation files have the `.mo` extension.

# Internationalization and localization settings

Django provides several settings for internationalization. The following settings are the most relevant ones:

- USE_I18N: A boolean that specifies whether Django's translation system is enabled. This is True by default.

- USE_L10N: A boolean indicating whether localized formatting is enabled. When active, localized formats are used to represent dates and numbers. This is False by default.

- USE_TZ: A boolean that specifies whether datetimes are timezone-aware. When you create a project with the startproject command, this is set to True.

- LANGUAGE_CODE: The default language code for the project. This is in standard language ID format, for example, 'en-us' for American English or 'en-gb' for British English. This setting requires USE_I18N set to True in order to take effect. You can find a list of valid language IDs at http:// www.i18nguy.com/unicode/language-identifiers.html.

- LANGUAGES: A tuple that contains available languages for the project. They come in two-tuples of **language code** and **language name**. You can see the list of available languages at django.conf.global_settings. When you choose which languages your site will be available in, you set LANGUAGES to a subset of that list.

- LOCALE_PATHS: A list of directories where Django looks for message files containing translations for this project.

- TIME_ZONE: A string that represents the time zone for the project. This is set to 'UTC' when you create a new project using the startproject command. You can set it to any other time zone such as 'Europe/Madrid'.

These are some of the internationalization and localization settings available. You can find the full list at https://docs.djangoproject.com/en/1.8/ref/ settings/#globalization-i18n-l10n.

# Internationalization management commands

Django includes the following commands to manage translations using manage.py or the django-admin utility:

- makemessages – This runs over the source tree to find all strings marked for translation and creates or updates the .po message files in the locale directory. A single .po file is created for each language.

- compilemessages – This compiles the existing .po message files to .mo files that are used to retrieve translations.

You will need the gettext toolset to be able to create, update, and compile message files. Most Linux distributions include the gettext toolkit. If you are using Mac OS X, probably the simplest way to install it is via Homebrew at http://brew. sh/ with the command brew install gettext. You might also need to force link it with the command brew link gettext --force. For Windows, follow the steps at https://docs.djangoproject.com/en/1.8/topics/i18n/ translation/#gettext-on-windows.

# How to add translations to a Django project

Let's take a look at the process to internationalize our project. We will need to do the following:

1. We mark strings for translation in our Python code and our templates.

2. We run the makemessages command to create or update message files that include all translations strings from our code.

3. We translate the strings contained in the message files and compile them using the compilemessages management command.

# How Django determines the current language

Django comes with a middleware that determines the current language based on request data. This is the LocaleMiddleware middleware that resides in django. middleware.locale. LocaleMiddleware performs the following tasks:

1. If you are using i18_patterns, that is, you use translated URL patterns, it looks for a language prefix in the requested URL to determine the current language.

2. If no language prefix is found, it looks for an existing LANGUAGE_SESSION_ KEY in the current user's session.

3. If the language is not set in the session, it looks for an existing cookie with the current language. A custom name for this cookie can be provided in the LANGUAGE_COOKIE_NAME setting. By default, the name for this cookie is django_language.

4. If no cookie is found, it looks for the Accept-Language HTTP header of the request.

5. If the Accept-Language header does not specify a language, Django uses the language defined in the LANGUAGE_CODE setting.

By default, Django will use the language defined in the LANGUAGE_CODE setting unless you are using LocaleMiddleware. The process described above only applies when using this middleware.

# Preparing our project for internationalization

Let's prepare our project to use different languages. We are going to create an English and a Spanish version for our shop. Edit the settings.py file of your project and add the following LANGUAGES setting to it. Place it next to the LANGUAGE_CODE setting:

```
LANGUAGES = (
    ('en', 'English'),
    ('es', 'Spanish'),
)
```

The LANGUAGES setting contains two tuples that consist of language code and name. Language codes can be locale-specific, such as en-us or en-gb, or generic, such as en. With this setting, we specify that our application will be only available in English and Spanish. If we don't define a custom LANGUAGES setting, the site will be available in all the languages Django is translated into.

Make your LANGUAGE_CODE setting look as follows:

```
LANGUAGE_CODE = 'en'
```

Add 'django.middleware.locale.LocaleMiddleware' to the MIDDLEWARE_CLASSES setting. Make sure that this middleware comes after SessionMiddleware, because LocaleMiddleware needs to use session data. It also has to be placed before CommonMiddleware, because the latter needs an active language to resolve the requested URL. The MIDDLEWARE_CLASSES setting should now look as follows:

```
MIDDLEWARE_CLASSES = (
    'django.contrib.sessions.middleware.SessionMiddleware',
    'django.middleware.locale.LocaleMiddleware',
    'django.middleware.common.CommonMiddleware',
    # ...
)
```

The order of middlewares is very important because each middleware can depend on data set by other middleware executed previously. Middleware is applied for requests in order of appearance in MIDDLEWARE_CLASSES, and in reverse order for responses.

Create the following directory structure inside the main project directory, next to the `manage.py` file:

```
locale/
    en/
    es/
```

The `locale` directory is the place where message files for your application will reside. Edit the `settings.py` file again and add the following setting to it:

```
LOCALE_PATHS = (
    os.path.join(BASE_DIR, 'locale/'),
)
```

The `LOCALE_PATHS` setting specifies the directories where Django has to look for translation files. Locale paths that appear first have the highest precedence.

When you use the `makemessages` command from your project directory, message files will be generated in the `locale/` path we created. However, for applications that contain a `locale/` directory, message files will be generated in that directory.

# Translating Python code

To translate literals in your Python code, you can mark strings for translation using the `gettext()` function included in `django.utils.translation`. This function translates the message and returns a string. The convention is to import this function as a shorter alias named _ (underscore character).

You can find all the documentation about translations at `https://docs.djangoproject.com/en/1.8/topics/i18n/translation/`.

## Standard translations

The following code shows how to mark a string for translation:

```
from django.utils.translation import gettext as _
output = _('Text to be translated.')
```

## Lazy translations

Django includes **lazy** versions for all of its translation functions, which have the suffix `_lazy()`. When using the lazy functions, strings are translated when the value is accessed rather than when the function is called (this is why they are translated **lazily**). The lazy translation functions come in handy when strings marked for translation are in paths that are executed when modules are loaded.

Using `gettext_lazy()` instead of `gettext()`, strings are translated when the value is accessed rather than when the function is called. Django offers a **lazy** version for all translation functions.

# Translations including variables

The strings marked for translation can include placeholders to include variables in the translations. The following code is an example of a translation string with a placeholder:

```
from django.utils.translation import gettext as _
month = _('April')
day = '14'
output = _('Today is %(month)s %(day)s') % {'month': month,
                                            'day': day}
```

By using placeholders, you can reorder the text variables. For example, an English translation for the previous example might be "*Today is April 14*", while the Spanish one is "*Hoy es 14 de Abril*". Always use string interpolation instead of positional interpolation when you have more than one parameter for the translation string. By doing so, you will be able to reorder the placeholder text.

# Plural forms in translations

For plural forms, you can use `ngettext()` and `ngettext_lazy()`. These functions translate singular and plural forms depending on an argument that indicates the number of objects. The following example shows how to use them:

```
output = ngettext('there is %(count)d product',
                  'there are %(count)d products',
                  count) % {'count': count}
```

Now that you know the basics about translating literals in our Python code, it's time to apply translations to our project.

# Translating your own code

Edit the `settings.py` file of your project, import the `gettext_lazy()` function, and change the LANGUAGES setting as follows to translate the language names:

```
from django.utils.translation import gettext_lazy as _

LANGUAGES = (
```

```
        ('en', _('English')),
        ('es', _('Spanish')),
    )
```

Here, we use the `gettext_lazy()` function instead of `gettext()` to avoid a circular import, thus translating the languages' names when they are accessed.

Open the shell and run the following command from your project directory:

**django-admin makemessages --all**

You should see the following output:

```
    processing locale es
    processing locale en
```

Take a look at the `locale/` directory. You should see a file structure like this:

```
    en/
        LC_MESSAGES/
            django.po
    es/
        LC_MESSAGES/
            django.po
```

A `.po` message file has been created for each language. Open `es/LC_MESSAGES/django.po` with a text editor. At the end of the file, you should be able to see the following:

```
    #: settings.py:104
    msgid "English"
    msgstr ""

    #: settings.py:105
    msgid "Spanish"
    msgstr ""
```

Each translation string is preceded by a comment showing details about the file and line where it was found. Each translation includes two strings:

- `msgid`: The translation string as it appears in the source code.
- `msgstr`: The language translation, which is empty by default. This is where you have to enter the actual translation for the given string.

Fill in the `msgstr` translations for the given `msgid` string as follows:

```
#: settings.py:104
msgid "English"
msgstr "Inglés"

#: settings.py:105
msgid "Spanish"
msgstr "Español"
```

Save the modified message file, open the shell, and run the following command:

**django-admin compilemessages**

If everything goes well, you should see an output like the following:

```
processing file django.po in myshop/locale/en/LC_MESSAGES
processing file django.po in myshop/locale/es/LC_MESSAGES
```

The output gives you information about the message files that are being compiled. Take a look at the `locale` directory of the `myshop` project again. You should see the following files:

```
en/
    LC_MESSAGES/
        django.mo
        django.po
es/
    LC_MESSAGES/
        django.mo
        django.po
```

You can see that a `.mo` compiled message file has been generated for each language.

We have translated the language names themselves. Now let's translate the model field names that are displayed in the site. Edit the `models.py` file of the `orders` application and add names marked for translation for the `Order` model fields as follows:

```
from django.utils.translation import gettext_lazy as _

class Order(models.Model):
    first_name = models.CharField(_('first name'),
                                  max_length=50)
    last_name = models.CharField(_('last name'),
                                 max_length=50)
    email = models.EmailField(_('e-mail'),)
```

```
address = models.CharField(_('address'),
                            max_length=250)
postal_code = models.CharField(_('postal code'),
                                max_length=20)
city = models.CharField(_('city'),
                          max_length=100)
#...
```

We have added names for the fields that are displayed when a user is placing a new order. These are `first_name`, `last_name`, `email`, `address`, `postal_code`, and `city`. Remember that you can also use the `verbose_name` attribute to name the fields.

Create the following directory structure inside the `orders` application directory:

```
locale/
    en/
    es/
```

By creating a `locale` directory, translation strings of this application will be stored in a message file under this directory instead of the main messages file. In this way, you can generate separated translation files for each application.

Open the shell from the project directory and run the following command:

**`django-admin makemessages --all`**

You should see the following output:

```
processing locale es
processing locale en
```

Open the `es/LC_MESSAGES/django.po` file using a text editor. You will see the translations strings for the `Order` model. Fill in the following `msgstr` translations for the given `msgid` strings:

```
#: orders/models.py:10
msgid "first name"
msgstr "nombre"

#: orders/models.py:12
msgid "last name"
msgstr "apellidos"

#: orders/models.py:14
msgid "e-mail"
msgstr "e-mail"
```

```
#: orders/models.py:15
msgid "address"
msgstr "dirección"

#: orders/models.py:17
msgid "postal code"
msgstr "código postal"

#: orders/models.py:19
msgid "city"
msgstr "ciudad"
```

After you have finished adding the translations, save the file.

Besides a text editor, you can use Poedit to edit translations. Poedit is a software to edit translations, and it uses gettext. It is available for Linux, Windows, and Mac OS X. You can download Poedit from http://poedit.net/.

Let's also translate the forms of our project. OrderCreateForm of the orders application does not have to be translated, since it is a ModelForm and it uses the verbose_name attribute of the Order model fields for the form field labels. We are going to translate the forms of the cart and coupons applications.

Edit the forms.py file inside the cart application directory and add a label attribute to the quantity field of the CartAddProductForm, then mark this field for translation as follows:

```
from django import forms
from django.utils.translation import gettext_lazy as _

PRODUCT_QUANTITY_CHOICES = [(i, str(i)) for i in range(1, 21)]

class CartAddProductForm(forms.Form):
    quantity = forms.TypedChoiceField(
                                choices=PRODUCT_QUANTITY_CHOICES,
                                coerce=int,
                                label=_('Quantity'))
    update = forms.BooleanField(required=False,
                                initial=False,
                                widget=forms.HiddenInput)
```

Edit the `forms.py` file of the `coupons` application and translate the `CouponApplyForm` form as follows:

```python
from django import forms
from django.utils.translation import gettext_lazy as _

class CouponApplyForm(forms.Form):
    code = forms.CharField(label=_('Coupon'))
```

We have added a label to the `code` field and marked it for translation.

# Translating templates

Django offers the `{% trans %}` and `{% blocktrans %}` template tags to translate strings in templates. In order to use the translation template tags, you have to add `{% load i18n %}` at the top of your template to load them.

## The {% trans %} template tag

The `{% trans %}` template tag allows you to mark a string, a constant, or variable content for translation. Internally, Django executes `gettext()` on the given text. This is how to mark a string for translation in a template:

```
{% trans "Text to be translated" %}
```

You can use `as` to store the translated content in a variable that you can use throughout your template. The following example stores the translated text in a variable called `greeting`:

```
{% trans "Hello!" as greeting %}
<h1>{{ greeting }}</h1>
```

The `{% trans %}` tag is useful for simple translation strings, but it cannot handle content for translation that includes variables.

## The {% blocktrans %} template tag

The `{% blocktrans %}` template tag allows you to mark content that includes literals and variable content using placeholders. The following example shows you how to use the `{% blocktrans %}` tag including a `name` variable in the content for translation:

```
{% blocktrans %}Hello {{ name }}!{% endblocktrans %}
```

You can use `with` to include template expressions such as accessing object attributes or applying template filters to variables. You always have to use placeholders for these. You cannot access expressions or object attributes inside the `blocktrans` block. The following example shows you how to use `with` to include an object attribute on which the `capfirst` filter is applied:

```
{% blocktrans with name=user.name|capfirst %}
  Hello {{ name }}!
{% endblocktrans %}
```

> Use the `{% blocktrans %}` tag instead of `{% trans %}` when you need to include variable content in your translation string.

## Translating the shop templates

Edit the `shop/base.html` template of the `shop` application. Make sure you load the `i18n` tag at the top of the template and mark strings for translation as follows:

```
{% load i18n %}
{% load static %}
<!DOCTYPE html>
<html>
<head>
  <meta charset="utf-8" />
  <title>
    {% block title %}{% trans "My shop" %}{% endblock %}
  </title>
  <link href="{% static "css/base.css" %}" rel="stylesheet">
</head>
<body>
  <div id="header">
    <a href="/" class="logo">{% trans "My shop" %}</a>
  </div>
  <div id="subheader">
    <div class="cart">
      {% with total_items=cart|length %}
        {% if cart|length > 0 %}
          {% trans "Your cart" %}:
          <a href="{% url "cart:cart_detail" %}">
            {% blocktrans with total_items_plural=total_
items|pluralize
total_price=cart.get_total_price %}
```

```
            {{ total_items }} item{{ total_items_plural }},
            ${{ total_price }}
          {% endblocktrans %}
        </a>
      {% else %}
        {% trans "Your cart is empty." %}
      {% endif %}
    {% endwith %}
  </div>
  </div>
  <div id="content">
    {% block content %}
    {% endblock %}
  </div>
</body>
</html>
```

Notice the {% blocktrans %} tag to display the cart's summary. The cart's summary was previously as follows:

```
{{ total_items }} item{{ total_items|pluralize }},
${{ cart.get_total_price }}
```

We utilized {% blocktrans with ... %} to use placeholders for total_items|pluralize (template tag applied here) and cart.get_total_price (object method accessed here), resulting in:

```
{% blocktrans with total_items_plural=total_items|pluralize
total_price=cart.get_total_price %}
  {{ total_items }} item{{ total_items_plural }},
  ${{ total_price }}
{% endblocktrans %}
```

Next, edit the shop/product/detail.html template of the shop application and load the i18n tags at the top of it but after the {% extends %} tag, which always has to be the first tag in the template:

```
{% load i18n %}
```

Then, find the following line:

```
<input type="submit" value="Add to cart">
```

Replace it with the following one:

```
<input type="submit" value="{% trans "Add to cart" %}">
```

Now translate the `orders` application templates. Edit the `orders/order/create.html` template of the `orders` application and mark text for translation as follows:

```
{% extends "shop/base.html" %}
{% load i18n %}

{% block title %}
  {% trans "Checkout" %}
{% endblock %}

{% block content %}
  <h1>{% trans "Checkout" %}</h1>

  <div class="order-info">
    <h3>{% trans "Your order" %}</h3>
    <ul>
      {% for item in cart %}
        <li>
          {{ item.quantity }}x {{ item.product.name }}
          <span>${{ item.total_price }}</span>
        </li>
      {% endfor %}
      {% if cart.coupon %}
        <li>
          {% blocktrans with code=cart.coupon.code
discount=cart.coupon.discount %}
            "{{ code }}" ({{ discount }}% off)
          {% endblocktrans %}
          <span>- ${{ cart.get_discount|floatformat:"2" }}</span>
        </li>
      {% endif %}
    </ul>
    <p>{% trans "Total" %}: ${{
cart.get_total_price_after_discount|floatformat:"2" }}</p>
  </div>

  <form action="." method="post" class="order-form">
    {{ form.as_p }}
    <p><input type="submit" value="{% trans "Place order" %}"></p>
    {% csrf_token %}
  </form>
{% endblock %}
```

Take a look at the following files in the code that come along with this chapter to see how strings are marked for translation:

- The `shop` application: the `shop/product/list.html` template
- The `orders` application: the `orders/order/created.html` template
- The `cart` application: the `cart/detail.html` template

Let's update the message files to include the new translation strings. Open the shell and run the following command:

```
django-admin makemessages --all
```

The `.po` files inside the `locale` directory of the `myshop` project and you'll see that the `orders` application now contains all the strings we marked for translation.

Edit the `.po` translation files of the project and the `orders` application and include Spanish translations. You can refer to the translated `.po` files in the source code that comes along with this chapter.

Open the shell from the project directory and run the following commands:

```
cd orders/
django-admin compilemessages
cd ../
```

We have compiled the translation files for the `order` application.

Run the following command so that translations for applications that do not contain a `locale` directory are included in the project's messages file:

```
django-admin compilemessages
```

# Using the Rosetta translation interface

Rosetta is a third-party application that allows you to edit translations using the same interface as the Django administration site. Rosetta makes it easy to edit `.po` files and it updates compiled translation files. Let's add it into our project.

Install Rosetta via pip using this command:

```
pip install django-rosetta==0.7.6
```

Then, add `'rosetta'` to the INSTALLED_APPS setting in your project's `settings.py` file.

You need to add Rosetta's URLs to your main URL configuration. Edit the main `urls.py` file of your project and add the following URL pattern to it:

```
url(r'^rosetta/', include('rosetta.urls')),
```

Make sure you place it before the `shop.urls` pattern to avoid a wrong pattern match.

Open `http://127.0.0.1:8000/admin/` and log in using your superuser. Then, navigate to `http://127.0.0.1:8000/rosetta/` in your browser. You should see a list of existing languages like this:

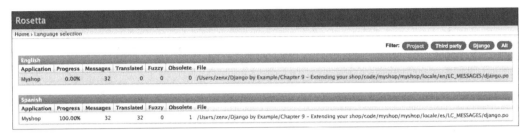

In the **Filter** section, click **All** to display all the available message files, including those that belong to the `orders` application. Click the **Myshop** link under the **Spanish** section to edit Spanish translations. You should see a list of translation strings as follows:

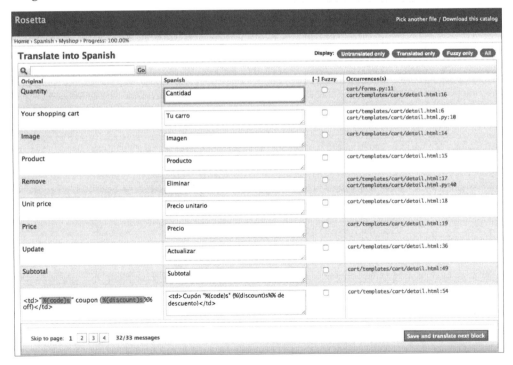

You can enter the translations under the **Spanish** column. The **Occurrences** column displays the files and line of code where each translation string was found.

Translations that include placeholders will appear like this:

```
%(total_items)s item%              %(total_items)s producto%(total_items_plural)s,
(total_items_plural)s, $%(total_price)s    $%(total_price)s
```

Rosetta uses a different background color to display placeholders. When you translate content, make sure you keep placeholders untranslated. For example, take the following string:

```
%(total_items)s item%(total_items_plural)s, $%(total_price)s
```

It is translated into Spanish like this:

```
%(total_items)s producto%(total_items_plural)s, $%(total_price)s
```

You can take a look at the source code that comes along with this chapter to use the same Spanish translations for your project.

When you finish editing translations, click the **Save and translate next block** button to save the translations to the `.po` file. Rosetta compiles the message file when you save translations, so there is no need for you to run the `compilemessages` command. However, Rosetta requires write access to the `locale` directories to write the message files. Make sure the directories have valid permissions.

If you want other users to be able to edit translations, open `http://127.0.0.1:8000/admin/auth/group/add/` in your browser and create a new group named `translators`. Then access `http://127.0.0.1:8000/admin/auth/user/` to edit the users you want to grant permissions to so they can edit translations. When editing a user, under the **Permissions** section, add the `translators` group to the **Chosen Groups** for each user. Rosetta is only available to superusers or users that belong to the `translators` group.

You can read Rosetta's documentation at `http://django-rosetta.readthedocs.org/en/latest/`.

> When you add new translations in your production environment, if you serve Django with a real web server, you will have to reload your server after running the `compilemessages` command or after saving the translations with Rosetta for changes to take effect.

# Fuzzy translations

You might have noticed that there is a **Fuzzy** column in Rosetta. This is not a Rosetta feature; it is provided by gettext. If the fuzzy flag is active for a translation, it will not be included in the compiled message files. This flag is for translation strings that require revision from the translator. When .po files are updated with new translation strings, it is possible that some translation strings are automatically flagged as fuzzy. This happens when gettext finds some msgid that has been slightly modified and gettext pairs it with what it thinks it was the old translation and flags it as fuzzy for review. The translator should then review fuzzy translations, remove the fuzzy flag, and compile the message file again.

# URL patterns for internationalization

Django offers internationalization capabilities for URLs. It includes two main features for internationalized URLs:

- **Language prefix in URL patterns**: Adding a language prefix to URLs to serve each language version under a different base URL
- **Translated URL patterns**: Marking URL patterns for translation so that the same URL is different for each language

A reason for translating URLs is to optimize your site for search engines. By adding a language prefix to your patterns, you will be able to index an URL for each language instead of a single URL for all of them. Furthermore, by translating URLs into each language, you will provide search engines with URLs that will rank better for each language.

## Adding a language prefix to URL patterns

Django allows you to add a language prefix to your URL patterns. For example, the English version of your site can be served under a path starting by /en/ and the Spanish version under /es/.

To use languages in URL patterns, you have to make sure that django.middleware. locale.LocaleMiddleware appears in the MIDDLEWARE_CLASSES setting in the settings.py file. Django will use it to identify the current language from the requested URL.

Let's add a language prefix to our URL patterns. Edit the main urls.py file of the myshop project and add the following import:

```
from django.conf.urls.i18n import i18n_patterns
```

Then, add `i18n_patterns()` as follows:

```
urlpatterns = i18n_patterns(
    url(r'^admin/', include(admin.site.urls)),
    url(r'^cart/', include('cart.urls', namespace='cart')),
    url(r'^orders/', include('orders.urls', namespace='orders')),
    url(r'^payment/', include('payment.urls',
        namespace='payment')),
    url(r'^paypal/', include('paypal.standard.ipn.urls')),
    url(r'^coupons/', include('coupons.urls',
        namespace='coupons')),
    url(r'^rosetta/', include('rosetta.urls')),
    url(r'^', include('shop.urls', namespace='shop')),
)
```

You can combine URL patterns under `patterns()` and under `i18n_patterns()` so that some patterns include a language prefix and others don't. However, it's best to use translated URLs only to avoid the possibility that a carelessly translated URL matches a non-translated URL pattern.

Run the development server and open `http://127.0.0.1:8000/` in your browser. Since you are using the `LocaleMiddleware` Django will perform the steps described in the *How Django determines the current language* section to determine the current language and then it will redirect you to the same URL including the language prefix. Take a look at the URL in your browser; it should now look like `http://127.0.0.1:8000/en/`. The current language will be the one set by the `Accept-Language` header of your browser if it is Spanish or English, or the default `LANGUAGE_CODE` (English) defined in your settings otherwise.

# Translating URL patterns

Django supports translated strings in URL patterns. You can use a different translation for each language for a single URL pattern. You can mark URL patterns for translation the same way you would do with literals, using the `ugettext_lazy()` function.

Edit the main `urls.py` file of the `myshop` project and add translation strings to the regular expressions of the URL patterns for the `cart`, `orders`, `payment`, and `coupons` applications as follows:

```
from django.utils.translation import gettext_lazy as _

urlpatterns = i18n_patterns(
    url(r'^admin/', include(admin.site.urls)),
    url(_(r'^cart/'), include('cart.urls', namespace='cart')),
```

```
        url(_(r'^orders/'), include('orders.urls',
                                    namespace='orders')),
        url(_(r'^payment/'), include('payment.urls',
                                     namespace='payment')),
        url(r'^paypal/', include('paypal.standard.ipn.urls')),
        url(_(r'^coupons/'), include('coupons.urls',
                                     namespace='coupons')),
        url(r'^rosetta/', include('rosetta.urls')),
        url(r'^', include('shop.urls', namespace='shop')),
    )
```

Edit the urls.py file of the orders application and mark URL patterns for
translation like this:

```
from django.conf.urls import url
from .import views
from django.utils.translation import gettext_lazy as _

urlpatterns = [
    url(_(r'^create/$'), views.order_create, name='order_create'),
    # ...
]
```

Edit the urls.py file of the payment application and change the code into this:

```
from django.conf.urls import url
from . import views
from django.utils.translation import gettext_lazy as _

urlpatterns = [
    url(_(r'^process/$'), views.payment_process, name='process'),
    url(_(r'^done/$'), views.payment_done, name='done'),
    url(_(r'^canceled/$'),
        views.payment_canceled,
        name='canceled'),
]
```

We don't need to translate the URL patterns of the shop application since they are
built with variables and do not include any other literals.

Open the shell and run the next command to update the message files with the new
translations:

```
django-admin makemessages --all
```

Make sure the development server is running. Open `http://127.0.0.1:8000/en/` `rosetta/` in your browser and click the **Myshop** link under the **Spanish** section. You can use the display filter to see only the strings that have not been translated yet. Make sure you keep the special characters of regular expressions in your URL translations. Translating URLs is a delicate task; if you alter the regular expression, you can break the URL.

# Allowing users to switch language

Since we are serving content that is available in multiple languages, we should let our users switch the site's language. We are going to add a language selector to our site. The language selector will consist of a list of available languages, which are displayed using links.

Edit the `shop/base.html` template and find the following lines:

```
<div id="header">
  <a href="/" class="logo">{% trans "My shop" %}</a>
</div>
```

Replace them with the following code:

```
<div id="header">
  <a href="/" class="logo">{% trans "My shop" %}</a>

  {% get_current_language as LANGUAGE_CODE %}
  {% get_available_languages as LANGUAGES %}
  {% get_language_info_list for LANGUAGES as languages %}
  <div class="languages">
    <p>{% trans "Language" %}:</p>
    <ul class="languages">
      {% for language in languages %}
        <li>
          <a href="/{{ language.code }}/" {% if language.code ==
LANGUAGE_CODE %} class="selected"{% endif %}>
            {{ language.name_local }}
          </a>
        </li>
      {% endfor %}
    </ul>
  </div>
</div>
```

This is how we build our language selector:

1.  First we load the internationalization tags using {% load i18n %}.

2.  We use the {% get_current_language %} tag to retrieve the current language.

3.  We get the languages defined in the LANGUAGES setting using the {% get_available_languages %} template tag.

4.  We use the tag {% get_language_info_list %} to provide easy access to the language attributes.

5.  We build an HTML list to display all available languages and we add a selected class attribute to the current active language.

We use the template tags provided by i18n based on the languages available in the settings of your project. Now open http://127.0.0.1:8000/ in your browser and take a look. You should see the language selector at the top right of the site as follows:

Users can now easily switch their language.

# Translating models with django-parler

Django does not provide a solution for translating models out of the box. You have to implement your own solution to manage content stored in different languages or use a third-party module for model translation. There are several third-party applications that allow you to translate model fields. Each of them takes a different approach to storing and accessing translations. One of these applications is django-parler. This module offers a very effective way to translate models and it integrates smoothly with Django's administration site.

django-parler generates a separate database table for each model that contains translations. This table includes all the translated fields and a foreign key for the original object the translation belongs to. It also contains a language field, since each row stores the content for one single language.

# Installing django-parler

Install django-parler via pip using the following command:

```
pip install django-parler==1.5.1
```

Then, edit the `settings.py` file of your project and add `'parler'` to the `INSTALLED_APPS` setting. Add also the following code to your settings file:

```
PARLER_LANGUAGES = {
    None: (
        {'code': 'en',},
        {'code': 'es',},
    ),
    'default': {
        'fallback': 'en',
        'hide_untranslated': False,
    }
}
```

This setting defines the available languages en and es for django-parler. We specify the default language en and we indicate that django-parler should not hide untranslated content.

# Translating model fields

Let's add translations for our product catalog. django-parler provides a `TranslatedModel` model class and a `TranslatedFields` wrapper to translate model fields. Edit the `models.py` file inside the `shop` application directory and add the following import:

```
from parler.models import TranslatableModel, TranslatedFields
```

Then, change the `Category` model to make the `name` and `slug` fields translatable. We are keeping also the non-translated fields for now:

```
class Category(TranslatableModel):
    name = models.CharField(max_length=200, db_index=True)
    slug = models.SlugField(max_length=200,
                            db_index=True,
                            unique=True)
    translations = TranslatedFields(
        name = models.CharField(max_length=200,
                                db_index=True),
        slug = models.SlugField(max_length=200,
                                db_index=True,
                                unique=True)
    )
```

The `Category` model inherits now from `TranslatedModel` instead of `models.Model`. and both the `name` and `slug` fields are included in the `TranslatedFields` wrapper.

Edit the `Product` model to add translations for the `name`, `slug`, and `description` fields as follows. Also keep the non-translated fields for now:

```
class Product(TranslatableModel):
    name = models.CharField(max_length=200, db_index=True)
    slug = models.SlugField(max_length=200, db_index=True)
    description = models.TextField(blank=True)
    translations = TranslatedFields(
        name = models.CharField(max_length=200, db_index=True),
        slug = models.SlugField(max_length=200, db_index=True),
        description = models.TextField(blank=True)
    )
    category = models.ForeignKey(Category,
                                    related_name='products')
    image = models.ImageField(upload_to='products/%Y/%m/%d',
                                    blank=True)
    price = models.DecimalField(max_digits=10, decimal_places=2)
    stock = models.PositiveIntegerField()
    available = models.BooleanField(default=True)
    created = models.DateTimeField(auto_now_add=True)
    updated = models.DateTimeField(auto_now=True)
```

django-parler generates another model for each translatable model. In the following image, you can see the fields of the `Product` model and what the generated `ProductTranslation` model will look like:

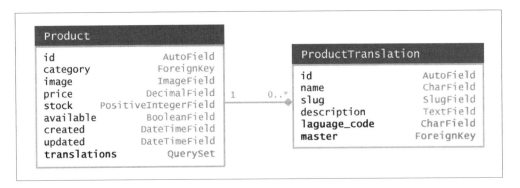

The `ProductTranslation` model generated by django-parler includes the `name`, `slug`, and `description` translatable fields, a `language_code` field, and a `ForeignKey` for the master `Product` object. There is a one-to-many relationship from `Product` to `ProductTranslation`. A `ProductTranslation` object will exist for each available language of each `Product` object.

Since Django uses a separate table for translations, there are some Django features that we cannot use. It is not possible to use a default ordering by a translated field. You can filter by translated fields in queries, but you cannot include a translatable field in the `ordering` Meta options. Edit the `models.py` file of the `shop` application and comment out the `ordering` attribute of the `Category` Meta class:

```
class Meta:
    # ordering = ('name',)
    verbose_name = 'category'
    verbose_name_plural = 'categories'
```

We also have to comment out the `index_together` attribute of the `Product` Meta class, since the current version of django-parler does not provide support to validate it. Edit the `Product` Meta class and make it look like this:

```
class Meta:
        ordering = ('-created',)
    # index_together = (('id', 'slug'),)
```

You can read more about django-parler's compatibility with Django at `http://django-parler.readthedocs.org/en/latest/compatibility.html`.

# Creating a custom migration

When you create new models with translations, you need to execute `makemigrations` to generate migrations for the models and then migrate to sync changes to the database. However, when making existing fields translatable, you probably have existing data in your database that you want to keep. We are going to migrate our current data into the new translation models. Therefore, we have added the translated fields but we have intentionally kept the original fields.

The steps to add translations to existing fields are the following:

1.  We create the migration for the new translatable model fields, keeping the original fields.

2.  We build a custom migration to copy data from existing fields into translation models.

3.  We remove the existing fields from the original models.

Run the following command to create the migration for the translation fields we have added to the `Category` and `Product` models:

```
python manage.py makemigrations shop --name "add_translation_model"
```

You should see the following output:

```
Migrations for 'shop':
  0002_add_translation_model.py:
    - Create model CategoryTranslation
    - Create model ProductTranslation
    - Change Meta options on category
    - Alter index_together for product (0 constraint(s))
    - Add field master to producttranslation
    - Add field master to categorytranslation
    - Alter unique_together for producttranslation (1 constraint(s))
    - Alter unique_together for categorytranslation (1 constraint(s))
```

## Migrating existing data

Now we need to create a custom migration to copy existing data into the new translation models. Create an empty migration using this command:

```
python manage.py makemigrations --empty shop --name "migrate_
translatable_fields"
```

You will get the following output:

```
Migrations for 'shop':
  0003_migrate_translatable_fields.py
```

Edit the `shop/migrations/0003_migrate_translatable_fields.py` file and add the following code to it:

```
# -*- coding: utf-8 -*-
from __future__ import unicode_literals
    from django.db import models, migrations
from django.apps import apps
from django.conf import settings
from django.core.exceptions import ObjectDoesNotExist

translatable_models = {
    'Category': ['name', 'slug'],
    'Product': ['name', 'slug', 'description'],
}
```

```python
def forwards_func(apps, schema_editor):
    for model, fields in translatable_models.items():
        Model = apps.get_model('shop', model)
        ModelTranslation = apps.get_model('shop',
                                '{}Translation'.format(model))

        for obj in Model.objects.all():
            translation_fields = {field: getattr(obj, field) for field
in fields}
            translation = ModelTranslation.objects.create(
                            master_id=obj.pk,
                            language_code=settings.LANGUAGE_CODE,
                            **translation_fields)

def backwards_func(apps, schema_editor):
    for model, fields in translatable_models.items():
        Model = apps.get_model('shop', model)
        ModelTranslation = apps.get_model('shop',
                                '{}Translation'.format(model))

        for obj in Model.objects.all():
            translation = _get_translation(obj, ModelTranslation)
            for field in fields:
                setattr(obj, field, getattr(translation, field))
            obj.save()

def _get_translation(obj, MyModelTranslation):
    translations = MyModelTranslation.objects.filter(master_id=obj.pk)
    try:
        # Try default translation
        return translations.get(language_code=settings.LANGUAGE_CODE)
    except ObjectDoesNotExist:
        # Hope there is a single translation
        return translations.get()

class Migration(migrations.Migration):
    dependencies = [
        ('shop', '0002_add_translation_model'),
    ]
    operations = [
        migrations.RunPython(forwards_func, backwards_func),
    ]
```

This migration includes `forwards_func()` and `backwards_func()` functions that contain the code to be executed to apply/reverse the migration.

The migration process works as follows:

1. We define the models and their translatable fields in the `translatable_models` dictionary.

2. To apply the migration, we iterate over the models that include translations to get the model and its translatable model classes with `app.get_model()`.

3. We iterate over all existing objects in the database and create a translation object for the LANGUAGE_CODE defined in the project's settings. We include a `ForeignKey` to the original object and a copy for each translatable field from the original fields.

The backward function executes the reverse process, retrieving the default translation object and copying the translatable fields' values back into the original object.

We have created a migration to add translation fields, then a migration to copy content from existing fields into the new translation models.

Finally, we need to remove the original fields we don't need anymore. Edit the `models.py` file of the `shop` application and remove the `name` and `slug` fields of the `Category` model. The `Category` model fields should now look as follows:

```
class Category(TranslatableModel):
    translations = TranslatedFields(
        name = models.CharField(max_length=200, db_index=True),
        slug = models.SlugField(max_length=200,
                                db_index=True,
                                unique=True)
    )
```

Remove the `name`, `slug`, and `description` fields of the `Product` model. It should now look like this:

```
class Product(TranslatableModel):
    translations = TranslatedFields(
        name = models.CharField(max_length=200, db_index=True),
        slug = models.SlugField(max_length=200, db_index=True),
        description = models.TextField(blank=True)
    )
    category = models.ForeignKey(Category,
                                 related_name='products')
    image = models.ImageField(upload_to='products/%Y/%m/%d',
                              blank=True)
```

```
price = models.DecimalField(max_digits=10, decimal_places=2)
stock = models.PositiveIntegerField()
available = models.BooleanField(default=True)
created = models.DateTimeField(auto_now_add=True)
updated = models.DateTimeField(auto_now=True)
```

Now we have to create a final migration that reflects this model change. However, if we try to run the manage.py utility, we will get an error because we haven't adapted the administration site for the translatable models yet. Let's fix the administration site first.

# Integrating translations in the administration site

Django-parler integrates smoothly with the Django administration site. It includes a TranslatableAdmin class that overrides the ModelAdmin class provided by Django to manage model translations.

Edit the admin.py file of the shop application and add the following import to it:

```
from parler.admin import TranslatableAdmin
```

Modify the CategoryAdmin and ProductAdmin classes to inherit from TranslatableAdmin instead of ModelAdmin. Django-parler doesn't support the prepopulated_fields attribute yet, but it does support the get_prepopulated_fields() method that provides the same functionality. Let's change this accordingly. The admin.py file should now look like this:

```
from django.contrib import admin
from .models import Category, Product
from parler.admin import TranslatableAdmin

class CategoryAdmin(TranslatableAdmin):
    list_display = ['name', 'slug']

    def get_prepopulated_fields(self, request, obj=None):
        return {'slug': ('name',)}

admin.site.register(Category, CategoryAdmin)

class ProductAdmin(TranslatableAdmin):
    list_display = ['name', 'slug', 'category', 'price', 'stock',
                    'available', 'created', 'updated']
    list_filter = ['available', 'created', 'updated', 'category']
    list_editable = ['price', 'stock', 'available']
```

```
    def get_prepopulated_fields(self, request, obj=None):
        return {'slug': ('name',)}

admin.site.register(Product, ProductAdmin)
```

We have adapted the administration site to work with the new translated models. We can now sync the database with the model changes we made.

# Applying migrations for model translation

We removed the old fields from our models before adapting the administration site. Now we need to create a migration for this change. Open the shell and run the following command:

**python manage.py makemigrations shop --name "remove_untranslated_fields"**

You will see the following output:

```
Migrations for 'shop':
  0004_remove_untranslated_fields.py:
    - Remove field name from category
    - Remove field slug from category
    - Remove field description from product
    - Remove field name from product
    - Remove field slug from product
```

With this migration, we are going to remove the original fields and keep the translatable fields.

In summary, we have created the following migrations:

1.  Added translatable fields to models.
2.  Migrated existing data from the original fields to the translatable fields.
3.  Removed the original fields from the models.

Run the following command to apply the three migrations we have created:

**python manage.py migrate shop**

You will an output that includes the following lines:

```
Applying shop.0002_add_translation_model... OK
Applying shop.0003_migrate_translatable_fields... OK
Applying shop.0004_remove_untranslated_fields... OK
```

Our models are now synchronized with the database. Let's translate an object.

Run the development server using `python manage.py runserver` and open `http://127.0.0.1:8000/en/admin/shop/category/add/` in your browser. You will see that the **Add category** page includes two different tabs, one for **English** and one for **Spanish** translations:

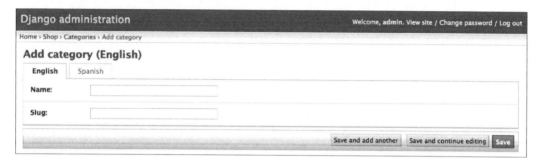

You can now add a translation and click the **Save** button. Make sure you save the changes before you change the tab or you will lose them.

## Adapting views for translations

We have to adapt our `shop` views to use translations QuerySets. Run `python manage.py shell` from the command line and take a look at how you can retrieve and query translation fields. To get a field's content for the current active language, you just have to access the field the same way you access any normal model field:

```
>>> from shop.models import Product
>>> product=Product.objects.first()
>>> product.name
'Black tea'
```

When you access translated fields, they are resolved using the current language. You can set a different current language for an object so that you access that specific translation:

```
>>> product.set_current_language('es')
>>> product.name
'Té negro'
>>> product.get_current_language()
'es'
```

When performing a QuerySet using `filter()`, you can filter using the related translation objects with the `translations__` syntax as follows:

```
>>> Product.objects.filter(translations__name='Black tea')
[<Product: Black tea>]
```

You can also use the `language()` manager to set a specific language for the objects retrieved as follows:

```
>>> Product.objects.language('es').all()
[<Product: Té negro>, <Product: Té en polvo>, <Product: Té rojo>,
<Product: Té verde>]
```

As you can see, the way to access and query translated fields is quite straightforward.

Let's adapt the product catalog views. Edit the `views.py` file of the `shop` application and in the `product_list` view, find the following line:

```
category = get_object_or_404(Category, slug=category_slug)
```

Replace it with the following ones:

```
language = request.LANGUAGE_CODE
category = get_object_or_404(Category,
                             translations__language_code=language,
                             translations__slug=category_slug)
```

Then, edit the `product_detail` view and find the following lines:

```
product = get_object_or_404(Product,
                            id=id,
                            slug=slug,
                            available=True)
```

Replace them with the following code:

```
language = request.LANGUAGE_CODE
get_object_or_404(Product,
                  id=id,
                  translations__language_code=language,
                  translations__slug=slug,
                  available=True)
```

The `product_list` and `product_detail` views are now adapted to retrieve objects using translated fields. Run the development server and open `http://127.0.0.1:8000/es/` in your browser. You should see the product list page, including all products translated into Spanish:

Now each product's URL is built using the `slug` field translated into the current language. For example, the URL for a product in Spanish is `http://127.0.0.1:8000/es/2/te-rojo/`, whereas in English the URL is `http://127.0.0.1:8000/en/2/red-tea/`. If you navigate to a product detail page, you will see the translated URL and the contents for the selected language, like the following example:

If you want to know more about django-parler, you can find the full documentation at `http://django-parler.readthedocs.org/en/latest/`.

You have learned how to translate Python code, templates, URL patterns, and model fields. To complete the internationalization and localization process, we need to display localized formatting for dates, times, and numbers.

# Format localization

Depending on the user's locale, you might want to display dates, times, and numbers in different formats. The localized formatting can be activated by changing the `USE_L10N` setting to `True` in the `settings.py` file of your project.

When `USE_L10N` is enabled, Django will try to use a locale specific format whenever it outputs a value in a template. You can see that decimal numbers in the English version of your site are displayed with a dot separator for decimal places, while in the Spanish version they are displayed using a comma. This is due to the locale formats specified for the `es` locale by Django. You can take a look at the Spanish formatting configuration at `https://github.com/django/django/blob/stable/1.8.x/django/conf/locale/es/formats.py`.

Normally, you will set the `USE_L10N` setting to `True` and let Django apply the format localization for each locale. However, there might be situations in which you don't want to use localized values. This is especially relevant when outputting JavaScript or JSON that has to provide a machine-readable format.

Django offers a `{% localize %}` template tag that allows you to turn on/off localization for template fragments. This gives you control over localized formatting. You will have to load the `l10n` tags to be able to use this template tag. The following is an example of how to turn on and off localization in a template:

```
{% load l10n %}

{% localize on %}
  {{ value }}
{% endlocalize %}

{% localize off %}
  {{ value }}
{% endlocalize %}
```

Django also offers the `localize` and `unlocalize` template filters to force or avoid localization of a value. These filters can be applied as follows:

```
{{ value|localize }}
{{ value|unlocalize }}
```

You can also create custom format files to specify locale formatting. You can find further information about format localization at `https://docs.djangoproject.com/en/1.8/topics/i18n/formatting/`.

# Using django-localflavor to validate form fields

django-localflavor is a third-party module that contains a collection of specific utils, such as form fields or model fields that are specific for each country. It's very useful to validate local regions, local phone numbers, identity card numbers, social security numbers, and so on. The package is organized into a series of modules named after ISO 3166 country codes.

Install django-localflavor using the following command:

```
pip install django-localflavor==1.1
```

Edit the `settings.py` file of your project and add `'localflavor'` to the `INSTALLED_APPS` setting.

We are going to add a United States (U.S.) zip code field so that a valid U.S. zip code is required to create a new order.

Edit the `forms.py` file of the `orders` application and make it look as follows:

```
from django import forms
from .models import Order
from localflavor.us.forms import USZipCodeField

class OrderCreateForm(forms.ModelForm):
    postal_code = USZipCodeField()
    class Meta:
        model = Order
        fields = ['first_name', 'last_name', 'email', 'address',
                  'postal_code', 'city',]
```

We import the `USZipCodeField` field from the `us` package of `localflavor` and use it for the `postal_code` field of the `OrderCreateForm` form. Open `http://127.0.0.1:8000/en/orders/create/` in your browser and try to enter a 3-letter postal code. You will get the following validation error that is raised by `USZipCodeField`:

```
Enter a zip code in the format XXXXX or XXXXX-XXXX.
```

This is just a brief example of how to use a custom field from localflavor in your own project for validation purposes. The local components provided by localflavor are very useful to adapt your application to specific countries. You can read the django-localflavor documentation and see all available local components for each country at `https://django-localflavor.readthedocs.org/en/latest/`.

Next, we are going to build a recommendation engine into our shop.

# Building a recommendation engine

A recommendation engine is a system that predicts the **preference** or **rating** that a user would give to an item. The system selects relevant items for the users based on their behavior and the knowledge it has about them. Nowadays, recommendation systems are used in many online services. They help users by selecting the stuff they might be interested in from the vast amount of available data irrelevant to them. Offering good recommendations enhances user engagement. E-commerce sites also benefit from offering relevant product recommendations by increasing their average sale.

We are going to create a simple yet powerful recommendation engine that suggests products that are usually bought together. We will suggest products based on historic sales, thus identifying products that are usually bought together. We are going to suggest complementary products in two different scenarios:

- **Product detail page**: We will display a list of products that are usually bought with the given product. This will be displayed like: **Users who bought this also bought X, Y, Z**. We need a data structure that allows us to store the number of times that each product has been bought together with the product being displayed.

- **Cart detail page**: Based on the products users add to the cart, we are going to suggest products that are usually bought together with these ones. In this case, the score we calculate to obtain related products has to be aggregated.

We are going to use Redis to store products that are purchased together. Remember that you already used Redis in *Chapter 6, Tracking User Actions*. If you haven't installed Redis yet, you can find installation instructions in that chapter.

# Recommending products based on previous purchases

Now, we will recommend products to users based on what they have added to the cart. We are going to store a key in Redis for each product bought in our site. The product key will contain a Redis sorted set with scores. We will increment the score by 1 for each product bought together every time a new purchase is completed.

When an order is successfully paid for, we store a key for each product bought, including a sorted set of products that belong to the same order. The sorted set allows us to give scores for products that are bought together.

Edit the settings.py file of your project and add the following settings to it:

```
REDIS_HOST = 'localhost'
REDIS_PORT = 6379
REDIS_DB = 1
```

These are the settings required to establish a connection with the Redis server. Create a new file inside the shop application directory and name it recommender.py. Add the following code to it:

```
import redis
from django.conf import settings
from .models import Product

# connect to redis
r = redis.StrictRedis(host=settings.REDIS_HOST,
                      port=settings.REDIS_PORT,
                      db=settings.REDIS_DB)

class Recommender(object):

    def get_product_key(self, id):
        return 'product:{}:purchased_with'.format(id)

    def products_bought(self, products):
        product_ids = [p.id for p in products]
        for product_id in product_ids:
            for with_id in product_ids:
                # get the other products bought with each product
                if product_id != with_id:
                    # increment score for product purchased together
                    r.zincrby(self.get_product_key(product_id),
                        with_id,
                        amount=1)
```

This is the `Recommender` class that will allow us to store product purchases and retrieve product suggestions for a given product or products. The `get_product_key()` method receives an `id` of a `Product` object and builds the Redis key for the sorted set where related products are stored, which looks like `product:[id]:purchased_with`.

The `products_bought()` method receives a list of `Product` objects that have been bought together (that is, belong to the same order). In this method, we perform the following tasks:

1. We get the product IDs for the given `Product` objects.

2. We iterate over the product IDs. For each `id`, we iterate over the product IDs and skip the same product so that we get the products that are bought together with each product.

3. We get the Redis product key for each product bought using the `get_product_id()` method. For a product with an ID of `33`, this method returns the key `product:33:purchased_with`. This is the key for the sorted set that contains the product IDs of products that were bought together with this one.

4. We increment the score of each product `id` contained in the sorted set by `1`. The score represents the times another product has been bought together with the given product.

So we have a method to store and score the products that were bought together. Now we need a method to retrieve the products that are bought together for a list of given products. Add the following `suggest_products_for()` method to the `Recommender` class:

```
def suggest_products_for(self, products, max_results=6):
    product_ids = [p.id for p in products]
    if len(products) == 1:
        # only 1 product
        suggestions = r.zrange(
                        self.get_product_key(product_ids[0]),
                        0, -1, desc=True)[:max_results]
    else:
        # generate a temporary key
        flat_ids = ''.join([str(id) for id in product_ids])
        tmp_key = 'tmp_{}'.format(flat_ids)
        # multiple products, combine scores of all products
        # store the resulting sorted set in a temporary key
        keys = [self.get_product_key(id) for id in product_ids]
        r.zunionstore(tmp_key, keys)
```

```
        # remove ids for the products the recommendation is for
        r.zrem(tmp_key, *product_ids)
        # get the product ids by their score, descendant sort
        suggestions = r.zrange(tmp_key, 0, -1,
                               desc=True)[:max_results]
        # remove the temporary key
        r.delete(tmp_key)
    suggested_products_ids = [int(id) for id in suggestions]

    # get suggested products and sort by order of appearance
    suggested_products = list(Product.objects.filter(id__in=suggested_
products_ids))
    suggested_products.sort(key=lambda x: suggested_products_ids.
index(x.id))
    return suggested_products
```

The `suggest_products_for()` method receives the following parameters:

- `products`: This is a list of `Product` objects to get recommendations for. It can contain one or more products.

- `max_results`: This is an integer that represents the maximum number of recommendations to return.

In this method, we perform the following actions:

1. We get the product IDs for the given `Product` objects.

2. If only one product is given, we retrieve the ID of the products that were bought together with the given product, ordered by the total number of times that they were bought together. To do so, we use Redis' ZRANGE command. We limit the number of results to the number specified in the `max_results` attribute (6 by default).

3. If more than one product is given, we generate a temporary Redis key built with the IDs of the products.

4. We combine and sum all scores for the items contained in the sorted set of each of the given products. This is done using the Redis' ZUNIONSTORE command. The ZUNIONSTORE command performs a union of the sorted sets with the given keys, and stores the aggregated sum of scores of the elements in a new Redis key. You can read more about this command at `http://redis.io/commands/ZUNIONSTORE`. We save the aggregated scores in the temporary key.

5. Since we are aggregating scores, we might obtain the same products we are getting recommendations for. We remove them from the generated sorted set using the ZREM command.

6. We retrieve the IDs of the products from the temporary key, ordered by their score using the ZRANGE command. We limit the number of results to the number specified in the max_results attribute. Then we remove the temporary key.

7. Finally, we get the Product objects with the given id and we order the products by the same order as the them.

For practical purposes, let's also add a method to clear the recommendations. Add the following method to the Recommender class:

```
def clear_purchases(self):
    for id in Product.objects.values_list('id', flat=True):
        r.delete(self.get_product_key(id))
```

Let's try our recommendation engine. Make sure you include several Product objects in the database and initialize the Redis server using the following command from the shell:

**src/redis-server**

Open another shell, execute python manage.py shell, and write the following code to retrieve several products:

```
from shop.models import Product
black_tea = Product.objects.get(translations__name='Black tea')
red_tea = Product.objects.get(translations__name='Red tea')
green_tea = Product.objects.get(translations__name='Green tea')
tea_powder = Product.objects.get(translations__name='Tea powder')
```

Then, add some test purchases to the recommendation engine:

```
from shop.recommender import Recommender
r = Recommender()
r.products_bought([black_tea, red_tea])
r.products_bought([black_tea, green_tea])
r.products_bought([red_tea, black_tea, tea_powder])
r.products_bought([green_tea, tea_powder])
r.products_bought([black_tea, tea_powder])
r.products_bought([red_tea, green_tea])
```

We have stored the following scores:

```
black_tea: red_tea (2), tea_powder (2), green_tea (1)
red_tea: black_tea (2), tea_powder (1), green_tea (1)
green_tea: black_tea (1), tea_powder (1), red_tea(1)
tea_powder: black_tea (2), red_tea (1), green_tea (1)
```

Let's take a look at the recommended products for a single product:

```
>>> r.suggest_products_for([black_tea])
[<Product: Tea powder>, <Product: Red tea>, <Product: Green tea>]
>>> r.suggest_products_for([red_tea])
[<Product: Black tea>, <Product: Tea powder>, <Product: Green tea>]
>>> r.suggest_products_for([green_tea])
[<Product: Black tea>, <Product: Tea powder>, <Product: Red tea>]
>>> r.suggest_products_for([tea_powder])
[<Product: Black tea>, <Product: Red tea>, <Product: Green tea>]
```

As you can see, the order for recommended products is based on their score. Let's get recommendations for multiple products with aggregated scores:

```
>>> r.suggest_products_for([black_tea, red_tea])
[<Product: Tea powder>, <Product: Green tea>]
>>> r.suggest_products_for([green_tea, red_tea])
[<Product: Black tea>, <Product: Tea powder>]
>>> r.suggest_products_for([tea_powder, black_tea])
[<Product: Red tea>, <Product: Green tea>]
```

You can see that the order of the suggested products matches the aggregated scores. For example, products suggested for black_tea and red_tea are tea_powder (2+1) and green_tea (1+1).

We have verified that our recommendation algorithm works as expected. Let's display recommendations for products on our site.

Edit the views.py file of the shop application and add the following import:

```
from .recommender import Recommender
```

Add the following code to the `product_detail` view just before the `render()` function:

```
r = Recommender()
recommended_products = r.suggest_products_for([product], 4)
```

We get a maximum of four product suggestions. The `product_detail` view should now look as follows:

```
from .recommender import Recommender

def product_detail(request, id, slug):
    product = get_object_or_404(Product,
                                id=id,
                                slug=slug,
                                available=True)
    cart_product_form = CartAddProductForm()
    r = Recommender()
    recommended_products = r.suggest_products_for([product], 4)
    return render(request,
                  'shop/product/detail.html',
                  {'product': product,
                   'cart_product_form': cart_product_form,
                   'recommended_products': recommended_products})
```

Now edit the `shop/product/detail.html` template of the `shop` application and add the following code after `{{ product.description|linebreaks }}`:

```
{% if recommended_products %}
  <div class="recommendations">
    <h3>{% trans "People who bought this also bought" %}</h3>
    {% for p in recommended_products %}
      <div class="item">
        <a href="{{ p.get_absolute_url }}">
          <img src="{% if p.image %}{{ p.image.url }}{% else %}{%
static "img/no_image.png" %}{% endif %}">
        </a>
        <p><a href="{{ p.get_absolute_url }}">{{ p.name }}</a></p>
      </div>
    {% endfor %}
  </div>
{% endif %}
```

Run the development server with the command `python manage.py runserver` and open `http://127.0.0.1:8000/en/` in your browser. Click on any product to see its details page. You should see that recommended products are displayed below the product, as shown in the following image:

We are also going to include product recommendations in the cart. The recommendation will be based on the products that the user has added to the cart. Edit the `views.py` inside the `cart` application directory and add the following import:

```python
from shop.recommender import Recommender
```

Then, edit the `cart_detail` view to make it look as follows:

```python
def cart_detail(request):
    cart = Cart(request)
    for item in cart:
        item['update_quantity_form'] = CartAddProductForm(
                            initial={'quantity': item['quantity'],
                                     'update': True})
    coupon_apply_form = CouponApplyForm()

    r = Recommender()
    cart_products = [item['product'] for item in cart]
    recommended_products = r.suggest_products_for(cart_products,
                                                  max_results=4)
```

```
return render(request,
              'cart/detail.html',
              {'cart': cart,
               'coupon_apply_form': coupon_apply_form,
               'recommended_products': recommended_products})
```

Edit the `cart/detail.html` template of the `cart` application and add the following code just after the `</table>` HTML tag:

```
{% if recommended_products %}
  <div class="recommendations cart">
    <h3>{% trans "People who bought this also bought" %}</h3>
    {% for p in recommended_products %}
      <div class="item">
        <a href="{{ p.get_absolute_url }}">
          <img src="{% if p.image %}{{ p.image.url }}{% else %}{%
static "img/no_image.png" %}{% endif %}">
        </a>
        <p><a href="{{ p.get_absolute_url }}">{{ p.name }}</a></p>
      </div>
    {% endfor %}
  </div>
{% endif %}
```

Open `http://127.0.0.1:8000/en/` in your browser and add a couple of products to your cart. When you navigate to `http://127.0.0.1:8000/en/cart/`, you should see the aggregated product recommendations for the items in the cart as follows:

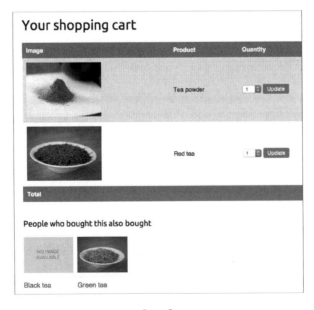

Congratulations! You have built a complete recommendation engine using Django and Redis.

# Summary

In this chapter, you created a coupon system using sessions. You learned how internationalization and localization work. You also built a recommendation engine using Redis.

In the next chapter, you will start a new project. You will build an e-learning platform with Django using class-based views and you will create a custom content management system.

# 10
# Building an e-Learning Platform

In the previous chapter, you added internationalization to your online shop project. You also built a coupon system and a product recommendation engine. In this chapter, you will create a new project. You will build an e-Learning platform creating a custom content management system.

In this chapter, you will learn how to:

- Create fixtures for your models
- Use model inheritance
- Create custom model fields
- Use class-based views and mixins
- Build formsets
- Manage groups and permissions
- Create a content management system

## Creating an e-Learning platform

Our last practical project will be an e-Learning platform. In this chapter, we are going to build a flexible **Content Management System (CMS)** that allows instructors to create courses and manage their contents.

First, create a virtual environment for your new project and activate it with the following commands:

```
mkdir env
virtualenv env/educa
source env/educa/bin/activate
```

Install Django in your virtual environment with the following command:

```
pip install Django==1.8.6
```

We are going to manage image uploads in our project, so we also need to install Pillow with the following command:

```
pip install Pillow==2.9.0
```

Create a new project using the following command:

```
django-admin startproject educa
```

Enter the new `educa` directory and create a new application using the following commands:

```
cd educa
django-admin startapp courses
```

Edit the `settings.py` file of the `educa` project and add `courses` to the `INSTALLED_APPS` setting as follows:

```
INSTALLED_APPS = (
    'courses',
    'django.contrib.admin',
    'django.contrib.auth',
    'django.contrib.contenttypes',
    'django.contrib.sessions',
    'django.contrib.messages',
    'django.contrib.staticfiles',
)
```

The `courses` application is now active for the project. Let's define the models for courses and course contents.

# Building the course models

Our e-Learning platform will offer courses in various subjects. Each course will be divided into a configurable number of modules, and each module will contain a configurable number of contents. There will be contents of various types: text, file, image, or video. The following example shows what the data structure of our course catalog will look like:

```
Subject 1
  Course 1
    Module 1
      Content 1 (image)
```

```
        Content 3 (text)
    Module 2
        Content 4 (text)
        Content 5 (file)
        Content 6 (video)
    ...
```

Let's build the course models. Edit the `models.py` file of the `courses` application and add the following code to it:

```python
from django.db import models
from django.contrib.auth.models import User

class Subject(models.Model):
    title = models.CharField(max_length=200)
    slug = models.SlugField(max_length=200, unique=True)

    class Meta:
        ordering = ('title',)

    def __str__(self):
        return self.title

class Course(models.Model):
    owner = models.ForeignKey(User,
                                related_name='courses_created')
    subject = models.ForeignKey(Subject,
                                related_name='courses')
    title = models.CharField(max_length=200)
    slug = models.SlugField(max_length=200, unique=True)
    overview = models.TextField()
    created = models.DateTimeField(auto_now_add=True)

    class Meta:
        ordering = ('-created',)

    def __str__(self):
        return self.title

class Module(models.Model):
    course = models.ForeignKey(Course, related_name='modules')
    title = models.CharField(max_length=200)
    description = models.TextField(blank=True)

    def __str__(self):
        return self.title
```

These are the initial `Subject`, `Course`, and `Module` models. The `Course` model fields are as follows:

- `owner`: The instructor that created this course.
- `subject`: The subject that this course belongs to. A `ForeignKey` field that points to the `Subject` model.
- `title`: The title of the course.
- `slug`: The slug of the course. This will be used in URLs later.
- `overview`: This is a `TextField` column to include an overview about the course.
- `created`: The date and time when the course was created. It will be automatically set by Django when creating new objects because of `auto_now_add=True`.

Each course is divided into several modules. Therefore, the `Module` model contains a `ForeignKey` field that points to the `Course` model.

Open the shell and run the following command to create the initial migration for this app:

**python manage.py makemigrations**

You will see the following output:

```
Migrations for 'courses':
  0001_initial.py:
    - Create model Course
    - Create model Module
    - Create model Subject
    - Add field subject to course
```

Then, run the following command to apply all migrations to the database:

**python manage.py migrate**

You should see an output including all applied migrations, including those of Django. The output will contain the following line:

```
Applying courses.0001_initial... OK
```

This tells us that the models of our `courses` app have been synced to the database.

# Registering the models in the administration site

We are going to add the course models to the administration site. Edit the `admin.py` file inside the `courses` application directory and add the following code to it:

```
from django.contrib import admin
from .models import Subject, Course, Module

@admin.register(Subject)
class SubjectAdmin(admin.ModelAdmin):
    list_display = ['title', 'slug']
    prepopulated_fields = {'slug': ('title',)}

class ModuleInline(admin.StackedInline):
    model = Module

@admin.register(Course)
class CourseAdmin(admin.ModelAdmin):
    list_display = ['title', 'subject', 'created']
    list_filter = ['created', 'subject']
    search_fields = ['title', 'overview']
    prepopulated_fields = {'slug': ('title',)}
    inlines = [ModuleInline]
```

The models for the course application are now registered in the administration site. We use the `@admin.register()` decorator instead of the `admin.site.register()` function. Both provide the same functionality.

# Providing initial data for models

Sometimes you might want to pre-populate your database with hard-coded data. This is useful to automatically include initial data in the project setup instead of having to add it manually. Django comes with a simple way to load and dump data from the database into files that are called fixtures.

Django supports fixtures in JSON, XML, or YAML formats. We are going to create a fixture to include some initial `Subject` objects for our project.

First, create a superuser using the following command:

```
python manage.py createsuperuser
```

Then, run the development server using the following command:

```
python manage.py runserver
```

Now, open `http://127.0.0.1:8000/admin/courses/subject/` in your browser. Create several subjects using the administration site. The list display page should look as follows:

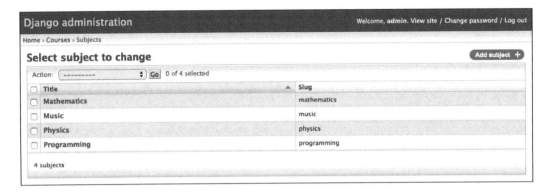

Run the following command from the shell:

```
python manage.py dumpdata courses --indent=2
```

You will see an output similar to the following:

```
[
  {
    "fields": {
      "title": "Programming",
      "slug": "programming"
    },
    "model": "courses.subject",
    "pk": 1
  },
  {
    "fields": {
      "title": "Mathematics",
      "slug": "mathematics"
    },
    "model": "courses.subject",
    "pk": 2
  },
  {
```

```
      "fields": {
        "title": "Physics",
        "slug": "physics"
      },
      "model": "courses.subject",
      "pk": 3
    },
    {
      "fields": {
        "title": "Music",
        "slug": "music"
      },
      "model": "courses.subject",
      "pk": 4
    }
  ]
```

The dumpdata command dumps data from the database into the standard output, serialized in JSON by default. The resulting data structure includes information about the model and its fields for Django to be able to load it into the database.

You can provide names of applications to the command or specify models for outputting data using the app.Model format. You can also specify the format using the --format flag. By default, dumpdata outputs the serialized data to the standard output. However, you can indicate an output file using the --output flag. The --indent flag allows you to specify indentation. For more information on dumpdata parameters, run python manage.py dumpdata --help.

Save this dump to a fixtures file into a fixtures/ directory in the orders application using the following commands:

```
mkdir courses/fixtures
python manage.py dumpdata courses --indent=2 --output=courses/fixtures/subjects.json
```

Use the administration site to remove the subjects you created. Then load the fixture into the database using the following command:

```
python manage.py loaddata subjects.json
```

All Subject objects included in the fixture are loaded into the database.

By default, Django looks for files in the `fixtures/` directory of each application, but you can specify the complete path to the fixture file for the `loaddata` command. You can also use the `FIXTURE_DIRS` setting to tell Django additional directories to look for fixtures.

 Fixtures are not only useful for initial data but also to provide sample data for your application or data required for your tests.

You can read about how to use fixtures for testing at `https://docs.djangoproject.com/en/1.8/topics/testing/tools/#topics-testing-fixtures`.

If you want to load fixtures in model migrations, take a look at Django's documentation about data migrations. Remember that we created a custom migration in *Chapter 9*, *Extending Your Shop* to migrate existing data after modifying models for translations. You can find the documentation for migrating data at `https://docs.djangoproject.com/en/1.8/topics/migrations/#data-migrations`.

# Creating models for diverse content

We plan to add different types of content to the course modules such as texts, images, files, and videos. We need a versatile data model that allows us to store diverse content. In *Chapter 6*, *Tracking User Actions*, you have learned about the convenience of using generic relations to create foreign keys that can point to objects of any model. We are going to create a `Content` model that represents the modules contents and define a generic relation to associate any kind of content.

Edit the `models.py` file of the `courses` application and add the following imports:

```
from django.contrib.contenttypes.models import ContentType
from django.contrib.contenttypes.fields import GenericForeignKey
```

Then add the following code to the end of the file:

```
class Content(models.Model):
    module = models.ForeignKey(Module, related_name='contents')
    content_type = models.ForeignKey(ContentType)
    object_id = models.PositiveIntegerField()
    item = GenericForeignKey('content_type', 'object_id')
```

This is the `Content` model. A module contains multiple contents, so we define a `ForeignKey` field to the `Module` model. We also set up a generic relation to associate objects from different models that represent different types of content. Remember that we need three different fields to set up a generic relationship. In our `Content` model, these are:

- `content_type`: A `ForeignKey` field to the `ContentType` model
- `object_id`: This is `PositiveIntegerField` to store the primary key of the related object
- `item`: A `GenericForeignKey` field to the related object by combining the two previous fields

Only the `content_type` and `object_id` fields have a corresponding column in the database table of this model. The `item` field allows you to retrieve or set the related object directly, and its functionality is built on top of the other two fields.

We are going to use a different model for each type of content. Our content models will have some common fields, but they will differ in the actual contents they can store.

# Using model inheritance

Django supports model inheritance. It works in a similar way to standard class inheritance in Python. Django offers the following three options to use model inheritance:

- **Abstract models**: Useful when you want to put some common information into several models. No database table is created for the abstract model.
- **Multi-table model inheritance**: Applicable when each model in the hierarchy is considered a complete model by itself. A database table is created for each model.
- **Proxy models**: Useful when you need to change the behavior of a model, for example, including additional methods, changing the default manager, or using different meta options. No database table is created for proxy models.

Let's take a closer look at each of them.

# Abstract models

An abstract model is a base class in which you define fields you want to include in all child models. Django doesn't create any database table for abstract models. A database table is created for each child model, including the fields inherited from the abstract class and the ones defined in the child model.

To mark a model as abstract, you need to include `abstract=True` in its `Meta` class. Django will recognize that it is an abstract model and will not create a database table for it. To create child models, you just need to subclass the abstract model. The following is an example of an abstract `Content` model and a child `Text` model:

```python
from django.db import models

class BaseContent(models.Model):
    title = models.CharField(max_length=100)
    created = models.DateTimeField(auto_now_add=True)

    class Meta:
        abstract = True

class Text(BaseContent):
    body = models.TextField()
```

In this case, Django would create a table for the `Text` model only, including the `title`, `created`, and `body` fields.

# Multi-table model inheritance

In multi-table inheritance, each model corresponds to a database table. Django creates a `OneToOneField` field for the relationship in the child's model to its parent.

To use multi-table inheritance, you have to subclass an existing model. Django will create a database table for both the original model and the sub-model. The following example shows multi-table inheritance:

```python
from django.db import models

class BaseContent(models.Model):
    title = models.CharField(max_length=100)
    created = models.DateTimeField(auto_now_add=True)

class Text(BaseContent):
    body = models.TextField()
```

Django would include an automatically generated `OneToOneField` field in the `Text` model and create a database table for each model.

# Proxy models

Proxy models are used to change the behavior of a model, for example, including additional methods or different meta options. Both models operate on the database table of the original model. To create a proxy model, add `proxy=True` to the `Meta` class of the model.

The following example illustrates how to create a proxy model:

```
from django.db import models
from django.utils import timezone

class BaseContent(models.Model):
    title = models.CharField(max_length=100)
    created = models.DateTimeField(auto_now_add=True)

class OrderedContent(BaseContent):
    class Meta:
        proxy = True
        ordering = ['created']

    def created_delta(self):
        return timezone.now() - self.created
```

Here, we define an `OrderedContent` model that is a proxy model for the `Content` model. This model provides a default ordering for QuerySets and an additional `created_delta()` method. Both models, `Content` and `OrderedContent`, operate on the same database table, and objects are accessible via the ORM through either model.

# Creating the content models

The `Content` model of our `courses` application contains a generic relation to associate different types of content to it. We will create a different model for each type of content. All content models will have some fields in common, and additional fields to store custom data. We are going to create an abstract model that provides the common fields for all content models.

Edit the `models.py` file of the `courses` application and add the following code to it:

```
class ItemBase(models.Model):
    owner = models.ForeignKey(User,
                                related_name='%(class)s_related')
    title = models.CharField(max_length=250)
    created = models.DateTimeField(auto_now_add=True)
    updated = models.DateTimeField(auto_now=True)
```

```
        class Meta:
            abstract = True

        def __str__(self):
            return self.title


    class Text(ItemBase):
        content = models.TextField()

    class File(ItemBase):
        file = models.FileField(upload_to='files')

    class Image(ItemBase):
        file = models.FileField(upload_to='images')

    class Video(ItemBase):
        url = models.URLField()
```

In this code, we define an abstract model named `ItemBase`. Therefore, we have set `abstract=True` in its `Meta` class. In this model, we define the `owner`, `title`, `created`, and `updated` fields. These common fields will be used for all types of content. The `owner` field allows us to store which user created the content. Since this field is defined in an abstract class, we need different `related_name` for each sub-model. Django allows us to specify a placeholder for the `model` class name in the `related_name` attribute as `%(class)s`. By doing so, `related_name` for each child model will be generated automatically. Since we use `'%(class)s_related'` as `related_name`, the reverse relation for child models will be `text_related`, `file_related`, `image_related`, and `video_related` respectively.

We have defined four different content models, which inherit from the `ItemBase` abstract model. These are:

- `Text`: To store text content.
- `File`: To store files, such as PDF.
- `Image`: To store image files.
- `Video`: To store videos. We use an `URLField` field to provide a video URL in order to embed it.

Each child model contains the fields defined in the `ItemBase` class in addition to its own fields. A database table will be created for the `Text`, `File`, `Image`, and `Video` models respectively. There will be no database table associated to the `ItemBase` model since it is an abstract model.

Edit the `Content` model you created previously and modify its `content_type` field as follows:

```
content_type = models.ForeignKey(ContentType,
                    limit_choices_to={'model__in':('text',
                                       'video',
                                       'image',
                                       'file')})
```

We add a `limit_choices_to` argument to limit the `ContentType` objects that can be used for the generic relationship. We use the `model__in` field lookup to filter the query to the `ContentType` objects with a `model` attribute that is `'text'`, `'video'`, `'image'` or, `'file'`.

Let's create a migration to include the new models we have added. Run the following command from the command line:

**python manage.py makemigrations**

You should see the following output:

```
Migrations for 'courses':
  0002_content_file_image_text_video.py:
    - Create model Content
    - Create model File
    - Create model Image
    - Create model Text
    - Create model Video
```

Then, run the following command to apply the new migration:

**python manage.py migrate**

The output you see should end as follows:

```
Running migrations:
  Rendering model states... DONE
  Applying courses.0002_content_file_image_text_video... OK
```

We have created models that are suitable to add diverse content to the course modules. However, there is still something missing in our models. The course modules and contents should follow a particular order. We need a field that allows us to order them easily.

# Creating custom model fields

Django comes with a complete collection of model fields that you can use to build your models. However, you can also create your own model fields to store custom data or alter the behavior of existing fields.

We need a field that allows us to specify an order for objects. If you think about an easy way to do this with a field provided by Django, you will probably think of adding a `PositiveIntegerField` to your models. This is a good starting point. We can create a custom field that inherits from `PositiveIntegerField` and provides additional behavior.

There are two relevant functionalities that we will build into our order field:

- Automatically assign an order value when no specific order is provided. When no order is provided while storing an object, our field should automatically assign the next order based on the last existing ordered object. If there are two objects with order 1 and 2 respectively, when saving a third object, we should automatically assign the order 3 to it if no specific order is given.

- Order objects with respect to other fields. Course modules will be ordered with respect to the course they belong to and module contents with respect to the module they belong to.

Create a new `fields.py` file inside the `courses` application directory and add the following code to it:

```python
from django.db import models
from django.core.exceptions import ObjectDoesNotExist

class OrderField(models.PositiveIntegerField):

    def __init__(self, for_fields=None, *args, **kwargs):
        self.for_fields = for_fields
        super(OrderField, self).__init__(*args, **kwargs)

    def pre_save(self, model_instance, add):
        if getattr(model_instance, self.attname) is None:
            # no current value
            try:
                qs = self.model.objects.all()
                if self.for_fields:
                    # filter by objects with the same field values
                    # for the fields in "for_fields"
```

```
            query = {field: getattr(model_instance, field) for
    field in self.for_fields}
                qs = qs.filter(**query)
                # get the order of the last item
                last_item = qs.latest(self.attname)
                value = last_item.order + 1
            except ObjectDoesNotExist:
                value = 0
            setattr(model_instance, self.attname, value)
            return value
        else:
            return super(OrderField,
                    self).pre_save(model_instance, add)
```

This is our custom `OrderField`. It inherits from the `PositiveIntegerField` field provided by Django. Our `OrderField` field takes an optional `for_fields` parameter that allows us to indicate the fields that the order has to be calculated with respect to.

Our field overrides the `pre_save()` method of the `PositiveIntegerField` field, which is executed before saving the field into the database. In this method, we perform the following actions:

1.  We check if a value already exists for this field in the model instance. We use `self.attname`, which is the attribute name given to the field in the model. If the attribute's value is different than None, we calculate the order we should give it as follows:

    1.  We build a QuerySet to retrieve all objects for the field's model. We retrieve the model class the field belongs to by accessing `self.model`.

    2.  We filter the QuerySet by the fields' current value for the model fields that are defined in the `for_fields` parameter of the field, if any. By doing so, we calculate the order with respect to the given fields.

    3.  We retrieve the object with the highest order with `last_item = qs.latest(self.attname)` from the database. If no object is found, we assume this object is the first one and assign the order 0 to it.

    4.  If an object is found, we add 1 to the highest order found.

    5.  We assign the calculated order to the field's value in the model instance using `setattr()` and return it.

2.  If the model instance has a value for the current field, we don't do anything.

When you create custom model fields, make them generic. Avoid hardcoding data that depends on a specific model or field. Your field should work in any model.

You can find more information about writing custom model fields at `https://docs.djangoproject.com/en/1.8/howto/custom-model-fields/`.

Let's add the new field to our models. Edit the `models.py` file of the `courses` application and import the new field as follows:

```
from .fields import OrderField
```

Then, add the following `OrderField` field to the `Module` model:

```
order = OrderField(blank=True, for_fields=['course'])
```

We name the new field `order`, and we specify that the ordering is calculated with respect to the course by setting `for_fields=['course']`. This means that the order for a new module will be assigned adding 1 to the last module of the same `Course` object. Now you can edit the `__str__()` method of the `Module` model to include its order as follows:

```
def __str__(self):
    return '{}. {}'.format(self.order, self.title)
```

Module contents also need to follow a particular order. Add an `OrderField` field to the `Content` model as follows:

```
order = OrderField(blank=True, for_fields=['module'])
```

This time, we specify that the order is calculated with respect to the `module` field. Finally, let's add a default ordering for both models. Add the following `Meta` class to the `Module` and `Content` models:

```
class Meta:
    ordering = ['order']
```

The `Module` and `Content` models should now look as follows:

```
class Module(models.Model):
    course = models.ForeignKey(Course, related_name='modules')
    title = models.CharField(max_length=200)
    description = models.TextField(blank=True)
    order = OrderField(blank=True, for_fields=['course'])
```

```
    class Meta:
        ordering = ['order']

    def __str__(self):
        return '{}. {}'.format(self.order, self.title)


class Content(models.Model):
    module = models.ForeignKey(Module, related_name='contents')
    content_type = models.ForeignKey(ContentType,
                    limit_choices_to={'model__in':('text',
                                                    'video',
                                                'file')})
    object_id = models.PositiveIntegerField()
    item = GenericForeignKey('content_type', 'object_id')
    order = OrderField(blank=True, for_fields=['module'])

    class Meta:
        ordering = ['order']
```

Let's create a new model migration that reflects the new order fields. Open the shell and run the following command:

```
python manage.py makemigrations courses
```

You will see the following output:

```
You are trying to add a non-nullable field 'order' to content without
a default; we can't do that (the database needs something to populate
existing rows).
Please select a fix:
 1) Provide a one-off default now (will be set on all existing rows)
 2) Quit, and let me add a default in models.py
Select an option:
```

Django is telling us that since we added a new field for an existing model, we have to provide a default value for existing rows in the database. If the field had `null=True`, it would accept null values and Django would create the migration without asking for a default value. We can specify a default value or cancel the migration and add a `default` attribute to the `order` field in the `models.py` file before creating the migration.

Enter 1 and press *Enter* to provide a default value for existing records. You will see the following output:

```
Please enter the default value now, as valid Python
The datetime and django.utils.timezone modules are available, so you
can do e.g. timezone.now()
>>>
```

Enter 0 so that this is the default value for existing records and press *Enter*. Django will ask you for a default value for the Module model too. Choose the first option and enter 0 as default value again. Finally, you will see an output similar to the following one:

```
Migrations for 'courses':
  0003_auto_20150701_1851.py:
    - Change Meta options on content
    - Change Meta options on module
    - Add field order to content
    - Add field order to module
```

Then, apply the new migrations with the following command:

**python manage.py migrate**

The output of the command will inform you that the migration was successfully applied as follows:

```
Applying courses.0003_auto_20150701_1851... OK
```

Let's test our new field. Open the shell using python manage.py shell and create a new course as follows:

```
>>> from django.contrib.auth.models import User
>>> from courses.models import Subject, Course, Module
>>> user = User.objects.latest('id')
>>> subject = Subject.objects.latest('id')
>>> c1 = Course.objects.create(subject=subject, owner=user,
title='Course 1', slug='course1')
```

We have created a course in the database. Now, let's add modules to the course and see how the modules' order is automatically calculated. We create an initial module and check its order:

```
>>> m1 = Module.objects.create(course=c1, title='Module 1')
>>> m1.order
0
```

`OrderField` sets its value to `0`, since this is the first `Module` object created for the given course. Now we create a second module for the same course:

```
>>> m2 = Module.objects.create(course=c1, title='Module 2')
>>> m2.order
1
```

`OrderField` calculates the next order value adding `1` to the highest order for existing objects. Let's create a third module forcing a specific order:

```
>>> m3 = Module.objects.create(course=c1, title='Module 3', order=5)
>>> m3.order
5
```

If we specify a custom order, the `OrderField` field does not interfere and the value given to the `order` is used.

Let's add a fourth module:

```
>>> m4 = Module.objects.create(course=c1, title='Module 4')
>>> m4.order
6
```

The order for this module has been automatically set. Our `OrderField` field does not guarantee that all order values are consecutive. However, it respects existing order values and always assigns the next order based on the highest existing order.

Let's create a second course and add a module to it:

```
>>> c2 = Course.objects.create(subject=subject, title='Course 2',
slug='course2', owner=user)
>>> m5 = Module.objects.create(course=c2, title='Module 1')
>>> m5.order
0
```

To calculate the new module's order, the field only takes into consideration existing modules that belong to the same course. Since this is the first module of the second course, the resulting order is `0`. This is because we specified `for_fields=['course']` in the `order` field of the `Module` model.

Congratulations! You have successfully created your first custom model field.

# Creating a content management system

Now that we have created a versatile data model, we are going to build a content management system (CMS). The CMS will allow instructors to create courses and manage their content. We need to provide the following functionality:

- Login to the CMS.
- List the courses created by the instructor.
- Create, edit, and delete courses.
- Add modules to a course and re-order them.
- Add different types of content to each module and re-order contents.

## Adding the authentication system

We are going to use Django's authentication framework in our platform. Both instructors and students will be an instance of Django's User model. Thus, they will be able to login to the site using the authentication views of django.contrib.auth.

Edit the main urls.py file of the educa project and include the login and logout views of Django's authentication framework:

```
from django.conf.urls import include, url
from django.contrib import admin
from django.contrib.auth import views as auth_views

urlpatterns = [
    url(r'^accounts/login/$', auth_views.login, name='login'),
    url(r'^accounts/logout/$', auth_views.logout, name='logout'),
    url(r'^admin/', include(admin.site.urls)),
]
```

## Creating the authentication templates

Create the following file structure inside the courses application directory:

```
templates/
    base.html
    registration/
        login.html
        logged_out.html
```

Before building the authentication templates, we need to prepare the base template for our project. Edit the `base.html` template file and add the following content to it:

```
{% load staticfiles %}
<!DOCTYPE html>
<html>
<head>
  <meta charset="utf-8" />
  <title>{% block title %}Educa{% endblock %}</title>
  <link href="{% static "css/base.css" %}" rel="stylesheet">
</head>
<body>
  <div id="header">
    <a href="/" class="logo">Educa</a>
    <ul class="menu">
      {% if request.user.is_authenticated %}
        <li><a href="{% url "logout" %}">Sign out</a></li>
      {% else %}
        <li><a href="{% url "login" %}">Sign in</a></li>
      {% endif %}
    </ul>
  </div>
  <div id="content">
    {% block content %}
    {% endblock %}
  </div>

  <script src="https://ajax.googleapis.com/ajax/libs/jquery/2.1.4/jquery.min.js"></script>
  <script>
    $(document).ready(function() {
      {% block domready %}
      {% endblock %}
    });
  </script>
</body>
</html>
```

This is the base template that will be extended by the rest of the templates. In this template, we define the following blocks:

- `title`: The block for other templates to add a custom title for each page.

- `content`: The main block for content. All templates that extend the base template should add content to this block.

- `domready`: Located inside the `$document.ready()` function of jQuery. It allows us to execute code when the DOM has finished loading.

The CSS styles used in this template are located in the `static/` directory of the `courses` application, in the code that comes along with this chapter. You can copy the `static/` directory into the same directory of your project to use them.

Edit the `registration/login.html` template and add the following code to it:

```
{% extends "base.html" %}

{% block title %}Log-in{% endblock %}

{% block content %}
  <h1>Log-in</h1>
  <div class="module">
    {% if form.errors %}
      <p>Your username and password didn't match. Please try again.</
p>
    {% else %}
      <p>Please, use the following form to log-in:</p>
    {% endif %}
    <div class="login-form">
      <form action="{% url 'login' %}" method="post">
        {{ form.as_p }}
        {% csrf_token %}
        <input type="hidden" name="next" value="{{ next }}" />
        <p><input type="submit" value="Log-in"></p>
      </form>
    </div>
  </div>
{% endblock %}
```

This is a standard login template for Django's `login` view. Edit the `registration/logged_out.html` template and add the following code to it:

```
{% extends "base.html" %}

{% block title %}Logged out{% endblock %}

{% block content %}
  <h1>Logged out</h1>
  <div class="module">
    <p>You have been successfully logged out. You can <a href="{% url
"login" %}">log-in again</a>.</p>
  </div>
{% endblock %}
```

This is the template that will be displayed to the user after logout. Run the development server with the command `python manage.py runserver` and open `http://127.0.0.1:8000/accounts/login/` in your browser. You should see the login page like this:

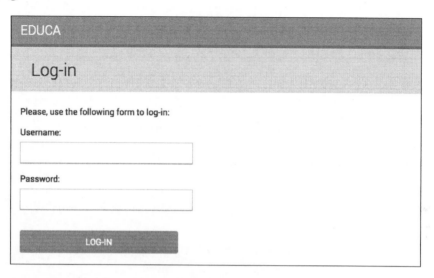

# Creating class-based views

We are going to build views to create, edit, and delete courses. We will use class-based views for this. Edit the `views.py` file of the `courses` application and add the following code to it:

```
from django.views.generic.list import ListView
from .models import Course

class ManageCourseListView(ListView):
    model = Course
    template_name = 'courses/manage/course/list.html'

    def get_queryset(self):
        qs = super(ManageCourseListView, self).get_queryset()
        return qs.filter(owner=self.request.user)
```

This is the `ManageCourseListView` view. It inherits from Django's generic `ListView`. We override the `get_queryset()` method of the view to retrieve only courses created by the current user. To prevent users from editing, updating, or deleting courses they didn't create, we will also need to override the `get_queryset()` method in the create, update, and delete views. When you need to provide a specific behavior for several class-based views, it is recommended to use *mixins*.

# Using mixins for class-based views

Mixins are a special kind of multiple inheritance for a class. You can use them to provide common discrete functionality that, added to other mixins, allows you to define the behavior of a class. There are two main situations to use mixins:

- You want to provide multiple optional features for a class
- You want to use a particular feature in several classes

You can find documentation about how to use mixins with class-based views at `https://docs.djangoproject.com/en/1.8/topics/class-based-views/mixins/`.

Django comes with several mixins that provide additional functionality to your class-based views. You can find all mixins at `https://docs.djangoproject.com/en/1.8/ref/class-based-views/mixins/`.

We are going to create a mixin class that includes a common behavior and use it for the course's views. Edit the `views.py` file of the `courses` application and modify it as follows:

```python
from django.core.urlresolvers import reverse_lazy
from django.views.generic.list import ListView
from django.views.generic.edit import CreateView, UpdateView, \
                                       DeleteView
from .models import Course


class OwnerMixin(object):
    def get_queryset(self):
        qs = super(OwnerMixin, self).get_queryset()
        return qs.filter(owner=self.request.user)


class OwnerEditMixin(object):
    def form_valid(self, form):
        form.instance.owner = self.request.user
        return super(OwnerEditMixin, self).form_valid(form)


class OwnerCourseMixin(OwnerMixin):
    model = Course


class OwnerCourseEditMixin(OwnerCourseMixin, OwnerEditMixin):
    fields = ['subject', 'title', 'slug', 'overview']
    success_url = reverse_lazy('manage_course_list')
    template_name = 'courses/manage/course/form.html'
```

```
class ManageCourseListView(OwnerCourseMixin, ListView):
    template_name = 'courses/manage/course/list.html'

class CourseCreateView(OwnerCourseEditMixin, CreateView):
    pass

class CourseUpdateView(OwnerCourseEditMixin, UpdateView):
    pass

class CourseDeleteView(OwnerCourseMixin, DeleteView):
    template_name = 'courses/manage/course/delete.html'
    success_url = reverse_lazy('manage_course_list')
```

In this code, we create the `OwnerMixin` and `OwnerEditMixin` mixins. We will use these mixins together with the `ListView`, `CreateView`, `UpdateView`, and `DeleteView` views provided by Django. `OwnerMixin` implements the following method:

- `get_queryset()`: This method is used by the views to get the base QuerySet. Our mixin will override this method to filter objects by the `owner` attribute to retrieve objects that belong to the current user (`request.user`).

`OwnerEditMixin` implements the following method:

- `form_valid()`: This method is used by views that use Django's `ModelFormMixin` mixin, i.e., views with forms or modelforms such as `CreateView` and `UpdateView`. `form_valid()` is executed when the submitted form is valid. The default behavior for this method is saving the instance (for modelforms) and redirecting the user to `success_url`. We override this method to automatically set the current user in the `owner` attribute of the object being saved. By doing so, we set the owner for an object automatically when it is saved.

Our `OwnerMixin` class can be used for views that interact with any model that contains an `owner` attribute.

We also define an `OwnerCourseMixin` class that inherits `OwnerMixin` and provides the following attribute for child views:

- `model`: The model used for QuerySets. Used by all views.

We define a `OwnerCourseEditMixin` mixin with the following attributes:

- `fields`: The fields of the model to build the model form of the `CreateView` and `UpdateView` views.

- `success_url`: Used by `CreateView` and `UpdateView` to redirect the user after the form is successfully submitted. We use a URL with the name `manage_course_list` that we are going to create later.

Finally, we create the following views that subclass `OwnerCourseMixin`:

- `ManageCourseListView`: Lists the courses created by the user. It inherits from `OwnerCourseMixin` and `ListView`.

- `CourseCreateView`: Uses a modelform to create a new `Course` object. It uses the fields defined in `OwnerCourseEditMixin` to build a model form and also subclasses `CreateView`.

- `CourseUpdateView`: Allows editing an existing `Course` object. It inherits from `OwnerCourseEditMixin` and `UpdateView`.

- `CourseDeleteView`: Inherits from `OwnerCourseMixin` and the generic `DeleteView`. Defines `success_url` to redirect the user after the object is deleted.

# Working with groups and permissions

We have created the basic views to manage courses. Currently, any user could access these views. We want to restrict these views so that only instructors have permission to create and manage courses. Django's authentication framework includes a permission system that allows you to assign permissions to users and groups. We are going to create a group for instructor users and assign permissions to create, update, and delete courses.

Run the development server using the command `python manage.py runserver` and open `http://127.0.0.1:8000/admin/auth/group/add/` in your browser to create a new `Group` object. Add the name *Instructors* and choose all permissions of the `courses` application except those of the `Subject` model as follows:

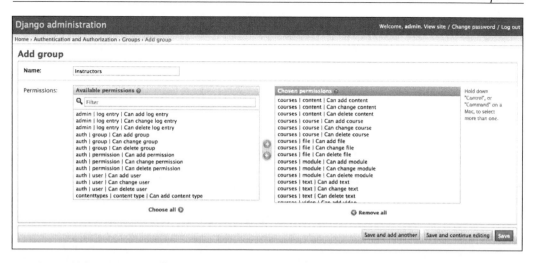

As you can see, there are three different permissions for each model: **Can add**, **can change**, and **Can delete**. After choosing permissions for this group, click the **Save** button.

Django creates permissions for models automatically, but you can also create custom permissions. You can read more about adding custom permissions at `https://docs.djangoproject.com/en/1.8/topics/auth/customizing/#custom-permissions`.

Open `http://127.0.0.1:8000/admin/auth/user/add/` and create a new user. Edit the user and add the **Instructors** group to it as follows:

Users inherit the permissions of the groups they belong to, but you can also add individual permissions to a single user using the administration site. Users that have `is_superuser` set to `True` have all permissions automatically.

# Restricting access to class-based views

We are going to restrict access to the views so that only users with the appropriate permissions can add, change, or delete `Course` objects. The authentication framework includes a `permission_required` decorator to restrict access to views. Django 1.9 will include permission mixins for class-based views. However, Django 1.8 does not include them. Therefore, we are going to use permission mixins provided by a third-party module named django-braces.

# Using mixins from django-braces

Django-braces is a third-party module that contains a collection of generic mixins for Django. These mixins provide additional features for class-based views. You can see a list of all mixins provided by django-braces at `http://django-braces.readthedocs.org/en/latest/`.

Install django-braces via pip using the command:

```
pip install django-braces==1.8.1
```

We are going to use the following two mixins from django-braces to limit access to views:

- `LoginRequiredMixin`: Replicates the `login_required` decorator's functionality.
- `PermissionRequiredMixin`: Grants access to the view to users that have a specific permission. Remember that superusers automatically have all permissions.

Edit the `views.py` file of the `courses` application and add the following import:

```
from braces.views import LoginRequiredMixin,
                         PermissionRequiredMixin
```

Make `OwnerCourseMixin` inherit `LoginRequiredMixin` like this:

```
class OwnerCourseMixin(OwnerMixin, LoginRequiredMixin):
    model = Course
    fields = ['subject', 'title', 'slug', 'overview']
    success_url = reverse_lazy('manage_course_list')
```

Then, add a `permission_required` attribute to the create, update, and delete views, as follows:

```
class CourseCreateView(PermissionRequiredMixin,
                       OwnerCourseEditMixin,
                       CreateView):
    permission_required = 'courses.add_course'

class CourseUpdateView(PermissionRequiredMixin,
                       OwnerCourseEditMixin,
                       UpdateView):
    template_name = 'courses/manage/course/form.html'
    permission_required = 'courses.change_course'
```

```
class CourseDeleteView(PermissionRequiredMixin,
                       OwnerCourseMixin,
                       DeleteView):
    template_name = 'courses/manage/course/delete.html'
    success_url = reverse_lazy('manage_course_list')
    permission_required = 'courses.delete_course'
```

`PermissionRequiredMixin` checks that the user accessing the view has the permission specified in the `permission_required` attribute. Our views are now only accessible to users that have proper permissions.

Let's create URLs for these views. Create a new file inside the `courses` application directory and name it `urls.py`. Add the following code to it:

```
from django.conf.urls import url
from . import views

urlpatterns = [
    url(r'^mine/$',
        views.ManageCourseListView.as_view(),
        name='manage_course_list'),
    url(r'^create/$',
        views.CourseCreateView.as_view(),
        name='course_create'),
    url(r'^(?P<pk>\d+)/edit/$',
        views.CourseUpdateView.as_view(),
        name='course_edit'),
    url(r'^(?P<pk>\d+)/delete/$',
        views.CourseDeleteView.as_view(),
        name='course_delete'),
]
```

These are the URL patterns for the list, create, edit, and delete course views. Edit the main `urls.py` file of the `educa` project and include the URL patterns of the `courses` application as follows:

```
urlpatterns = [
    url(r'^accounts/login/$', auth_views.login, name='login'),
    url(r'^accounts/logout/$', auth_views.logout, name='logout'),
    url(r'^admin/', include(admin.site.urls)),
    url(r'^course/', include('courses.urls')),
]
```

We need to create the templates for these views. Create the following directories and files inside the `templates/` directory of the `courses` application:

```
courses/
    manage/
        course/
            list.html
            form.html
            delete.html
```

Edit the `courses/manage/course/list.html` template and add the following code to it:

```
{% extends "base.html" %}

{% block title %}My courses{% endblock %}

{% block content %}
  <h1>My courses</h1>

  <div class="module">
    {% for course in object_list %}
      <div class="course-info">
        <h3>{{ course.title }}</h3>
        <p>
          <a href="{% url "course_edit" course.id %}">Edit</a>
          <a href="{% url "course_delete" course.id %}">Delete</a>
        </p>
      </div>
    {% empty %}
      <p>You haven't created any courses yet.</p>
    {% endfor %}
    <p>
      <a href="{% url "course_create" %}" class="button">Create new
course</a>
    </p>
  </div>
{% endblock %}
```

This is the template for the `ManageCourseListView` view. In this template, we list the courses created by the current user. We include links to edit or delete each course, and a link to create new courses.

Run the development server using the command `python manage.py runserver`. Open `http://127.0.0.1:8000/accounts/login/?next=/course/mine/` in your browser and log in with a user that belongs to the `Instructors` group. After logging in, you will be redirected to the URL `http://127.0.0.1:8000/course/mine/` and you should see the following page:

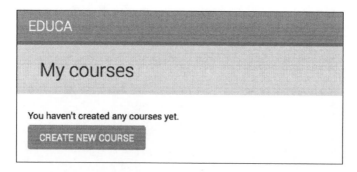

This page will display all courses created by the current user.

Let's create the template that displays the form for the create and update course views. Edit the `courses/manage/course/form.html` template and write the following code:

```
{% extends "base.html" %}

{% block title %}
  {% if object %}
    Edit course "{{ object.title }}"
  {% else %}
    Create a new course
  {% endif %}
{% endblock %}

{% block content %}
  <h1>
    {% if object %}
      Edit course "{{ object.title }}"
    {% else %}
      Create a new course
    {% endif %}
  </h1>
  <div class="module">
    <h2>Course info</h2>
    <form action="." method="post">
      {{ form.as_p }}
```

```
        {% csrf_token %}
        <p><input type="submit" value="Save course"></p>
    </form>
  </div>
{% endblock %}
```

The `form.html` template is used for both the `CourseCreateView` and `CourseUpdateView` views. In this template, we check if an `object` variable is in the context. If `object` exists in the context, we know that we are updating an existing course, and we use it in the page title. Otherwise, we are creating a new `Course` object.

Open `http://127.0.0.1:8000/course/mine/` in your browser and click the **Create new course** button. You will see the following page:

Fill in the form and click the **Save course** button. The course will be saved and you will be redirected to the course list page. It should look as follows:

Then, click the **Edit** link for the course you have just created. You will see the form again, but this time you are editing an existing `Course` object instead of creating one.

Finally, edit the `courses/manage/course/delete.html` template and add the following code:

```
{% extends "base.html" %}

{% block title %}Delete course{% endblock %}

{% block content %}
  <h1>Delete course "{{ object.title }}"</h1>

  <div class="module">
    <form action="" method="post">
      {% csrf_token %}
      <p>Are you sure you want to delete "{{ object }}"?</p>
      <input type="submit" class"button" value="Confirm">
    </form>
  </div>
{% endblock %}
```

This is the template for the `CourseDeleteView` view. This view inherits from `DeleteView` provided by Django, which expects user confirmation to delete an object.

Open your browser and click the **Delete** link of your course. You should see the following confirmation page:

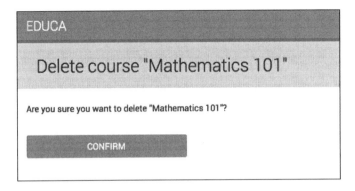

Click the **CONFIRM** button. The course will be deleted and you will be redirected to the course list page again.

Instructors can now create, edit, and delete courses. Next, we need to provide them with a content management system to add modules and contents to courses. We will start by managing course modules.

# Using formsets

Django comes with an abstraction layer to work with multiple forms on the same page. These groups of forms are known as formsets. Formsets manage multiple instances of certain Form or ModelForm. All forms are submitted at once and the formset takes care of things like the initial number of forms to display, limiting the maximum number of forms that can be submitted, and validating all forms.

Formsets include an is_valid() method to validate all forms at once. You can also provide initial data for the forms and specify how many additional empty forms to display.

You can learn more about formsets at https://docs.djangoproject.com/en/1.8/topics/forms/formsets/, and about model formsets at https://docs.djangoproject.com/en/1.8/topics/forms/modelforms/#model-formsets.

# Managing course modules

Since a course is divided into a variable number of modules, it makes sense to use formsets here. Create a `forms.py` file in the `courses` application directory and add the following code to it:

```
from django import forms
from django.forms.models import inlineformset_factory
from .models import Course, Module

ModuleFormSet = inlineformset_factory(Course,
                                      Module,
                                      fields=['title',
                                              'description'],
                                      extra=2,
                                      can_delete=True)
```

This is the `ModuleFormSet` formset. We build it using the `inlineformset_factory()` function provided by Django. Inline formsets is a small abstraction on top of formsets that simplifies working with related objects. This function allows us to build a model formset dynamically for the `Module` objects related to a `Course` object.

We use the following parameters to build the formset:

- `fields`: The fields that will be included in each form of the formset.

- `extra`: Allows us to set up the number of empty extra forms to display in the formset.

- `can_delete`: If you set this to `True`, Django will include a Boolean field for each form that will be rendered as a checkbox input. It allows you to mark the objects you want to delete.

Edit the `views.py` file of the `courses` application and add the following code to it:

```
from django.shortcuts import redirect, get_object_or_404
from django.views.generic.base import TemplateResponseMixin, View
from .forms import ModuleFormSet

class CourseModuleUpdateView(TemplateResponseMixin, View):
    template_name = 'courses/manage/module/formset.html'
    course = None

    def get_formset(self, data=None):
        return ModuleFormSet(instance=self.course,
                             data=data)
```

```
        def dispatch(self, request, pk):
            self.course = get_object_or_404(Course,
                                            id=pk,
                                            owner=request.user)
            return super(CourseModuleUpdateView,
                         self).dispatch(request, pk)

        def get(self, request, *args, **kwargs):
            formset = self.get_formset()
            return self.render_to_response({'course': self.course,
                                            'formset': formset})

        def post(self, request, *args, **kwargs):
            formset = self.get_formset(data=request.POST)
            if formset.is_valid():
                formset.save()
                return redirect('manage_course_list')
            return self.render_to_response({'course': self.course,
                                            'formset': formset})
```

The `CourseModuleUpdateView` view handles the formset to add, update, and delete modules for a specific course. This view inherits from the following mixins and views:

- `TemplateResponseMixin`: This mixin takes charge of rendering templates and returning an HTTP response. It requires a `template_name` attribute that indicates the template to be rendered and provides the `render_to_response()` method to pass it a context and render the template.

- `View`: The basic class-based view provided by Django.

In this view, we implement the following methods:

- `get_formset()`: We define this method to avoid repeating the code to build the formset. We create a `ModuleFormSet` object for the given `Course` object with optional data.

- `dispatch()`: This method is provided by the `View` class. It takes an HTTP request and its parameters and attempts to delegate to a lowercase method that matches the HTTP method used: A GET request is delegated to the `get()` method and a POST request to `post()` respectively. In this method, we use the `get_object_or_404()` shortcut function to get the `Course` object for the given `id` parameter that belongs to the current user. We include this code in the `dispatch()` method because we need to retrieve the course for both GET and POST requests. We save it into the `course` attribute of the view to make it accessible to other methods.

- `get()`: Executed for GET requests. We build an empty `ModuleFormSet` formset and render it to the template together with the current `Course` object using the `render_to_response()` method provided by `TemplateResponseMixin`.

- `post()`: Executed for POST requests. In this method, we perform the following actions:

  1. We build a `ModuleFormSet` instance using the submitted data.

  2. We execute the `is_valid()` method of the formset to validate all of its forms.

  3. If the formset is valid, we save it by calling the `save()` method. At this point, any changes made, such as adding, updating, or marking modules for deletion, are applied to the database. Then, we redirect users to the `manage_course_list` URL. If the formset is not valid, we render the template to display any errors instead.

Edit the `urls.py` file of the `courses` application and add the following URL pattern to it:

```
url(r'^(?P<pk>\d+)/module/$',
    views.CourseModuleUpdateView.as_view(),
    name='course_module_update'),
```

Create a new directory inside the `courses/manage/` template directory and name it `module`. Create a `courses/manage/module/formset.html` template and add the following code to it:

```html
{% extends "base.html" %}

{% block title %}
  Edit "{{ course.title }}"
{% endblock %}

{% block content %}
  <h1>Edit "{{ course.title }}"</h1>
  <div class="module">
    <h2>Course modules</h2>
    <form action="" method="post">
      {{ formset }}
      {{ formset.management_form }}
      {% csrf_token %}
      <input type="submit" class="button" value="Save modules">
    </form>
  </div>
{% endblock %}
```

In this template, we create a `<form>` HTML element, in which we include our formset. We also include the management form for the formset with the variable `{{ formset.management_form }}`. The management form includes hidden fields to control the initial, total, minimum, and maximum number of forms. As you can see, it's very easy to create a formset.

Edit the `courses/manage/course/list.html` template and add the following link for the `course_module_update` URL below the course edit and delete links:

```
<a href="{% url "course_edit" course.id %}">Edit</a>
<a href="{% url "course_delete" course.id %}">Delete</a>
<a href="{% url "course_module_update" course.id %}">Edit modules</a>
```

We have included the link to edit the course modules. Open `http://127.0.0.1:8000/course/mine/` in your browser and click the **Edit modules** link for a course. You should see a formset as follows:

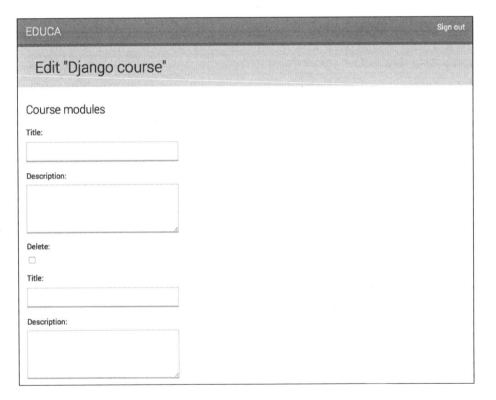

The formset includes a form for each `Module` object contained in the course. After these, two empty extra forms are displayed because we set `extra=2` for `ModuleFormSet`. When you save the formset, Django will include another two extra fields to add new modules.

# Adding content to course modules

Now, we need a way to add content to course modules. We have four different types of content: Text, Video, Image, and File. We can consider creating four different views to create content, one for each model. Yet, we are going to take a more generic approach and create a view that handles creating or updating objects of any content model.

Edit the `views.py` file of the `courses` application and add the following code to it:

```python
from django.forms.models import modelform_factory
from django.apps import apps
from .models import Module, Content


class ContentCreateUpdateView(TemplateResponseMixin, View):
    module = None
    model = None
    obj = None
    template_name = 'courses/manage/content/form.html'

    def get_model(self, model_name):
        if model_name in ['text', 'video', 'image', 'file']:
            return apps.get_model(app_label='courses',
                                  model_name=model_name)
        return None

    def get_form(self, model, *args, **kwargs):
        Form = modelform_factory(model, exclude=['owner',
                                                 'order',
                                                 'created',
                                                 'updated'])
        return Form(*args, **kwargs)

    def dispatch(self, request, module_id, model_name, id=None):
        self.module = get_object_or_404(Module,
                                        id=module_id,
                                        course__owner=request.user)
        self.model = self.get_model(model_name)
        if id:
            self.obj = get_object_or_404(self.model,
                                         id=id,
                                         owner=request.user)
        return super(ContentCreateUpdateView,
            self).dispatch(request, module_id, model_name, id)
```

This is the first part of `ContentCreateUpdateView`. It will allow us to create and update contents of different models. This view defines the following methods:

- `get_model()`: Here, we check that the given model name is one of the four content models: text, video, image, or file. Then we use Django's `apps` module to obtain the actual class for the given model name. If the given model name is not one of the valid ones, we return `None`.

- `get_form()`: We build a dynamic form using the `modelform_factory()` function of the form's framework. Since we are going to build a form for the `Text`, `Video`, `Image`, and `File` models, we use the `exclude` parameter to specify the common fields to exclude from the form and let all other attributes be included automatically. By doing so, we don't have to know which fields to include depending on the model.

- `dispatch()`: It receives the following URL parameters and stores the corresponding module, model, and content object as class attributes:
  - `module_id`: The `id` for the module that the content is/will be associated with.
  - `model_name`: The model name of the content to create/update.
  - `id`: The id of the object that is being updated. It's `None` to create new objects.

Add the following `get()` and `post()` methods to `ContentCreateUpdateView`:

```
def get(self, request, module_id, model_name, id=None):
    form = self.get_form(self.model, instance=self.obj)
    return self.render_to_response({'form': form,
                                    'object': self.obj})


def post(self, request, module_id, model_name, id=None):
    form = self.get_form(self.model,
                         instance=self.obj,
                         data=request.POST,
                         files=request.FILES)
    if form.is_valid():
        obj = form.save(commit=False)
        obj.owner = request.user
        obj.save()
        if not id:
            # new content
            Content.objects.create(module=self.module,
```

```
                              item=obj)
         return redirect('module_content_list', self.module.id)

        return self.render_to_response({'form': form,
                                        'object': self.obj})
```

These methods are as follows:

- `get()`: Executed when a GET request is received. We build the model form for the `Text`, `Video`, `Image`, or `File` instance that is being updated. Otherwise, we pass no instance to create a new object, since `self.obj` is `None` if no id is provided.

- `post()`: Executed when a POST request is received. We build the modelform passing any submitted data and files to it. Then we validate it. If the form is valid, we create a new object and assign `request.user` as its owner before saving it to the database. We check for the `id` parameter. If no `id` is provided, we know the user is creating a new object instead of updating an existing one. If this is a new object, we create a `Content` object for the given module and associate the new content to it.

Edit the `urls.py` file of the `courses` application and add the following URL patterns to it:

```
url(r'^module/(?P<module_id>\d+)/content/(?P<model_name>\w+)/
create/$',
    views.ContentCreateUpdateView.as_view(),
    name='module_content_create'),
url(r'^module/(?P<module_id>\d+)/content/(?P<model_name>\w+)/(?P<id>\
d+)/$',
    views.ContentCreateUpdateView.as_view(),
    name='module_content_update'),
```

The new URL patterns are:

- `module_content_create`: To create new text, video, image, or file objects and adding them to a module. It includes the `module_id` and `model_name` parameters. The first one allows linking the new content object to the given module. The latter specifies the content model to build the form for.

- `module_content_update`: To update an existing text, video, image, or file object. It includes the `module_id` and `model_name` parameters, and an `id` parameter to identify the content that is being updated.

Create a new directory inside the `courses/manage/` template directory and name it `content`. Create the template `courses/manage/content/form.html` and add the following code to it:

```
{% extends "base.html" %}

{% block title %}
  {% if object %}
    Edit content "{{ object.title }}"
  {% else %}
    Add a new content
  {% endif %}
{% endblock %}

{% block content %}
  <h1>
    {% if object %}
      Edit content "{{ object.title }}"
    {% else %}
      Add a new content
    {% endif %}
  </h1>
  <div class="module">
    <h2>Course info</h2>
    <form action="" method="post" enctype="multipart/form-data">
      {{ form.as_p }}
      {% csrf_token %}
      <p><input type="submit" value="Save content"></p>
    </form>
  </div>
{% endblock %}
```

This is the template for the `ContentCreateUpdateView` view. In this template, we check if an `object` variable is in the context. If `object` exists in the context, we know that we are updating an existing object. Otherwise, we are creating a new object.

We include `enctype="multipart/form-data"` to the `<form>` HTML element, because the form contains a file upload for the `File` and `Image` content models.

Run the development server. Create a module for an existing course and open
`http://127.0.0.1:8000/course/module/6/content/image/create/` in your
browser. Change the module id in the URL if necessary. You will see the form to
create an `Image` object as follows:

## Add a new content

### Course info

Title:

File:

Choose File   no file selected

SAVE CONTENT

Don't submit the form yet. If you try to do so, it will fail because we haven't defined
the `module_content_list` URL yet. We are going to create it in a bit.

We also need a view to delete contents. Edit the `views.py` file of the `courses`
application and add the following code:

```
class ContentDeleteView(View):

    def post(self, request, id):
        content = get_object_or_404(Content,
                            id=id,
                            module__course__owner=request.user)
        module = content.module
        content.item.delete()
        content.delete()
        return redirect('module_content_list', module.id)
```

The `ContentDeleteView` retrieves the `Content` object with the given `id`, it deletes
the related `Text`, `Video`, `Image`, or `File` object, and finally, it deletes the `Content`
object and redirects the user to the `module_content_list` URL to list the other
contents of the module.

Edit the `urls.py` file of the `courses` application and add the following URL pattern to it:

```
url(r'^content/(?P<id>\d+)/delete/$',
    views.ContentDeleteView.as_view(),
    name='module_content_delete'),
```

Now, instructors can create, update, and delete contents easily.

# Managing modules and contents

We have built views to create, edit, and delete course modules and contents. Now, we need a view to display all modules for a course and list contents for a specific module.

Edit the `views.py` file of the `courses` application and add the following code to it:

```
class ModuleContentListView(TemplateResponseMixin, View):
    template_name = 'courses/manage/module/content_list.html'

    def get(self, request, module_id):
        module = get_object_or_404(Module,
                                    id=module_id,
                                    course__owner=request.user)

        return self.render_to_response({'module': module})
```

This is `ModuleContentListView`. This view gets the `Module` object with the given `id` that belongs to the current user and renders a template with the given module.

Edit the `urls.py` file of the `courses` application and add the following URL pattern to it:

```
url(r'^module/(?P<module_id>\d+)/$',
    views.ModuleContentListView.as_view(),
    name='module_content_list'),
```

Create a new template inside the `templates/courses/manage/module/` directory and name it `content_list.html`. Add the following code to it:

```
{% extends "base.html" %}

{% block title %}
  Module {{ module.order|add:1 }}: {{ module.title }}
{% endblock %}
```

```
{% block content %}
{% with course=module.course %}
  <h1>Course "{{ course.title }}"</h1>
  <div class="contents">
    <h3>Modules</h3>
    <ul id="modules">
      {% for m in course.modules.all %}
        <li data-id="{{ m.id }}" {% if m == module %}
class="selected"{% endif %}>
          <a href="{% url "module_content_list" m.id %}">
            <span>
              Module <span class="order">{{ m.order|add:1 }}</span>
            </span>
            <br>
            {{ m.title }}
          </a>
        </li>
      {% empty %}
        <li>No modules yet.</li>
      {% endfor %}
    </ul>
    <p><a href="{% url "course_module_update" course.id %}">Edit
modules</a></p>
  </div>
  <div class="module">
    <h2>Module {{ module.order|add:1 }}: {{ module.title }}</h2>
    <h3>Module contents:</h3>

    <div id="module-contents">
      {% for content in module.contents.all %}
        <div data-id="{{ content.id }}">
          {% with item=content.item %}
            <p>{{ item }}</p>
            <a href="#">Edit</a>
            <form action="{% url "module_content_delete" content.id
%}" method="post">
              <input type="submit" value="Delete">
              {% csrf_token %}
            </form>
          {% endwith %}
        </div>
      {% empty %}
        <p>This module has no contents yet.</p>
      {% endfor %}
```

```
      </div>
      <hr>
      <h3>Add new content:</h3>
      <ul class="content-types">
          <li><a href="{% url "module_content_create" module.id "text"
  %}">Text</a></li>
          <li><a href="{% url "module_content_create" module.id "image"
  %}">Image</a></li>
          <li><a href="{% url "module_content_create" module.id "video"
  %}">Video</a></li>
          <li><a href="{% url "module_content_create" module.id "file"
  %}">File</a></li>
      </ul>
    </div>
  {% endwith %}
  {% endblock %}
```

This is the template that displays all modules for a course and the contents for the selected module. We iterate over the course modules to display them in a sidebar. We also iterate over the module's contents and access content.item to get the related Text, Video, Image, or File object. We also include links to create new text, video, image, or file contents.

We want to know which type of object each of the item object is: Text, Video, Image, or File. We need the model name to build the URL to edit the object. Besides this, we could display each item in the template differently, based on the type of content it is. We can get the model for an object from the model's Meta class, by accessing the object's _meta attribute. Nevertheless, Django doesn't allow accessing variables or attributes starting with underscore in templates to prevent retrieving private attributes or calling private methods. We can solve this by writing a custom template filter.

Create the following file structure inside the courses application directory:

```
templatetags/
    __init__.py
    course.py
```

Edit the course.py module and add the following code to it:

```python
from django import template

register = template.Library()


@register.filter
def model_name(obj):
```

```
try:
    return obj._meta.model_name
except AttributeError:
    return None
```

This is the `model_name` template filter. We can apply it in templates as `object|model_name` to get the model's name for an object.

Edit the `templates/courses/manage/module/content_list.html` template and add the following line after the `{% extends %}` template tag:

```
{% load course %}
```

This will load the `course` template tags. Then, replace the following lines:

```
<p>{{ item }}</p>
<a href="#">Edit</a>
```

...with the following ones:

```
<p>{{ item }} ({{ item|model_name }})</p>
<a href="{% url "module_content_update" module.id item|model_name
item.id %}">Edit</a>
```

Now, we display the item model in the template and use the model name to build the link to edit the object. Edit the `courses/manage/course/list.html` template and add a link to the `module_content_list` URL like this:

```
<a href="{% url "course_module_update" course.id %}">Edit modules</a>
{% if course.modules.count > 0 %}
  <a href="{% url "module_content_list" course.modules.first.id
%}">Manage contents</a>
{% endif %}
```

The new link allows users to access the contents of the first module of the course, if any.

Open `http://127.0.0.1:8000/course/mine/` and click the **Manage contents** link for a course that contains at least one module. You will see a page like the following one:

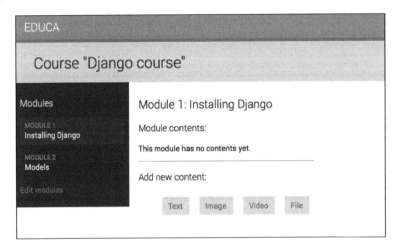

When you click on a module in the left sidebar, its contents are displayed in the main area. The template also includes links to add a new text, video, image, or file content for the module being displayed. Add a couple of different contents to the module and take a look at the result. The contents will appear after **Module contents** like the following example:

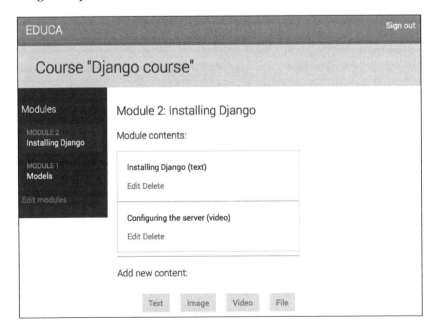

# Reordering modules and contents

We need to offer a simple way to re-order course modules and their contents. We will use a JavaScript drag-n-drop widget to let our users reorder the modules of a course by dragging them. When users finish dragging a module, we will launch an asynchronous request (AJAX) to store the new module order.

We need a view that receives the new order of modules' id encoded in JSON. Edit the `views.py` file of the `courses` application and add the following code to it:

```
from braces.views import CsrfExemptMixin, JsonRequestResponseMixin

class ModuleOrderView(CsrfExemptMixin,
                      JsonRequestResponseMixin,
                      View):
    def post(self, request):
        for id, order in self.request_json.items():
            Module.objects.filter(id=id,
                    course__owner=request.user).update(order=order)
        return self.render_json_response({'saved': 'OK'})
```

This is `ModuleOrderView`. We use the following mixins of django-braces:

- `CsrfExemptMixin`: To avoid checking for a CSRF token in POST requests. We need this to perform AJAX POST requests without having to generate `csrf_token`.

- `JsonRequestResponseMixin`: Parses the request data as JSON and also serializes the response as JSON and returns an HTTP response with the `application/json` content type.

We can build a similar view to order a module's contents. Add the following code to the `views.py` file:

```
class ContentOrderView(CsrfExemptMixin,
                       JsonRequestResponseMixin,
                       View):
    def post(self, request):
        for id, order in self.request_json.items():
            Content.objects.filter(id=id,
                        module__course__owner=request.user) \
                    .update(order=order)
        return self.render_json_response({'saved': 'OK'})
```

Now, edit the `urls.py` file of the `courses` application and add the following URL patterns to it:

```
url(r'^module/order/$',
    views.ModuleOrderView.as_view(),
    name='module_order'),
url(r'^content/order/$',
    views.ContentOrderView.as_view(),
    name='content_order'),
```

Finally, we need to implement the drag-n-drop functionality in the template. We will use the jQuery UI library for this. jQuery UI is built on top of jQuery and it provides a set of interface interactions, effects, and widgets. We will use its `sortable` element. First, we need to load jQuery UI in the base template. Open the `base.html` file located in the `templates/` directory of the `courses` application, and add jQuery UI below the script to load jQuery, as follows:

```
<script src="https://ajax.googleapis.com/ajax/libs/jquery/2.1.4/
jquery.min.js"></script>
<script src="https://ajax.googleapis.com/ajax/libs/jqueryui/1.11.4/
jquery-ui.min.js"></script>
```

We load the jQuery UI library just after the jQuery framework. Now, edit the `courses/manage/module/content_list.html` template and add the following code to it at the bottom of the template:

```
{% block domready %}
$('#modules').sortable({
    stop: function(event, ui) {
        modules_order = {};
        $('#modules').children().each(function(){
            // update the order field
            $(this).find('.order').text($(this).index() + 1);
            // associate the module's id with its order
            modules_order[$(this).data('id')] = $(this).index();
        });
        $.ajax({
            type: 'POST',
            url: '{% url "module_order" %}',
            contentType: 'application/json; charset=utf-8',
            dataType: 'json',
            data: JSON.stringify(modules_order)
        });
    }
});
```

```
$('#module-contents').sortable({
    stop: function(event, ui) {
        contents_order = {};
        $('#module-contents').children().each(function(){
            // associate the module's id with its order
            contents_order[$(this).data('id')] = $(this).index();
        });

        $.ajax({
            type: 'POST',
            url: '{% url "content_order" %}',
            contentType: 'application/json; charset=utf-8',
            dataType: 'json',
            data: JSON.stringify(contents_order),
        });
    }
});
{% endblock %}
```

This JavaScript code is in the {% block domready %} block and therefore it will be included inside the $(document).ready() event of jQuery that we defined in the base.html template. This guarantees that our JavaScript code is executed once the page has been loaded. We define a sortable element for the modules list in the sidebar and a different one for the module's content list. Both work in a similar manner. In this code, we perform the following tasks:

1. First, we define a sortable element for the modules HTML element. Remember that we use #modules, since jQuery uses CSS notation for selectors.

2. We specify a function for the stop event. This event is triggered every time the user finishes sorting an element.

3. We create an empty modules_order dictionary. The keys for this dictionary will be the modules' id, and the values will be the assigned order for each module.

4. We iterate over the #module children elements. We recalculate the displayed order for each module and get its data-id attribute, which contains the module's id. We add the id as key of the modules_order dictionary and the new index of module as the value.

5. We launch an AJAX POST request to the content_order URL, including the serialized JSON data of modules_order in the request. The corresponding ModuleOrderView takes care of updating the modules order.

The `sortable` element to order contents is quite similar to this one. Go back to your browser and reload the page. Now you will be able to click and drag both, modules and contents, to reorder them like the following example:

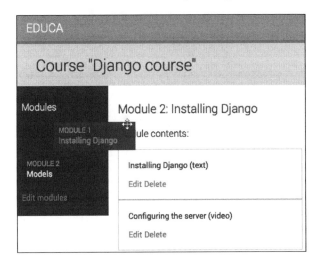

Great! Now you can re-order both course modules and module contents.

# Summary

In this chapter, you learned how to create a versatile content management system. You used model inheritance and created a custom model field. You also worked with class-based views and mixins. You created formsets and a system to manage diverse types of contents.

In the next chapter, you will create a student registration system. You will also render different kinds of contents, and you will learn how to work with Django's cache framework.

# 11
# Caching Content

In the previous chapter, you used model inheritance and generic relationships to create flexible course content models. You also built a course management system using class-based views, formsets and AJAX ordering for contents. In this chapter, you will:

- Create public views for displaying course information
- Build a student registration system
- Manage student enrollment in `courses`
- Render diverse course contents
- Cache content using the cache framework

We will start by creating a course catalog for students to browse existing courses and be able to enroll in them.

## Displaying courses

For our course catalog we have to build the following functionality:

- List all available courses, optionally filtered by subject
- Display a single course overview

Edit the `views.py` file of the courses application and add the following code:

```
from django.db.models import Count
from .models import Subject

class CourseListView(TemplateResponseMixin, View):
    model = Course
    template_name = 'courses/course/list.html'
```

```
def get(self, request, subject=None):
    subjects = Subject.objects.annotate(
                  total_courses=Count('courses'))
    courses = Course.objects.annotate(
                  total_modules=Count('modules'))
    if subject:
        subject = get_object_or_404(Subject, slug=subject)
        courses = courses.filter(subject=subject)
    return self.render_to_response({'subjects': subjects,
                                    'subject': subject,
                                    'courses': courses})
```

This is the `CourseListView`. It inherits from `TemplateResponseMixin` and `View`. In this view, we perform the following tasks:

1. We retrieve all subjects, including the total number of courses for each of them. We use the ORM's `annotate()` method with the `Count()` aggregation function for doing so.

2. We retrieve all available courses, including the total number of modules contained in each course.

3. If a subject slug URL parameter is given we retrieve the corresponding subject object and we limit the query to the courses that belong to the given subject.

4. We use the `render_to_response()` method provided by `TemplateResponseMixin` to render the objects to a template and return an HTTP response.

Let's create a detail view for displaying a single course overview. Add the following code to the `views.py` file:

```
from django.views.generic.detail import DetailView

class CourseDetailView(DetailView):
    model = Course
    template_name = 'courses/course/detail.html'
```

This view inherits from the generic `DetailView` provided by Django. We specify the `model` and `template_name` attributes. Django's `DetailView` expects a **primary key (pk)** or slug URL parameter to retrieve a single object for the given model. Then it renders the template specified in `template_name`, including the object in the context as object.

Edit the main `urls.py` file of the `educa` project and add the following URL pattern to it:

```
from courses.views import CourseListView

urlpatterns = [
    # ...
    url(r'^$', CourseListView.as_view(), name='course_list'),
]
```

We add the `course_list` URL pattern to the main `urls.py` file of the project because we want to display the list of courses in the URL `http://127.0.0.1:8000/` and all other URLs for the `courses` application have the `/course/` prefix.

Edit the `urls.py` file of the `courses` application and add the following URL patterns:

```
url(r'^subject/(?P<subject>[\w-]+)/$',
    views.CourseListView.as_view(),
    name='course_list_subject'),

url(r'^(?P<slug>[\w-]+)/$',
    views.CourseDetailView.as_view(),
    name='course_detail'),
```

We define the following URL patterns:

- `course_list_subject`: For displaying all courses for a subject
- `course_detail`: For displaying a single course overview

Let's build templates for the `CourseListView` and `CourseDetailView` views. Create the following file structure inside the templates/courses/ directory of the courses application:

- course/
- list.html
- detail.html

Edit the `courses/course/list.html` template and write the following code:

```
{% extends "base.html" %}

{% block title %}
    {% if subject %}
        {{ subject.title }} courses
    {% else %}
        All courses
    {% endif %}
```

```
{% endblock %}

{% block content %}
<h1>
    {% if subject %}
        {{ subject.title }} courses
    {% else %}
        All courses
    {% endif %}
</h1>
<div class="contents">
    <h3>Subjects</h3>
    <ul id="modules">
        <li {% if not subject %}class="selected"{% endif %}>
            <a href="{% url "course_list" %}">All</a>
        </li>
        {% for s in subjects %}
            <li {% if subject == s %}class="selected"{% endif %}>
                <a href="{% url "course_list_subject" s.slug %}">
                    {{ s.title }}
                    <br><span>{{ s.total_courses }} courses</span>
                </a>
            </li>
        {% endfor %}
    </ul>
</div>
<div class="module">
    {% for course in courses %}
        {% with subject=course.subject %}
            <h3><a href="{% url "course_detail" course.slug %}">{{
course.title }}</a></h3>
            <p>
                <a href="{% url "course_list_subject" subject.slug
%}">{{ subject }}</a>.
                {{ course.total_modules }} modules.
                Instructor: {{ course.owner.get_full_name }}
            </p>
        {% endwith %}
    {% endfor %}
</div>
{% endblock %}
```

This is the template for listing available courses. We create an HTML list to display all Subject objects and build a link to the course_list_subject URL for each of them. We add a selected HTML class to highlight the current subject, if any. We iterate over every Course object, displaying the total number of modules and the instructor name.

Run the development server using the command `python manage.py runserver` and open `http://127.0.0.1:8000/` in your browser. You should see a page similar to the following one:

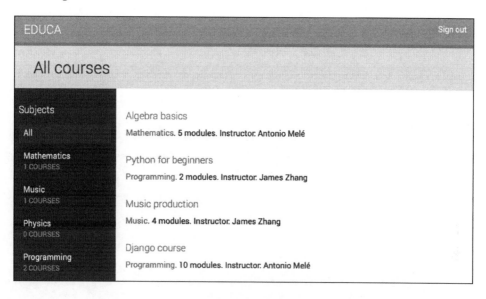

The left sidebar contains all subjects, including the total number of courses for each of them. You can click any subject to filter the courses being displayed.

Edit the `courses/course/detail.html` template and add the following code to it:

```
{% extends "base.html" %}

{% block title %}
    {{ object.title }}
{% endblock %}

{% block content %}
    {% with subject=course.subject %}
        <h1>
            {{ object.title }}
        </h1>
        <div class="module">
            <h2>Overview</h2>
            <p>
                <a href="{% url "course_list_subject" subject.slug
%}">{{ subject.title }}</a>.
                {{ course.modules.count }} modules.
```

```
            Instructor: {{ course.owner.get_full_name }}
        </p>
        {{ object.overview|linebreaks }}
    </div>
{% endwith %}
{% endblock %}
```

In this template, we display the overview and details for a single course. Open `http://127.0.0.1:8000/` in your browser and click one of the courses. You should see a page with the following structure:

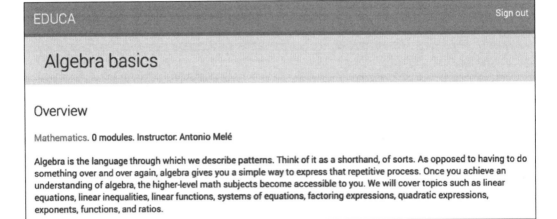

We have created a public area for displaying courses. Next, we need to allow users to register as students and enroll in courses.

# Adding student registration

Create a new application using the following command:

```
python manage.py startapp students
```

Edit the `settings.py` file of the `educa` project and add `'students'` to the `INSTALLED_APPS` setting as follows:

```
INSTALLED_APPS = (
    # ...
    'students',
)
```

# Creating a student registration view

Edit the `views.py` file of the students application and write the following code:

```
from django.core.urlresolvers import reverse_lazy
from django.views.generic.edit import CreateView
from django.contrib.auth.forms import UserCreationForm
from django.contrib.auth import authenticate, login

class StudentRegistrationView(CreateView):
    template_name = 'students/student/registration.html'
    form_class = UserCreationForm
    success_url = reverse_lazy('student_course_list')

    def form_valid(self, form):
        result = super(StudentRegistrationView,
                        self).form_valid(form)
        cd = form.cleaned_data
        user = authenticate(username=cd['username'],
                            password=cd['password1'])
        login(self.request, user)
        return result
```

This is the view that allows students to register in our site. We use the generic `CreateView` that provides the functionality for creating model objects. This view requires the following attributes:

- `template_name`: The path of the template to render for this view.

- `form_class`: The form for creating objects, which has to be a `ModelForm`. We use Django's `UserCreationForm` as registration form to create `User` objects.

- `success_url`: The URL to redirect the user to when the form is successfully submitted. We reverse the `student_course_list` URL, which we are going to create later for listing the courses students are enrolled in.

The `form_valid()` method is executed when valid form data has been posted. It has to return an HTTP response. We override this method to login the user after successfully signing up.

Create a new file inside the students application directory and add name it `urls.py`. Add the following code to it:

```
from django.conf.urls import url
from . import views

urlpatterns = [
```

```
      url(r'^register/$',
          views.StudentRegistrationView.as_view(),
          name='student_registration'),
  ]
```

The edit the main `urls.py` of the `educa` project and include the URLs for the students application by adding the following pattern to your URL configuration:

```
url(r'^students/', include('students.urls')),
```

Create the following file structure inside the `students` application:

```
templates/
    students/
        student/
            registration.html
```

Edit the `students/student/registration.html` template and add the following code to it:

```
{% extends "base.html" %}

{% block title %}
    Sign up
{% endblock %}

{% block content %}
    <h1>
        Sign up
    </h1>
    <div class="module">
        <p>Enter your details to create an account:</p>
        <form action="" method="post">
            {{ form.as_p }}
            {% csrf_token %}
            <p><input type="submit" value="Create my account"></p>
        </form>
    </div>
{% endblock %}
```

Finally edit the settings.py file of the `educa` project and add the following code to it:

```
from django.core.urlresolvers import reverse_lazy
LOGIN_REDIRECT_URL = reverse_lazy('student_course_list')
```

This is the setting used by the `auth` module to redirect the user to after a successful login, if no next parameter is present in the request.

Run the development server and open `http://127.0.0.1:8000/students/ register/` in your browser. You should see the registration form like this:

# Enrolling in courses

After users create an account, they should be able to enroll in `courses`. In order to store enrollments, we need to create a many-to-many relationship between the `Course` and `User` models. Edit the `models.py` file of the courses application and add the following field to the `Course` model:

```
students = models.ManyToManyField(User,
                                  related_name='courses_joined',
                                  blank=True)
```

From the shell, execute the following command to create a migration for this change:

**python manage.py makemigrations**

You will see an output similar to this:

```
Migrations for 'courses':
  0004_course_students.py:
    - Add field students to course
```

Then execute the next command to apply pending migrations:

```
python manage.py migrate
```

You should see the following output:

```
Operations to perform:
  Apply all migrations: courses
Running migrations:
  Rendering model states... DONE
  Applying courses.0004_course_students... OK
```

We can now associate students with the courses in which they are enrolled. Let's create the functionality for students to enroll in courses.

Create a new file inside the `students` application directory and name it `forms.py`. Add the following code to it:

```
from django import forms
from courses.models import Course

class CourseEnrollForm(forms.Form):
    course = forms.ModelChoiceField(queryset=Course.objects.all(),
                                    widget=forms.HiddenInput)
```

We are going to use this form for students to enroll in courses. The `course` field is for the course in which the user gets enrolled. Therefore, it's a `ModelChoiceField`. We use a `HiddenInput` widget because we are not going to show this field to the user. We are going to use this form in the `CourseDetailView` view to display an enroll button.

Edit the `views.py` file of the `students` application and add the following code:

```
from django.views.generic.edit import FormView
from braces.views import LoginRequiredMixin
from .forms import CourseEnrollForm

class StudentEnrollCourseView(LoginRequiredMixin, FormView):
    course = None
    form_class = CourseEnrollForm

    def form_valid(self, form):
        self.course = form.cleaned_data['course']
        self.course.students.add(self.request.user)
        return super(StudentEnrollCourseView,
                self).form_valid(form)
```

```
def get_success_url(self):
    return reverse_lazy('student_course_detail',
                        args=[self.course.id])
```

This is the `StudentEnrollCourseView`. It handles students enrolling in `courses`. The view inherits from the `LoginRequiredMixin` so that only logged in users can access the view. It also inherits from Django's `FormView`, since we handle a form submission. We use the `CourseEnrollForm` form for the `form_class` attribute and also define a `course` attribute for storing the given `Course` object. When the form is valid, we add the current user to the students enrolled in the course.

The `get_success_url()` method returns the URL the user will be redirected to if the form was successfully submitted. This method is equivalent to the `success_url` attribute. We reverse the `student_course_detail` URL, which we will create later in order to display the course contents.

Edit the `urls.py` file of the students application and add the following URL pattern to it:

```
url(r'^enroll-course/$',
    views.StudentEnrollCourseView.as_view(),
    name='student_enroll_course'),
```

Let's add the enroll button form to the course overview page. Edit the `views.py` file of the courses application and modify the `CourseDetailView` to make it look as follows:

```
from students.forms import CourseEnrollForm

class CourseDetailView(DetailView):
    model = Course
    template_name = 'courses/course/detail.html'

    def get_context_data(self, **kwargs):
        context = super(CourseDetailView,
                        self).get_context_data(**kwargs)
        context['enroll_form'] = CourseEnrollForm(
                                    initial={'course':self.object})
        return context
```

We use the `get_context_data()` method to include the enrollment form in the context for rendering the templates. We initialize the hidden course field of the form with the current `Course` object, so that it can be submitted directly.

Edit the `courses/course/detail.html` template and find the following line:

```
{{ object.overview|linebreaks }}
```

The preceding line should be replaced with the following ones:

```
{{ object.overview|linebreaks }}
{% if request.user.is_authenticated %}
    <form action="{% url "student_enroll_course" %}" method="post">
        {{ enroll_form }}
        {% csrf_token %}
        <input type="submit" class="button" value="Enroll now">
    </form>
{% else %}
    <a href="{% url "student_registration" %}" class="button">
        Register to enroll
    </a>
{% endif %}
```

This is the button for enrolling in courses. If the user is authenticated, we display the enrollment button including the hidden form that points to the `student_enroll_course` URL. If the user is not authenticated, we display a link to register in the platform.

Make sure the development server is running, open `http://127.0.0.1:8000/` in your browser and click a course. If you are logged in, you should see an **ENROLL NOW** button placed below the course overview, as follows:

---

Overview

Mathematics. 0 modules. Instructor: Antonio Melé

Algebra is the language through which we describe patterns. Think of it as a shorthand, of sorts. As opposed to having to do something over and over again, algebra gives you a simple way to express that repetitive process. Once you achieve an understanding of algebra, the higher-level math subjects become accessible to you. We will cover topics such as linear equations, linear inequalities, linear functions, systems of equations, factoring expressions, quadratic expressions, exponents, functions, and ratios.

ENROLL NOW

---

If you are not logged in, you will see a **Register to enroll** button instead.

# Accessing the course contents

We need a view for displaying the courses the students are enrolled in, and a view for accessing the actual course contents. Edit the `views.py` file of the students application and add the following code to it:

```
from django.views.generic.list import ListView
from courses.models import Course

class StudentCourseListView(LoginRequiredMixin, ListView):
    model = Course
    template_name = 'students/course/list.html'

    def get_queryset(self):
        qs = super(StudentCourseListView, self).get_queryset()
        return qs.filter(students__in=[self.request.user])
```

This is the view for students to list the courses they are enrolled in. It inherits from `LoginRequiredMixin` to make sure that only logged in users can access the view. It also inherits from the generic `ListView` for displaying a list of `Course` objects. We override the `get_queryset()` method for retrieving only the courses the user is enrolled in: We filter the QuerySet by the students `ManyToManyField` field for doing so.

Then add the following code to the `views.py` file:

```
from django.views.generic.detail import DetailView

class StudentCourseDetailView(DetailView):
    model = Course
    template_name = 'students/course/detail.html'

    def get_queryset(self):
        qs = super(StudentCourseDetailView, self).get_queryset()
        return qs.filter(students__in=[self.request.user])

    def get_context_data(self, **kwargs):
        context = super(StudentCourseDetailView,
                        self).get_context_data(**kwargs)
        # get course object
        course = self.get_object()
        if 'module_id' in self.kwargs:
            # get current module
            context['module'] = course.modules.get(
                                    id=self.kwargs['module_id'])
```

```
        else:
            # get first module
            context['module'] = course.modules.all()[0]
        return context
```

This is the `StudentCourseDetailView`. We override the `get_queryset()` method to limit the base QuerySet to courses in which the user is enrolled. We also override the `get_context_data()` method to set a course module in the context if the `module_id` URL parameter is given. Otherwise, we set the first module of the course. This way, students will be able to navigate through modules inside a course.

Edit the the `urls.py` file of the students application and add the following URL patterns to it:

```
url(r'^courses/$',
    views.StudentCourseListView.as_view(),
    name='student_course_list'),

url(r'^course/(?P<pk>\d+)/$',
    views.StudentCourseDetailView.as_view(),
    name='student_course_detail'),

url(r'^course/(?P<pk>\d+)/(?P<module_id>\d+)/$',
    views.StudentCourseDetailView.as_view(),
    name='student_course_detail_module'),
```

Create the following file structure inside the `templates/students/` directory of the `students` application:

```
course/

    detail.html

    list.html
```

Edit the `students/course/list.html` template and add the following code to it:

```
{% extends "base.html" %}

{% block title %}My courses{% endblock %}

{% block content %}
    <h1>My courses</h1>

    <div class="module">
        {% for course in object_list %}
            <div class="course-info">
```

```
            <h3>{{ course.title }}</h3>
            <p><a href="{% url "student_course_detail" course.id
%}">Access contents</a></p>
        </div>
    {% empty %}
        <p>
            You are not enrolled in any courses yet.
            <a href="{% url "course_list" %}">Browse courses</a>
to enroll in a course.
        </p>
    {% endfor %}
    </div>
{% endblock %}
```

This template displays the courses the user is enrolled in. Edit the `students/
course/detail.html` template and add the following code to it:

```
{% extends "base.html" %}

{% block title %}
    {{ object.title }}
{% endblock %}

{% block content %}
    <h1>
        {{ module.title }}
    </h1>
    <div class="contents">
        <h3>Modules</h3>
        <ul id="modules">
        {% for m in object.modules.all %}
            <li data-id="{{ m.id }}" {% if m == module %}
class="selected"{% endif %}>
                <a href="{% url "student_course_detail_module" object.
id m.id %}">
                    <span>
                        Module <span class="order">{{ m.order|add:1
}}</span>
                    </span>
                    <br>
                    {{ m.title }}
                </a>
            </li>
        {% empty %}
            <li>No modules yet.</li>
```

```
        {% endfor %}
        </ul>
    </div>
    <div class="module">
        {% for content in module.contents.all %}
            {% with item=content.item %}
                <h2>{{ item.title }}</h2>
                {{ item.render }}
            {% endwith %}
        {% endfor %}
    </div>
{% endblock %}
```

This is the template for enrolled students to access a course contents. First we build an HTML list including all course modules and highlighting the current module. Then we iterate over the current module contents, and access each content item to display it using {{ item.render }}. We are going to add the render() method to the content models next. This method will take care of rendering the content properly.

# Rendering different types of content

We need to provide a way to render each type of content. Edit the models.py file of the courses application directory and add the following render() method to the ItemBase model as follows:

```
from django.template.loader import render_to_string
from django.utils.safestring import mark_safe

class ItemBase(models.Model):
    # ...

    def render(self):
        return render_to_string('courses/content/{}.html'.format(
                self._meta.model_name), {'item': self})
```

This method uses the render_to_string() function for rendering a template and returning the rendered content as a string. Each kind of content is rendered using a template named after the content model. We use self._meta.model_name to build the appropriate template name for la. The render() methods provides a common interface for rendering diverse content.

Create the following file structure inside the `templates/courses/` directory of the courses application:

```
content/
    text.html
    file.html
    image.html
    video.html
```

Edit the `courses/content/text.html` template and write this code:

```
{{ item.content|linebreaks|safe }}
```

Edit the `courses/content/file.html` template and add the following:

```
<p><a href="{{ item.file.url }}" class="button">Download file</a></p>
```

Edit the `courses/content/image.html` template and write:

```
<p><img src="{{ item.file.url }}"></p>
```

For files uploaded with `ImageField` and `FileField` to work, we need to set up our project to serve media files with the development server. Edit the `settings.py` file of your project and add the following code to it:

```
MEDIA_URL = '/media/'
MEDIA_ROOT = os.path.join(BASE_DIR, 'media/')
```

Remember that `MEDIA_URL` is the base URL to serve uploaded media files and `MEDIA_ROOT` is the local path where the files are located.

Edit the main `urls.py` file of your project and add the following imports:

```
from django.conf import settings
from django.conf.urls.static import static
```

Then, write the following lines at the end of the file:

```
urlpatterns += static(settings.MEDIA_URL,
                      document_root=settings.MEDIA_ROOT)
```

Your project is now ready for uploading and serving media files using the development server. Remember that the development server is not suitable for production use. We will cover configuring a production environment in the next chapter.

We also have to create a template for rendering `Video` objects. We will use django-embed-video for embedding video content. Django-embed-video is a third-party Django application that allows you to embed videos in your templates, from sources like YouTube or Vimeo, by simply providing the video public URL.

Install the package with the following command:

```
pip install django-embed-video==1.0.0
```

Then, edit the `settings.py` file of your project and add `'embed_video'` to the `INSTALLED_APPS` setting. You can find django-embed-video's documentation at `http://django-embed-video.readthedocs.org/en/v1.0.0/`.

Edit the `courses/content/video.html` template and write the following code:

```
{% load embed_video_tags %}
{% video item.url 'small' %}
```

Now run the development server and access `http://127.0.0.1:8000/course/mine/` in your browser. Access the site with a user that belongs the Instructors group or a superuser, and add multiple contents to a course. For including video content, you can just copy any YouTube URL, for example `https://www.youtube.com/watch?v=bgV39DlmZ2U`, and include it it in the `url` field of the form. After adding contents to the course open `http://127.0.0.1:8000/`, click the course and click the **ENROLL NOW** button. You should get enrolled in the course and be redirected to the `student_course_detail` URL. The following image shows a sample course contents:

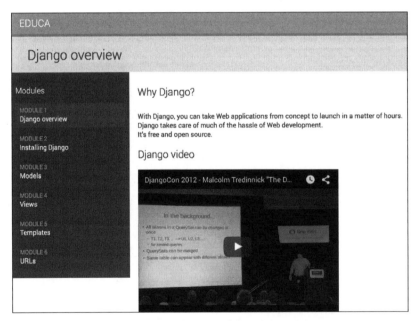

Great! You have created a common interface for rendering course contents, each of them being rendered in a particular way.

# Using the cache framework

HTTP requests to your web application usually entail database access, data processing, and template rendering. This is much more expensive in terms of processing than serving a static website.

The overhead in some requests can be significant when your site starts getting more and more traffic. This is where caching becomes precious. By caching queries, calculation results, or rendered content in an HTTP request, you will avoid cost-expensive operations in the following requests. This translates into shorter response times and less processing on the server side.

Django includes a robust cache system that allows you to cache data with different levels of granularity. You can cache a single query, the output of a specific view, parts of rendered template content, or your entire site. Items are stored in the cache system for a default time. You can specify the default timeout for cached data.

This is how you will usually use the cache framework when your application gets an HTTP request:

1.  Try to find the requested data in the cache.
2.  If found, return the cached data.
3.  If not found, perform the following steps:

    1.  Perform the query or processing required to obtain the data.
    2.  Save the generated data in the cache.
    3.  Return the data.

You can read detailed information about Django's cache system at `https://docs.djangoproject.com/en/1.8/topics/cache/`.

# Available cache backends

Django comes with several cache backends. These are:

*   `backends.memcached.MemcachedCache` or `backends.memcached.PyLibMCCache`: A memcached backend. memcached is a fast and efficient memory-based cache server. The backend to use depends on the memcached Python bindings you choose.

- `backends.db.DatabaseCache`: Use the database as cache system.
- `backends.filebased.FileBasedCache`: Use the file storage system. Serializes and stores each cache value as a separate file.
- `backends.locmem.LocMemCache`: Local memory cache backend. This the default cache backend.
- `backends.dummy.DummyCache`: A dummy cache backend intended only for development. It implements the cache interface without actually caching anything. This cache is per-process and thread-safe.

 For optimal performance, use a memory-based cache backend such as the Memcached backend.

# Installing memcached

We are going to use the memcached backend. Memcached runs in memory and it is allotted a specified amount of RAM. When the allotted RAM is full, Memcached starts removing the oldest data to store new data.

Download memcached from `http://memcached.org/downloads`. If you are using Linux, you can install memcached using the following command:

```
./configure && make && make test && sudo make install
```

If you are using Mac OS X, you can install Memcached with the Homebrew package manager using the command brew install Memcached. You can download Homebrew from `http://brew.sh`.

If you are using Windows, you can find a Windows binary version of memcached at `http://code.jellycan.com/memcached/`.

After installing Memcached, open a shell and start it using the following command:

```
memcached -l 127.0.0.1:11211
```

Memcached will run on port `11211` by default. However, you can specify a custom host and port by using the `-l` option. You can find more information about Memcached at `http://memcached.org`.

After installing Memcached, you have to install its Python bindings. You can do it with the following command:

```
pip install python3-memcached==1.51
```

# Cache settings

Django provides the following cache settings:

- CACHES: A dictionary containing all available caches for the project.
- CACHE_MIDDLEWARE_ALIAS: The cache alias to use for storage.
- CACHE_MIDDLEWARE_KEY_PREFIX: The prefix to use for cache keys. Set a prefix to avoid key collisions if you share the same cache between several sites.
- CACHE_MIDDLEWARE_SECONDS: The default number of seconds to cache pages.

The caching system for the project can be configured using the CACHES setting. This setting is a dictionary that allows you to specify the configuration for multiple caches. Each cache included in the CACHES dictionary can specify the following data:

- BACKEND: The cache backend to use.
- KEY_FUNCTION: A string containing a dotted path to a callable that takes a prefix, version, and key as arguments and returns a final cache key.
- KEY_PREFIX: A string prefix for all cache keys, to avoid collisions.
- LOCATION: The location of the cache. Depending on the cache backend, this might be a directory, a host and port, or a name for the in-memory backend.
- OPTIONS: Any additional parameters to be passed to the cache backend.
- TIMEOUT: The default timeout, in seconds, for storing the cache keys. 300 seconds by default, which is five minutes. If set to None cache keys will not expire.
- VERSION: The default version number for the cache keys. Useful for cache versioning.

# Adding memcached to your project

Let's configure the cache for our project. Edit the settings.py file of the educa project and add the following code to it:

```python
CACHES = {
    'default': {
        'BACKEND': 'django.core.cache.backends.memcached.
MemcachedCache',
        'LOCATION': '127.0.0.1:11211',
    }
}
```

We are using the `MemcachedCache` backend. We specify its location using `address:port` notation. If you have multiple `memcached` instances you can use a list for `LOCATION`.

## Montioring memcached

There is a third-party package called django-memcache-status that displays statistics for your `memcached` instances in the administration site. For compatibility with Python3, install it from the following fork with the following command:

```
pip install git+git://github.com/zenx/django-memcache-status.git
```

Edit the `settings.py` file and add `'memcache_status'` to the `INSTALLED_APPS` setting. Make sure memcached is running, start the development server in another shell window and open `http://127.0.0.1:8000/admin/` in your browser. Log in into the administration site using a superuser. You should see the following block:

memcached: default: 127.0.0.1:11211 (1) – 0% load

This graph shows the cache usage. The green color represents free cache while red indicates used space. If you click the title of the box, it shows detailed statistics about your `memcached` instance.

We have setup memcached for our project and are able to monitor it. Let's start caching data!

## Cache levels

Django provides the following levels of caching listed below by ascendant order of granularity:

- **Low-level cache API**: Provides the highest granularity. Allows you to cache specific queries or calculations.
- **Per-view cache**: Provides caching for individual views.
- **Template cache**: Allows you to cache template fragments.
- **Per-site cache**: The highest-level cache. It caches your entire site.

Think about your cache strategy before implementing caching. Focus first on expensive queries or calculations, which are not calculated in a per-user basis.

# Using the low-level cache API

The low-level cache API allows you to store objects in the cache with any granularity. It is located at `django.core.cache`. You can import it like this:

**from django.core.cache import cache**

This uses the default cache. It's equivalent to `caches['default']`. Accessing a specific cache is also possible via its alias:

```
from django.core.cache import caches
my_cache = caches['alias']
```

Let's take a look at how the cache API works. Open the shell with the command `python manage.py shell` and execute the following code:

```
>>> from django.core.cache import cache
>>> cache.set('musician', 'Django Reinhardt', 20)
```

We access the default cache backend and use `set(key, value, timeout)` to store a key named `'musician'` with a value that is the string `'Django Reinhardt'` for 20 seconds. If we don't specify a timeout, Django uses the default timeout specified for the cache backend in the CACHES setting. Now execute the following code:

```
>>> cache.get('musician')
'Django Reinhardt'
```

We retrieve the key from the cache. Wait for 20 seconds and execute the same code:

```
>>> cache.get('musician')
None
```

The `'musician'` cache key expired and the `get()` method returns None because the key is not in the cache anymore.

Always avoid storing a None value in a cache key because you won't be able to distinguish between the actual value and a cache miss.

Let's cache a QuerySet:

```
>>> from courses.models import Subject
>>> subjects = Subject.objects.all()
>>> cache.set('all_subjects', subjects)
```

We perform a queryset on the `Subject` model and store the returned objects in the `'all_subjects'` key. Let's retrieve the cached data:

```
>>> cache.get('all_subjects')
[<Subject: Mathematics>, <Subject: Music>, <Subject: Physics>,
<Subject: Programming>]
```

We are going to cache some queries in our views. Edit the `views.py` file of the courses application and add the following import:

```
from django.core.cache import cache
```

In the `get()` method of the `CourseListView`, replace the following line:

```
subjects = Subject.objects.annotate(
            total_courses=Count('courses'))
```

With the following ones:

```
subjects = cache.get('all_subjects')
if not subjects:
    subjects = Subject.objects.annotate(
                total_courses=Count('courses'))
    cache.set('all_subjects', subjects)
```

In this code, first we try to get the all_students key from the cache using `cache.get()`. This returns `None` if the given key is not found. If no key is found (not cached yet, or cached but timed out) we perform the query to retrieve all `Subject` objects and their number of courses, and we cache the result using `cache.set()`.

Run the development server and open `http://127.0.0.1:8000/` in your browser. When the view is executed, the cache key is not found and the QuerySet is executed. Open `http://127.0.0.1:8000/admin/` in your browser and expand the memcached statistics. You should see usage data for the cache similar to the following ones:

| memcached: default: 127.0.0.1:11211 (1) – 0% load | |
|---|---|
| Miss Ratio | 20% |
| Avg GET by item | 2 |
| Avg GET by seconds/minutes | 0/3 |
| Detailed Statistics: | |
| Auth Errors | 0 |
| Cmd Get | 5 |
| Rusage User | 0.003557 |
| Incr Misses | 0 |
| Get Hits | 4 |

Take a look at **Curr Items**, which should be **1**. This shows that there is one item currently stored in the cache. **Get Hits** shows how many get commands were successful and **Get Misses** shows the get requests for keys that are missing. The **Miss Ratio** is calculated using both of them.

Now navigate back to `http://127.0.0.1:8000/` using your browser and reload the page several times. If you take a look at the cache statistics now you will see several reads more (**Get Hits** and **Cmd Get** have increased).

# Caching based on dynamic data

Many times you will want to cache something that is based on dynamic data. In these cases, you have to build dynamic keys that contain all information required to uniquely identify the cached data. Edit the `views.py` file of the courses application and modify the `CourseListView` view to make it look like this:

```
class CourseListView(TemplateResponseMixin, View):
    model = Course
    template_name = 'courses/course/list.html'

    def get(self, request, subject=None):
        subjects = cache.get('all_subjects')
        if not subjects:
            subjects = Subject.objects.annotate(
                        total_courses=Count('courses'))
            cache.set('all_subjects', subjects)
        all_courses = Course.objects.annotate(
                        total_modules=Count('modules'))
```

```
        if subject:
            subject = get_object_or_404(Subject, slug=subject)
            key = 'subject_{}_courses'.format(subject.id)
            courses = cache.get(key)
            if not courses:
                courses = all_courses.filter(subject=subject)
                cache.set(key, courses)
        else:
            courses = cache.get('all_courses')
            if not courses:
                courses = all_courses
                cache.set('all_courses', courses)
        return self.render_to_response({'subjects': subjects,
                                        'subject': subject,
                                        'courses': courses})
```

In this case, we also cache both all courses and courses filtered by subject. We use the `all_courses` cache key for storing all courses if no subject is given. If there is a subject we build the key dynamically with `'subject_{}_courses'.format(subject.id)`.

It is important to note that we cannot use a cached QuerySet to build other QuerySets, since what we cached are actually the results of the QuerySet. So we cannot do:

```
    courses = cache.get('all_courses')
    courses.filter(subject=subject)
```

Instead we have to create the base QuerySet `Course.objects.annotate(total_modules=Count('modules'))`, which is not going to be executed until it is forced, and use it to further restrict the QuerySet with `all_courses.filter(subject=subject)` in case the data was not found in the cache.

# Caching template fragments

Caching template fragments is a higher level approach. You need to load the cache template tags in your template using `{% load cache %}`. Then you will be able to use the `{% cache %}` template tag to cache specific template fragments. You will usually use the template tag as follows:

```
{% cache 300 fragment_name %}
    ...
{% endcache %}
```

The {% cache %} tag has two required arguments: The timeout, in seconds, and a name for the fragment. If you need to cache content depending on dynamic data, you can do so by passing additional arguments to the {% cache %} template tag to uniquely identify the fragment.

Edit the /students/course/detail.html of the students application. Add the following code at the top of it, just after the {% extends %} tag:

```
{% load cache %}
```

Then, replace the following lines:

```
{% for content in module.contents.all %}
    {% with item=content.item %}
        <h2>{{ item.title }}</h2>
        {{ item.render }}
    {% endwith %}
{% endfor %}
```

With the following ones:

```
{% cache 600 module_contents module %}
    {% for content in module.contents.all %}
        {% with item=content.item %}
            <h2>{{ item.title }}</h2>
            {{ item.render }}
        {% endwith %}
    {% endfor %}
{% endcache %}
```

We cache this template fragment using the name module_contents and passing the current Module object to it. Thus, we uniquely identify the fragment. This is important to avoid caching a module's contents and serving the wrong content when a different module is requested.

If the USE_I18N setting is set to True, the per-site middleware cache will respect the active language. If you use the {% cache %} template tag you have use one of the translation-specific variables available in templates to achieve the same result, such as {% cache 600 name request.LANGUAGE_CODE %}.

# Caching views

You can cache the output of individual views using the `cache_page` decorator located at `django.views.decorators.cache`. The decorator requires a timeout argument (in seconds).

Let's use it in our views. Edit the `urls.py` file of the students application and add the following import:

```
from django.views.decorators.cache import cache_page
```

Then apply the `cache_page` decorator the `student_course_detail` and `student_course_detail_module` URL patterns, as follows:

```
url(r'^course/(?P<pk>\d+)/$',
    cache_page(60 * 15)(views.StudentCourseDetailView.as_view()),
    name='student_course_detail'),

url(r'^course/(?P<pk>\d+)/(?P<module_id>\d+)/$',
    cache_page(60 * 15)(views.StudentCourseDetailView.as_view()),
    name='student_course_detail_module'),
```

Now the result for the `StudentCourseDetailView` is cached for 15 minutes.

 The per-view cache uses the URL to build the cache key. Multiple URLs pointing to the same view will be cached separately.

# Using the per-site cache

This is the highest-level cache. It allows you to cache your entire site.

To allow the per-site cache edit the `settings.py` file of your project and add the `UpdateCacheMiddleware` and `FetchFromCacheMiddleware` classes to the `MIDDLEWARE_CLASSES` setting as follows:

```
MIDDLEWARE_CLASSES = (
    'django.contrib.sessions.middleware.SessionMiddleware',
    'django.middleware.cache.UpdateCacheMiddleware',
    'django.middleware.common.CommonMiddleware',
    'django.middleware.cache.FetchFromCacheMiddleware',
    'django.middleware.csrf.CsrfViewMiddleware',
    # ...
)
```

Remember that middlewares are executed in the given order during the request phase, and in reverse order during the response phase. `UpdateCacheMiddleware` is placed before `CommonMiddleware` because it runs during response time, when middlewares are executed in reverse order. `FetchFromCacheMiddleware` is placed after `CommonMiddleware` intentionally, because it needs to access request data set by the latter.

Then, add the following settings to the `settings.py` file:

```
CACHE_MIDDLEWARE_ALIAS = 'default'
CACHE_MIDDLEWARE_SECONDS = 60 * 15   # 15 minutes
CACHE_MIDDLEWARE_KEY_PREFIX = 'educa'
```

In these settings we use the default cache for our cache middleware and we set the global cache timeout to 15 minutes. We also specify a prefix for all cache keys to avoid collisions in case we use the same memcached backend for multiple projects. Our site will now cache and return cached content for all GET requests.

We have done this to test the per-site cache functionality. However, the per-site cache is not suitable for us, since the course management views need to show updated data to instantly reflect any changes. The best approach to follow in our project is to cache the templates or views that are used to display course contents to students.

We have seen an overview of the methods provided by Django to cache data. You should define your cache strategy wisely and prioritize the most expensive QuerySets or calculations.

# Summary

In this chapter, we have created public views for the courses and you have built a system for students to register and enroll in courses. We have installed memcached and have implemented different cache levels.

In the next chapter, we will build a RESTful API for your project.

# 12

# Building an API

In the previous chapter, you built a student registration system and enrollment in courses. You created views to display course contents and learned how to use Django's cache framework. In this chapter, you will learn how to do the following:

- Build a RESTful API
- Handle authentication and permissions for API views
- Create API view sets and routers

## Building a RESTful API

You might want to create an interface for other services to interact with your web application. By building an API, you can allow third parties to consume information and operate with your application programmatically.

There are several ways you can structure your API, but following REST principles is encouraged. The REST architecture comes from Representational State Transfer. RESTful APIs are resource-based. Your models represent resources and HTTP methods such as GET, POST, PUT, or DELETE are used to retrieve, create, update, or delete objects. HTTP response codes are also used in this context. Different HTTP response codes are returned to indicate the result of the HTTP request, e.g. 2XX response codes for success, 4XX for errors, and so on.

The most common formats to exchange data in RESTful APIs are JSON and XML. We will build a REST API with JSON serialization for our project. Our API will provide the following functionality:

- Retrieve subjects
- Retrieve available courses
- Retrieve course contents
- Enroll in a course

We can build an API from scratch with Django by creating custom views. However, there are several third-party modules that simplify creating an API for your project, the most popular among them being Django Rest Framework.

# Installing Django Rest Framework

Django Rest Framework allows you to easily build REST API's for your project. You can find all information about REST Framework at `http://www.django-rest-framework.org`.

Open the shell and install the framework with the following command:

```
pip install djangorestframework==3.2.3
```

Edit the `settings.py` file of the `educa` project and add `rest_framework` to the `INSTALLED_APPS` setting to activate the application, as follows:

```
INSTALLED_APPS = (
    # ...
    'rest_framework',
)
```

Then, add the following code to the `settings.py` file:

```
REST_FRAMEWORK = {
    'DEFAULT_PERMISSION_CLASSES': [
  'rest_framework.permissions.DjangoModelPermissionsOrAnonReadOnly'
    ]
}
```

You can provide a specific configuration for your API using the `REST_FRAMEWORK` setting. REST Framework offers a wide range of settings to configure default behaviors. The `DEFAULT_PERMISSION_CLASSES` setting specifies the default permissions to read, create, update, or delete objects. We set the `DjangoModelPermissionsOrAnonReadOnly` as the only default permission class. This class relies on Django's permissions system to allow users to create, update, or delete objects, while providing read-only access for anonymous users. You will learn more about permissions later.

For a complete list of available settings for REST framework, you can visit `http://www.django-rest-framework.org/api-guide/settings/`.

# Defining serializers

After setting up REST Framework, we need to specify how our data will be serialized. Output data has to be serialized into a specific format, and input data will be de-serialized for processing. The framework provides the following classes to build serializers for single objects:

- `Serializer`: Provides serialization for normal Python class instances
- `ModelSerializer`: Provides serialization for model instances
- `HyperlinkedModelSerializer`: The same as `ModelSerializer`, but represents object relationships with links rather than primary keys

Let's build our first serializer. Create the following file structure inside the `courses` application directory:

```
api/
    __init__.py
    serializers.py
```

We will build all the API functionality inside the `api` directory to keep everything well organized. Edit the `serializers.py` file and add the following code:

```
from rest_framework import serializers
from ..models import Subject

class SubjectSerializer(serializers.ModelSerializer):
    class Meta:
        model = Subject
        fields = ('id', 'title', 'slug')
```

This is the serializer for the `Subject` model. Serializers are defined in a similar fashion to Django's `Form` and `ModelForm` classes. The `Meta` class allows you to specify the model to serialize and the fields to be included for serialization. All model fields will be included if you don't set a `fields` attribute.

Let's try our serializer. Open the command line and start the Django shell with the command `python manage.py shell`. Run the following code:

```
from courses.models import Subject
from courses.api.serializers import SubjectSerializer
subject = Subject.objects.latest('id')
serializer = SubjectSerializer(subject)
serializer.data
```

In this example, we get a `Subject` object, create an instance of `SubjectSerializer`, and access the serialized data. You will get the following output:

```
{'slug': 'music', 'id': 4, 'title': 'Music'}
```

As you can see, the model data is translated into Python native data types.

# Understanding parsers and renderers

The serialized data has to be rendered in a specific format before you return it in an HTTP response. Likewise, when you get an HTTP request, you have to parse the incoming data and deserialize it before you can operate with it. REST Framework includes renderers and parsers to handle that.

Let's see how to parse incoming data. Given a JSON string input, you can use the `JSONParser` class provided by REST framework to convert it to a Python object. Execute the following code in the Python shell:

```
from io import BytesIO
from rest_framework.parsers import JSONParser
data = b'{"id":4,"title":"Music","slug":"music"}'
JSONParser().parse(BytesIO(data))
```

You will get the following output:

```
{'id': 4, 'title': 'Music', 'slug': 'music'}
```

REST Framework also includes `Renderer` classes that allow you to format API responses. The framework determines which renderer to use through content negotiation. It inspects the request's `Accept` header to determine the expected content type for the response. Optionally, the renderer is determined by the format suffix of the URL. For example, accessing  will trigger the `JSONRenderer` in order to return a JSON response.

Go back to the shell and execute the following code to render the `serializer` object from the previous serializer example:

```
from rest_framework.renderers import JSONRenderer
JSONRenderer().render(serializer.data)
```

You will see the following output:

```
b'{"id":4,"title":"Music","slug":"music"}'
```

We use the JSONRenderer to render the serialized data into JSON. By default, REST Framework uses two different renderers: JSONRenderer and BrowsableAPIRenderer. The latter provides a web interface to easily browse your API. You can change the default renderer classes with the DEFAULT_RENDERER_CLASSES option of the REST_FRAMEWORK setting.

You can find more information about renderers and parsers at http://www.django-rest-framework.org/api-guide/renderers/ and http://www.django-rest-framework.org/api-guide/parsers/ respectively.

# Building list and detail views

REST Framework comes with a set of generic views and mixins that you can use to build your API views. These provide functionality to retrieve, create, update, or delete model objects. You can see all generic mixins and views provided by REST Framework at http://www.django-rest-framework.org/api-guide/generic-views/.

Let's create list and detail views to retrieve Subject objects. Create a new file inside the courses/api/ directory and name it views.py. Add the following code to it:

```
from rest_framework import generics
from ..models import Subject
from .serializers import SubjectSerializer

class SubjectListView(generics.ListAPIView):
    queryset = Subject.objects.all()
    serializer_class = SubjectSerializer

class SubjectDetailView(generics.RetrieveAPIView):
    queryset = Subject.objects.all()
    serializer_class = SubjectSerializer
```

In this code, we are using the generic ListAPIView and RetrieveAPIView views of REST Framework. We include a pk URL parameter for the detail view to retrieve the object for the given primary key. Both views have the following attributes:

- queryset: The base QuerySet to use to retrieve objects
- serializer_class: The class to serialize objects

Let's add URL patterns for our views. Create a new file inside the `courses/api/` directory and name it `urls.py` and make it look as follows:

```
from django.conf.urls import url
from . import views

urlpatterns = [
    url(r'^subjects/$',
        views.SubjectListView.as_view(),
        name='subject_list'),
    url(r'^subjects/(?P<pk>\d+)/$',
        views.SubjectDetailView.as_view(),
        name='subject_detail'),
]
```

Edit the main `urls.py` file of the `educa` project and include the API patterns as follows:

```
urlpatterns = [
    # ...
    url(r'^api/', include('courses.api.urls', namespace='api')),
]
```

We use the `api` namespace for our API URLs. Ensure your server is running with the command `python manage.py runserver`. Open the shell and retrieve the URL `http://127.0.0.1:8000/api/subjects/` with cURL as follows:

```
$ curl http://127.0.0.1:8000/api/subjects/
```

You will get a response similar to the following one:

```
[{"id":2,"title":"Mathematics","slug":"mathematics"},{"id":4,"title":"Mus
ic","slug":"music"},{"id":3,"title":"Physics","slug":"physics"},{"id":1,"
title":"Programming","slug":"programming"}]
```

The HTTP response contains a list of `Subject` objects in JSON format. If your operating system doesn't come with cURL installed, you can download it from `http://curl.haxx.se/dlwiz/`. Instead of cURL, you can also use any other tool to send custom HTTP requests such as a browser extension such as Postman, which you can get at `https://www.getpostman.com`.

Open `http://127.0.0.1:8000/api/subjects/` in your browser. You will see REST Framework's browsable API as follows:

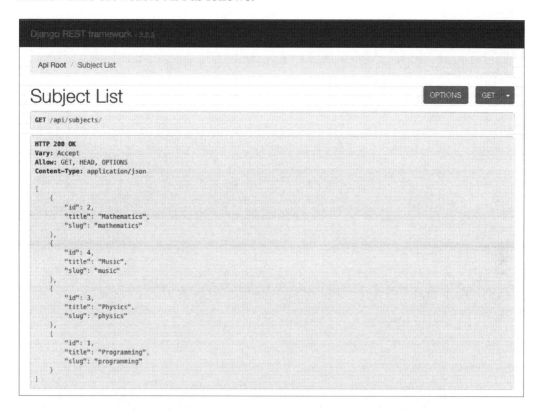

This HTML interface is provided by the `BrowsableAPIRenderer` renderer. It displays the result headers and content and allows you to perform requests. You can also access the API detail view for a `Subject` object by including its `id` in the URL. Open `http://127.0.0.1:8000/api/subjects/1/` in your browser. You will see a single `Subject` object rendered in JSON format.

# Creating nested serializers

We are going to create a serializer for the `Course` model. Edit the `api/serializers.py` file and add the following code to it:

```
from ..models import Course

class CourseSerializer(serializers.ModelSerializer):
    class Meta:
```

```
model = Course
fields = ('id', 'subject', 'title', 'slug', 'overview',
          'created', 'owner', 'modules')
```

Let's take a look at how a `Course` object is serialized. Open the shell, run `python manage.py shell`, and run the following code:

```
from rest_framework.renderers import JSONRenderer
from courses.models import Course
from courses.api.serializers import CourseSerializer
course = Course.objects.latest('id')
serializer = CourseSerializer(course)
JSONRenderer().render(serializer.data)
```

You will get a JSON object with the fields we included in `CourseSerializer`. You can see that the related objects of the `modules` manager are serialized as a list of primary keys, like this:

```
"modules": [17, 18, 19, 20, 21, 22]
```

We want to include more information about each module, so we need to serialize `Module` objects and nest them. Modify the previous code of the `api/serializers.py` file to make it look as follows:

```
from rest_framework import serializers
from ..models import Course, Module

class ModuleSerializer(serializers.ModelSerializer):
    class Meta:
        model = Module
        fields = ('order', 'title', 'description')

class CourseSerializer(serializers.ModelSerializer):
    modules = ModuleSerializer(many=True, read_only=True)

    class Meta:
        model = Course
        fields = ('id', 'subject', 'title', 'slug', 'overview',
                  'created', 'owner', 'modules')
```

We define a `ModuleSerializer` to provide serialization for the `Module` model. Then we add a `modules` attribute to `CourseSerializer` to nest the `ModuleSerializer` serializer. We set `many=True` to indicate that we are serializing multiple objects. The `read_only` parameter indicates that this field is read-only and should not be included in any input to create or update objects.

Open the shell and create an instance of `CourseSerializer` again. Render the serializer's `data` attribute with `JSONRenderer`. This time, the listed modules are being serialized with the nested `ModuleSerializer` serializer, like this:

```
"modules": [
    {
        "order": 0,
        "title": "Django overview",
        "description": "A brief overview about the Web Framework."
    },
    {
        "order": 1,
        "title": "Installing Django",
        "description": "How to install Django."
    },
    ...
]
```

You can read more about serializers at `http://www.django-rest-framework.org/api-guide/serializers/`.

# Building custom views

REST Framework provides an `APIView` class, which builds API functionality on top of Django's `View` class. The `APIView` class differs from `View` in using REST Framework's custom `Request` and `Response` objects and handling `APIException` exceptions to return the appropriate HTTP responses. It also has a built-in authentication and authorization system to manage access to views.

We are going to create a view for users to enroll in courses. Edit the `api/views.py` file and add the following code to it:

```python
from django.shortcuts import get_object_or_404
from rest_framework.views import APIView
from rest_framework.response import Response
from ..models import Course

class CourseEnrollView(APIView):
    def post(self, request, pk, format=None):
        course = get_object_or_404(Course, pk=pk)
        course.students.add(request.user)
        return Response({'enrolled': True})
```

The `CourseEnrollView` view handles user enrollment in courses. The preceding code is as follows:

- We create a custom view that subclasses `APIView`.

- We define a `post()` method for POST actions. No other HTTP method will be allowed for this view.

- We expect a `pk` URL parameter containing the ID of a course. We retrieve the course by the given `pk` parameter and raise a 404 exception if it's not found.

- We add the current user to the `students` many-to-many relationship of the `Course` object and return a successful response.

Edit the `api/urls.py` file and add the following URL pattern for the `CourseEnrollView` view:

```
url(r'^courses/(?P<pk>\d+)/enroll/$',
    views.CourseEnrollView.as_view(),
    name='course_enroll'),
```

Theoretically, we could now perform a POST request to enroll the current user in a course. However, we need to be able to identify the user and prevent unauthenticated users from accessing this view. Let's see how API authentication and permissions work.

# Handling authentication

REST Framework provides authentication classes to identify the user performing the request. If authentication is successful, the framework sets the authenticated `User` object in `request.user`. If no user is authenticated, an instance of Django's `AnonymousUser` is set instead.

REST Framework provides the following authentication backends:

- `BasicAuthentication`: HTTP Basic Authentication. The user and password are sent by the client in the `Authorization` HTTP header encoded with Base64. You can learn more about it at `https://en.wikipedia.org/wiki/Basic_access_authentication`.

- `TokenAuthentication`: Token-based authentication. A `Token` model is used to store user tokens. Users include the token in the `Authorization` HTTP header for authentication.

- `SessionAuthentication`: Uses Django's session backend for authentication. This backend is useful to perform authenticated AJAX requests to the API from your website's frontend.

You can build a custom authentication backend by subclassing the `BaseAuthentication` class provided by REST Framework and overriding the `authenticate()` method.

You can set authentication on a per-view basis, or set it globally with the `DEFAULT_AUTHENTICATION_CLASSES` setting.

 Authentication only identifies the user performing the request. It won't allow or deny access to views. You have to use permissions to restrict access to views.

You can find all the information about authentication at `http://www.django-rest-framework.org/api-guide/authentication/`.

Let's add `BasicAuthentication` to our view. Edit the `api/views.py` file of the `courses` application and add an `authentication_classes` attribute to `CourseEnrollView` as follows:

```
from rest_framework.authentication import BasicAuthentication

class CourseEnrollView(APIView):
    authentication_classes = (BasicAuthentication,)
    # ...
```

Users will be identified by the credentials set in the `Authorization` header of the HTTP request.

# Adding permissions to views

REST Framework includes a permission system to restrict access to views. Some of the built-in permissions of REST Framework are:

- `AllowAny`: Unrestricted access, regardless of if a user is authenticated or not.

- `IsAuthenticated`: Allows access to authenticated users only.

- `IsAuthenticatedOrReadOnly`: Complete access to authenticated users. Anonymous users are only allowed to execute read methods such as GET, HEAD, or OPTIONS.

- `DjangoModelPermissions`: Permissions tied to `django.contrib.auth`. The view requires a `queryset` attribute. Only authenticated users with model permissions assigned are granted permission.

- `DjangoObjectPermissions`: Django permissions on a per-object basis.

If users are denied permission, they will usually get one of the following HTTP error codes:

- `HTTP 401`: Unauthorized
- `HTTP 403`: Permission denied

You can read more information about permissions at `http://www.django-rest-framework.org/api-guide/permissions/`.

Edit the `api/views.py` file of the `courses` application and add a `permission_classes` attribute to `CourseEnrollView` as follows:

```
from rest_framework.authentication import BasicAuthentication
from rest_framework.permissions import IsAuthenticated

class CourseEnrollView(APIView):
    authentication_classes = (BasicAuthentication,)
    permission_classes = (IsAuthenticated,)
    # ...
```

We include the `IsAuthenticated` permission. This will prevent anonymous users from accessing the view. Now, we can perform a POST request to our new API method.

Make sure the development server is running. Open the shell and run the following command:

```
curl -i -X POST http://127.0.0.1:8000/api/courses/1/enroll/
```

You will get the following response:

```
HTTP/1.0 401 UNAUTHORIZED
...
{"detail": "Authentication credentials were not provided."}
```

We get a `401` HTTP code as expected, since we are not authenticated. Let's use basic authentication with one of our users. Run the following command:

```
curl -i -X POST -u student:password http://127.0.0.1:8000/api/
courses/1/enroll/
```

Replace `student:password` with the credentials of an existing user. You will get the following response:

```
HTTP/1.0 200 OK
...
{"enrolled": true}
```

You can access the administration site and check that the user is now enrolled in the course.

# Creating view sets and routers

`ViewSets` allow you to define the interactions of your API and let REST Framework build the URLs dynamically with a `Router` object. By using view sets, you can avoid repeating logic for multiple views. View sets include actions for the typical create, retrieve, update, delete operations, which are `list()`, `create()`, `retrieve()`, `update()`, `partial_update()`, and `destroy()`.

Let's create a view set for the `Course` model. Edit the `api/views.py` file and add the following code to it:

```
from rest_framework import viewsets
from .serializers import CourseSerializer

class CourseViewSet(viewsets.ReadOnlyModelViewSet):
    queryset = Course.objects.all()
    serializer_class = CourseSerializer
```

We subclass `ReadOnlyModelViewSet`, which provides the read-only actions `list()` and `retrieve()` to both list objects or retrieve a single object. Edit the `api/urls.py` file and create a router for our view set as follows:

```
from django.conf.urls import url, include
from rest_framework import routers
from . import views

router = routers.DefaultRouter()
router.register('courses', views.CourseViewSet)

urlpatterns = [
    # ...
    url(r'^', include(router.urls)),
]
```

We create a `DefaultRouter` object and register our view set with the `courses` prefix. The router takes charge of generating URLs automatically for our view set.

Open `http://127.0.0.1:8000/api/` in your browser. You will see that the router lists all view sets in its base URL, as shown in the following screenshot:

```
Api Root                                          OPTIONS    GET  ▾

GET /api/

HTTP 200 OK
Vary: Accept
Content-Type: application/json
Allow: GET, HEAD, OPTIONS

{
    "courses": "http://127.0.0.1:8000/api/courses/"
}
```

You can access `http://127.0.0.1:8000/api/courses/` to retrieve the list of courses.

You can learn more about view sets at `http://www.django-rest-framework.org/api-guide/viewsets/`. You can also find more information about routers at `http://www.django-rest-framework.org/api-guide/routers/`.

# Adding additional actions to view sets

You can add extra actions to view sets. Let's change our previous `CourseEnrollView` view into a custom view set action. Edit the `api/views.py` file and modify the `CourseViewSet` class to look as follows:

```python
from rest_framework.decorators import detail_route

class CourseViewSet(viewsets.ReadOnlyModelViewSet):
    queryset = Course.objects.all()
    serializer_class = CourseSerializer

    @detail_route(methods=['post'],
                  authentication_classes=[BasicAuthentication],
                  permission_classes=[IsAuthenticated])
    def enroll(self, request, *args, **kwargs):
        course = self.get_object()
        course.students.add(request.user)
        return Response({'enrolled': True})
```

We add a custom `enroll()` method that represents an additional action for this view set. The preceding code is as follows:

- We use the `detail_route` decorator of the framework to specify that this is an action to be performed on a single object.
- The decorator allows us to add custom attributes for the action. We specify that only the POST method is allowed for this view, and set the authentication and permission classes.
- We use `self.get_object()` to retrieve the `Course` object.
- We add the current user to the `students` many-to-many relationship and return a custom success response.

Edit the `api/urls.py` file and remove the following URL, since we don't need it anymore:

```
url(r'^courses/(?P<pk>[\d]+)/enroll/$',
    views.CourseEnrollView.as_view(),
    name='course_enroll'),
```

Then edit the `api/views.py` file and remove the `CourseEnrollView` class.

The URL to enroll in courses is now automatically generated by the router. The URL remains the same, since it's built dynamically using our action name `enroll`.

# Creating custom permissions

We want students to be able to access the contents of the courses they are enrolled in. Only students enrolled in a course should be able to access its contents. The best way to do this is with a custom permission class. Django provides a `BasePermission` class that allows you to define the following methods:

- `has_permission()`: View-level permission check
- `has_object_permission()`: Instance-level permission check

These methods should return `True` to grant access or `False` otherwise. Create a new file inside the `courses/api/` directory and name it `permissions.py`. Add the following code to it:

```python
from rest_framework.permissions import BasePermission

class IsEnrolled(BasePermission):
    def has_object_permission(self, request, view, obj):
        return obj.students.filter(id=request.user.id).exists()
```

We subclass the `BasePermission` class and override the `has_object_permission()`. We check that the user performing the request is present in the `students` relationship of the `Course` object. We are going to use the `IsEnrolled` permission next.

# Serializing course contents

We need to serialize course contents. The `Content` model includes a generic foreign key that allows us to associate objects of different content models. Yet, we have added a common `render()` method for all content models in the previous chapter. We can use this method to provide rendered contents to our API.

Edit the `api/serializers.py` file of the `courses` application and add the following code to it:

```python
from ..models import Content

class ItemRelatedField(serializers.RelatedField):
    def to_representation(self, value):
        return value.render()

class ContentSerializer(serializers.ModelSerializer):
    item = ItemRelatedField(read_only=True)

    class Meta:
        model = Content
        fields = ('order', 'item')
```

In this code, we define a custom field by subclassing the `RelatedField` serializer field provided by REST Framework and overriding the `to_representation()` method. We define the `ContentSerializer` serializer for the `Content` model and use the custom field for the `item` generic foreign key.

We need an alternate serializer for the `Module` model that includes its contents, and an extended `Course` serializer as well. Edit the `api/serializers.py` file and add the following code to it:

```python
class ModuleWithContentsSerializer(serializers.ModelSerializer):
    contents = ContentSerializer(many=True)

    class Meta:
        model = Module
        fields = ('order', 'title', 'description', 'contents')
```

```
class CourseWithContentsSerializer(serializers.ModelSerializer):
    modules = ModuleWithContentsSerializer(many=True)

    class Meta:
        model = Course
        fields = ('id', 'subject', 'title', 'slug',
                  'overview', 'created', 'owner', 'modules')
```

Let's create a view that mimics the behavior of the `retrieve()` action but includes the course contents. Edit the `api/views.py` file and add the following method to the `CourseViewSet` class:

```
from .permissions import IsEnrolled
from .serializers import CourseWithContentsSerializer

class CourseViewSet(viewsets.ReadOnlyModelViewSet):
    # ...
    @detail_route(methods=['get'],
                  serializer_class=CourseWithContentsSerializer,
                  authentication_classes=[BasicAuthentication],
                  permission_classes=[IsAuthenticated,
                                      IsEnrolled])
    def contents(self, request, *args, **kwargs):
        return self.retrieve(request, *args, **kwargs)
```

The description of this method is as follows:

- We use the `detail_route` decorator to specify that this action is performed on a single object.

- We specify that only the GET method is allowed for this action.

- We use the new `CourseWithContentsSerializer` serializer class that includes rendered course contents.

- We use both the `IsAuthenticated` and our custom `IsEnrolled` permissions. By doing so, we make sure that only users enrolled in the course are able to access its contents.

- We use the existing `retrieve()` action to return the course object.

Open `http://127.0.0.1:8000/api/courses/1/contents/` in your browser. If you access the view with the right credentials, you will see that each module of the course includes the rendered HTML for course contents, like this:

```
{
"order": 0,
"title": "Installing Django",
```

```
    "description": "",
    "contents": [
        {
            "order": 0,
            "item": "<p>Take a look at the following video for installing
Django:</p>\n"
        },
        {
            "order": 1,
            "item": "\n<iframe width=\"480\" height=\"360\" src=\"http://
www.youtube.com/embed/bgV39DlmZ2U?wmode=opaque\" frameborder=\"0\"
allowfullscreen></iframe>\n\n"
        }
    ]
}
```

You have built a simple API that allows other services to access the course application programmatically. REST Framework also allows you to manage creating and editing objects with the `ModelViewSet` view set. We have covered the main aspects of Django Rest Framework, but you will find further information about its features in its extensive documentation at `http://www.django-rest-framework.org/`.

# Summary

In this chapter, you created a RESTful API for other services to interact with your web application.

An additional *Chapter 13, Going Live* is available for download at `https://www.packtpub.com/sites/default/files/downloads/Django_By_Example_GoingLive.pdf`. It will teach you how to build a production environment using uWSGI and NGINX. You will also learn how to implement a custom middleware and create custom management commands.

You have reached the end of this book. Congratulations! You have learned the skills required to build successful web applications with Django. This book has guided you through the process of developing real-life projects and integrating Django with other technologies. Now you are ready to create your own Django project, whether it is a simple prototype or a large-scale web application.

Good luck with your next Django adventure!

# Index

## Thank you for buying
# Django By Example

## About Packt Publishing

Packt, pronounced 'packed', published its first book, *Mastering phpMyAdmin for Effective MySQL Management*, in April 2004, and subsequently continued to specialize in publishing highly focused books on specific technologies and solutions.

Our books and publications share the experiences of your fellow IT professionals in adapting and customizing today's systems, applications, and frameworks. Our solution-based books give you the knowledge and power to customize the software and technologies you're using to get the job done. Packt books are more specific and less general than the IT books you have seen in the past. Our unique business model allows us to bring you more focused information, giving you more of what you need to know, and less of what you don't.

Packt is a modern yet unique publishing company that focuses on producing quality, cutting-edge books for communities of developers, administrators, and newbies alike. For more information, please visit our website at www.packtpub.com.

## About Packt Open Source

In 2010, Packt launched two new brands, Packt Open Source and Packt Enterprise, in order to continue its focus on specialization. This book is part of the Packt Open Source brand, home to books published on software built around open source licenses, and offering information to anybody from advanced developers to budding web designers. The Open Source brand also runs Packt's Open Source Royalty Scheme, by which Packt gives a royalty to each open source project about whose software a book is sold.

## Writing for Packt

We welcome all inquiries from people who are interested in authoring. Book proposals should be sent to author@packtpub.com. If your book idea is still at an early stage and you would like to discuss it first before writing a formal book proposal, then please contact us; one of our commissioning editors will get in touch with you.

We're not just looking for published authors; if you have strong technical skills but no writing experience, our experienced editors can help you develop a writing career, or simply get some additional reward for your expertise.

## Django Design Patterns and Best Practices

ISBN: 978-1-78398-664-4          Paperback: 222 pages

Easily build maintainable websites with powerful and relevant Django design patterns

1. Unravel the common problems of web development in Django.

2. Learn the current best practices while working in Django 1.7 and Python 3.4.

3. Experience the challenges of working on an end-to-end social network project.

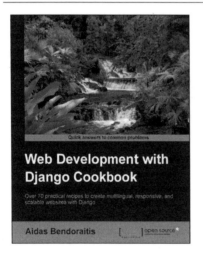

## Web Development with Django Cookbook

ISBN: 978-1-78328-689-8          Paperback: 294 pages

Over 70 practical recipes to create multilingual, responsive, and scalable websites with Django

1. Improve your skills by developing models, forms, views, and templates.

2. Create a rich user experience using Ajax and other JavaScript techniques.

3. A practical guide to writing and using APIs to import or export data.

Please check **www.PacktPub.com** for information on our titles

## Django Essentials

ISBN: 978-1-78398-370-4          Paperback: 172 pages

Develop simple web applications with the powerful Django framework

1. Get to know MVC pattern and the structure of Django.

2. Create your first webpage with Django mechanisms.

3. Enable user interaction with forms.

4. Program extremely rapid forms with Django features.

## Instant Django 1.5 Application Development Starter

ISBN: 978-1-78216-356-5          Paperback: 78 pages

Jump into Django with this hands-on guide to practical web application development with Python

1. Learn something new in an Instant! A short, fast, focused guide delivering immediate results.

2. Work with the database API to create a data-driven app.

3. Learn Django by creating a practical web application.

Please check **www.PacktPub.com** for information on our titles

29004227R00264

Made in the USA
Middletown, DE
03 February 2016